TRUST

FROM SOCRATES TO SPIN

KIERON O'HARA

INTRODUCED BY WILL HUTTON

ICON BOOKS

Published in the UK in 2004
by Icon Books Ltd., Grange Road,
Duxford, Cambridge CB2 4QF
Email: info@iconbooks.co.uk
www.iconbooks.co.uk

Sold in the UK, Europe, South Africa
and Asia by Faber and Faber Ltd.,
3 Queen Square, London WC1N 3AU
or their agents

Distributed in the UK, Europe, South Africa
and Asia by TBS Ltd., Frating Distribution Centre,
Colchester Road, Frating Green, Colchester CO7 7DW

Published in Australia in 2004
by Allen & Unwin Pty. Ltd., PO Box 8500,
83 Alexander Street, Crows Nest, NSW 2065

Distributed in Canada by Penguin Books Canada,
10 Alcorn Avenue, Suite 300, Toronto, Ontario M4V 3B2

ISBN 1 84046 531 X

Typesetting by Hands Fotoset

Printed and bound in the UK by
Clays of Bungay

Contents

List of Figures and Tables

Figures

List of Tables

* ANN SUMMERS
* BAGS FOR LIFE TH
* HESTON BLUMENT
* BNP COPPERS * CHRIST
* DONATIONS TO CHARI
* DRAMAS PORTRAYING
* ECONOMISTS * EMINEM * M
* FRIENDS OF THE GURKHAS A
* GREEN SHOOTS * G20 *
* THE IRISH ECONOMIC MIRAC
* KEEP CALM AND CARRY ON * LA
* MAKING YC
* MARKS & SPENCER S
* POLAR BEAR PICTURE SP
* QUANTITATIVE EASING * THE
* NICOLAS SARKOZY * STIN
* CAROL THATCHER *
* TORY JAM FANS * THA
* UKIP * UNIVERSITY OF G
* WET-LOOK
* WORKING UNTIL YOU DIE * X
* THE YEAR OF HUGH LA
* Z-LIS

Acknowledgements

Writing a book such as this is more than a one man job, even if there are only two index fingers actually hitting the word processor. Let me just take a couple of pages to thank those without whom not.

First and foremost, there would be no book at all without Professor Nigel Shadbolt of the University of Southampton. It was his suggestion that I begin research on trust in the context of the Internet; his ability to spot the killer issue remains undimmed by the passage of time. I have been working with Nigel for not far off 15 years now, during which time I have enjoyed a cheerfully parasitic existence off his intellectual breadth and leadership, which has enabled me to continue my philosophical explorations of the world without disappearing into the black hole of the *a priori*. He is also a good friend, a wonderful chap, and has stood me more slap-up meals than I've had hot dinners (hang on, that can't be right).

Let me also tip my hat to Pru Hobson-West of Nottingham University's Institute for the Study of Genetics, Biorisk and Society, who steered me carefully through much of my early research on the topic of trust, as I began to export my ideas away from the net and into real life. It's a bit more complicated out there, as Pru kept explaining to me with unfailing patience. Her encouragement was no little help either, especially during those 'beating my head against a wall' days. I somehow doubt whether she agrees with many of my conclusions, but her imprimatur can be detected in plenty of places along the way.

And thanks very much to Professor Brian Collins of RMCS,

Cranfield University, who has given me the benefit of his incredibly wide experience of the world of industry and politics. I hope that wider perspective is evident in the book. I was particularly impressed by the amount of time he has given me, despite his ridiculously busy schedule; just watching him in action is exhausting enough.

Tons of other people have chipped in, including Dave Stevens, Athina Karatzogianni, Sri Dasmahapatra, Leila Thorp and Elise Graves. Many thanks; many apologies to anyone I've forgotten. Thanks also to the guys at Icon Books, notably Andrew Furlow, who warped my original proposal out of all recognition and turned it into something readable.

Finally, the Department of Electronics and Computer Science at Southampton University has been a very congenial place to work in, and the glorious effect of release from the everyday academic pressures of admin and teaching cannot be underestimated. I hope this little tome comes up to the very high standards of one of the finest university departments in the country. While working on this book, I was supported by the Advanced Knowledge Technologies (AKT) Interdisciplinary Research Collaboration (IRC), which is sponsored by the UK Engineering and Physical Sciences Research Council under grant number GR/N15764/01. The AKT IRC comprises the Universities of Aberdeen, Edinburgh, Sheffield, Southampton and the Open University, and can be found at http://www.aktors.org; I describe this excellent project briefly in a previous book for Icon, *Plato and the Internet*.

For Mum
with love

Foreword

Trust – and its absence – preoccupies and concerns us. Trust knits society together, and makes it possible for people to get on with their everyday lives. Without it, society would become impossible. Very often, we simply have no choice but to trust others, yet this doesn't automatically mean that our anxieties are allayed. When we get on a train, we implicitly trust the engineers who have carried out safety checks, but this doesn't mean that we are entirely comfortable with having to do so. As parents, we want our children to develop their independence, and so have no choice but to trust the teachers or chat room moderators who look after them. But putting this trust in other adults may make us feel very uneasy. Having no choice but to trust can be painful.

Conversely, trust often seems sorely lacking. The extension of media interrogation into every corner of public life, coupled with the vast expansion of information sources led by the World Wide Web, means that we find it increasingly difficult to draw comfort from the expertise and authority of professionals, politicians and other public figures. Many of us feel that life would have been easier, trust less frail, in bygone eras when we felt happily able to defer to the senior figures in our community. Today, endemic cynicism and suspicion, especially within the media, mean that our more liberated and individualistic era is not necessarily a more satisfied one.

So do we want more trust or less? Would we rather not know what goes on inside the corridors of power, so as to create a comfort blanket of blind faith in the powers that be? Or on the other hand, might we be happier if we circumvented trust altogether, and accelerated our advance towards a culture of litigation, explicit guarantees and even greater individual liability? These are the dilemmas that an exploration of trust leads us towards.

The answer is surely that trust needs to be appropriately placed. Onora O'Neill, in her well known Reith Lectures on trust, correctly argues that 'To restore trust we need not only trustworthy persons and institutions, but assessable reasons for trusting and mistrusting'.[1] It's no good arguing for more trust – we need to be arguing for more appropriate trust, and for better means of assessing risk.

This, of course, goes to the heart of the modern condition. René Descartes' philosophical breakthrough nearly four centuries ago lay in his *doubting* of the outside world. The development of the critical, Enlightenment mind owed everything to suspicion of authority, not blind deference to it. Immanuel Kant even defined the European Enlightenment as such: 'Enlightenment is man's emergence from his self-incurred immaturity. Immaturity is the inability to use one's own understanding without the guidance of another.'[2] Self-reliance and distrust spawned the secular, public institutions which we hold most dear today – numerous independent media, a culture of scientific enquiry, the liberal rejection of aristocratic forms of authority and so forth. Distrust has made us Europeans who we are.

Moreover, the growing body of social scientific evidence on trust shows that countries with high levels of it are not necessarily enviable social models. The United States is currently an obvious example, a nation driven by such unshakeable faith in its own rectitude that dissent is increasingly marginalised. On the other hand, high trust nations such as Sweden and Finland manage to channel a sound social democratic compact into areas of their social economy where all benefit, without this resting on religious or nationalist forms of trust. In Scandinavia, the knowledge that jobs are secure, families to be looked after and decent norms of public conduct intact means that trust becomes an informed and rational decision, not a blind and irrational leap.

This is the art. To cope with the modern condition of uncertainty and risk, but to do so by building social democratic structures that enable us to trust one another as educated citizens, employees and neighbours. This is the enlightened critical road to a trusting society, as opposed to the fundamentalist or nationalist path, in which leaders present themselves in a mystical, charismatic fashion. Leadership, which our Prime Minister increasingly views as a goal in its own right, can become a dangerous concept, if allowed to become cult-like and monological.

A clear model of what reasonable trust looks like must be the guide. We need updated corporate governance structures which make it possible for employees and managers to enter informed moral agreements, to prevent great companies fragmenting into either webs of short-term transactional contracts or hotbeds of deceit. We need the explicit constitutional structures in place that enable us to decide when a politician is worthy of trust, or else we are left with flipping irrationally between trusting an increasingly irresponsible media or trusting the merchants of political spin.

There is nothing especially new about this. Coping with risk and opaque institutions is, as I say, characteristic of progressive modern societies. But there appears to be a new and more vigorous desire to clarify the too often slippery and mysterious entity that is trust. This book makes an excellent contribution on this front, and I welcome it.

Will Hutton, 2003

[1] Onora O'Neill, *A Question of Trust: The BBC Reith Lectures 2002* (Cambridge University Press, Cambridge , 2002), p. 98.

[2] 'An Answer to the Question what is Enlightenment', in Immanuel Kant, *Political Writings* (ed. H. Reiss, trans. H. Nisbet; Cambridge University Press, Cambridge, 1991).

Introduction

In the summer of 2003, well after the major drafts of this book were already written, a crisis arose for the UK government of Tony Blair. Not much, one would think, to be surprised about there – after all, all governments are periodically beset by crises, even one as ordinarily sure-footed as Mr Blair's. Except that this crisis was subtly different.

For Mr Blair's *competence* was not in question. Indeed, in so far as the crisis involved external events over which Mr Blair had control, he came out of the imbroglio rather well; he had, against an initially sceptical public opinion, fought and won a war against a major military dictatorship, and had even cajoled both the public and his rebellious backbench MPs round to a, perhaps grudging, support for his actions. Claims by the parliamentary awkward squad that thousands of civilians would die, or that street-fighting in Baghdad would continue for months, resulting in the destruction of that great and ancient city, turned out to be as wild as they sounded. In April and May, Mr Blair's star, if not necessarily high in the sky yet, was waxing nicely.

Then control slipped, as a murky set of developments took

place. Mr Blair's case for war had depended, to a reckless extent, on the claim that the President of Iraq, Saddam Hussein, had access to weapons of mass destruction (WMD), and that these could be deployed against troops of the US/UK coalition (that also included a tiny figleaf of representatives of other nations) within 45 minutes. Possession of such weapons would be a breach of the United Nations resolution which, in American and British eyes at least, legitimised the invasion. Such weapons were not found; neither have they been at the time of writing; even if they existed, the possibility of their deployment within three-quarters of an hour seems to have been dramatically exaggerated.

Amazingly, as the mutterings about the failure to find WMD grew louder, Mr Blair forbore to defend himself by pointing out that Saddam Hussein had been in breach of UN resolutions for donkey's years; or that in Saddam's hands a *rifle* would be a weapon of mass destruction, never mind more sinister ordnance; and that he had done the world a mercy by helping get rid of a truly evil man. He could even have admitted that the coalition might not find WMD; a decent defence of his position could still rely upon the massive quantity of evidence that such WMD existed. Support for Mr Blair's contention would include, for example, pretty well all the evidence assembled by the UN weapons inspector Hans Blix, the lack of any evidence for the destruction of the WMD discovered by previous weapons inspectors, US and UK military intelligence, the testimony of Iraqi deserters, and – not least – the complete inexplicability of Saddam Hussein's actions if he had in fact got rid of his weapons earlier (had he provided documentary proof, he could have ensured UN sanctions were lifted, and prevented the devastating war for which he was so unprepared strategically, which, on 9 April 2003, finally removed him from power, and which, in a blaze of American missiles, deprived him of his two notorious sons Uday and Qusay).

But Mr Blair's odd strategy of insisting that WMD would be found led to allegations that the intelligence upon which he relied was incorrect, and even that the dossiers of information that he had released to the public and his party to convince them of the righteousness of war had been somehow altered by his spin doctor Alastair Campbell. The Foreign Secretary, Jack Straw, claimed that the compilation and release of the dossiers had not been subject to undue pressure, but that the government information machine had broken down; the whole incident, far from being a conspiracy, was actually, in his word, a 'horlicks' (the otherwise puzzling citation of a malted milk bedtime drink in this context may give non-British readers a hint of the level of political debate in the UK; Mr Straw alludes delicately to the word 'bollocks', meaning originally 'testicles' and then a muddle or a mess).

So the government was not best pleased when the BBC continued to claim that the dossiers had been doctored. The Ministry of Defence unofficially named the BBC's source, a seasoned weapons expert called Dr Kelly, who then claimed that, though he was indeed the BBC's source, he had not said what the BBC had reported him as having said. Dr Kelly was summoned to appear before a House of Commons committee of MPs, who gave him a fairly rough time; his answers were unconvincing and evasive. The argument between the government and the BBC spiralled, while government spokesmen sought to marginalise Dr Kelly, and mendaciously to downplay his influence and expertise.

Then Dr Kelly was found dead, his wrists slashed.

This is the source of Mr Blair's crisis. As every headline in the usually politically moribund month of July trumpeted, this was a crisis of *trust*. Mr Blair, who has always been seen as a manipulator of the truth and a master of the media, relies heavily on trust. He is not popular. He is the leader of a traditionally left-wing party, in a traditionally right-wing country; his electoral strategy depends on presenting himself as in control of his party, and as the natural inheritor and interpreter of the legacy of Margaret Thatcher. His left-wing activists have to trust him to insert left-wing policies into the general market orientation of his government (as for example when he enacted a minimum wage); the right-wing voters have to trust him to keep taxes down against the wishes of his party. If either of those groups of people withdraw their trust, Mr Blair will be vulnerable. An enquiry into Dr Kelly's death is underway, and Mr Blair's career may depend on the result.

And yet, it is an odd phenomenon; Mr Blair's crisis is not about anything hard and fast, economic or political. It is nothing to do with unemployment, the level of sterling, the European Union, the congestion on Britain's roads, the environment, poverty, crime, inequality or inflation. Trust is – surely – hardly an actor on the political stage, more a mood, an almost unconscious assessment. How can it be quantified? What can Mr Blair do to restore it? What can his enemies do to chip away at it still further?

Trust for perhaps the first time has become the dominant political issue in the UK, although it has been the focus of some debate there and elsewhere for a decade or so. The book is about the ways in which trust operates, about the assumptions that are made about it, about the diagnoses for its failure. It is a survey, and a wide one at that, taking us from Biblical times to the cutting edge of technology, from philosophy to economics; such a survey will of necessity be incomplete, but if I can't clear the ground, I hope at least to machete a way through the thickets of commentary towards a greater understanding of the context and significance of the new political debates about trust.

Trust is central to all important social relations. Any attempt to place boundaries round the discussion will inevitably lead to artificiality. Hence the limits (from Socrates to Spin) set by the subtitle of this book are not meant to be historical; our argument will find much material that precedes Socrates, and it should remain relevant long after spin doctors are consigned to memory glorious or inglorious. Rather I hope by the subtitle's breadth to suggest that, to get anything like a decent account of trust, we will have to plunder many sources: the philosophy of Socrates and Aristotle, Hobbes and Kant; the sociology of Durkheim, Weber and Putnam; literature; economics; scientific methodology; the most ancient of history and the most current of current affairs.

CHAPTER ONE

By Atropos Divorced

The penultimate circle of Hell

Dante's *Divine Comedy*, written about 1300, is a wonderful allegorical description of the medieval spiritual world. Divided into three parts, the *Inferno*, the *Purgatorio* and the *Paradiso*, it tells of the poet's journey through, respectively, Hell, Purgatory and Heaven. The *Inferno* portrays Hell as a series of concentric circles, leading downwards. Each circle hosts the spirits of those who have committed a particular sin, tormented with various apposite and gruesome punishments. For instance, the second circle down contains the lustful, to be forever blown about by a howling wind, as they submitted to the dictates of their sinful appetites during life. Flatterers are buried in the slop and ordure they have excreted upon the Earth in life, and so on. As one moves down through the circles, the sins get worse, and in the very centre, frozen in a lake of ice, is Lucifer himself.

The exact geography of Hell is perhaps of passing interest in our more secular age, but Dante's classification and ordering of sin is still intriguing. Murderers, for example, and rapists, find themselves in the seventh circle, with the violent. But in the ninth circle, outdone only by the pure evil of Satan himself, are those who have betrayed a trust.

Indeed, so terrible a sin is betrayal that there is even a special, almost Blairite, 'fast track' system.

> ... oft-times the soul
> Drops hither, ere by Atropos divorced.[1]

Atropos is the Fate that cuts the thread of life; when sinners die, their souls, no longer supported by the thread, fall into Hell. Usually, they have to make their own way down to their eternal torments, but betrayers, so evil are they, whizz straight to the ninth circle. Indeed some particularly egregious specimens even fall straight there *before* they die, their bodies being taken over by fiends. The betrayers of their kindred, of their countries, of their guests and of their lords spend eternity frozen into the ice at the bottom of Hell.

At first sight, it seems bizarre that the crimes *we* consider most serious, such as murder and violence, are treated more leniently than betrayals of trust. Even though murderers' eternal tortures are sufficiently terrible to placate all but the most bloodthirsty tabloid newspaper editors, the relative position of murderers and betrayers goes against most of our intuitions. One might say that Hell's surprising topography is a symptom of the deep divide between our modern sensibilities and Dante's medieval mind.

Yet maybe Dante wasn't as morally askew as we might think. Consider how often trust features in our daily lives. The days of leaving our front doors unlocked are, sadly, over. But we open them to strangers, gas meter readers, postmen, policemen. We drive around at 70 mph and more, turning our cars into lethal metal missiles, and trusting *with our lives* other drivers to stick to the rules of the road, and to stay on the other side of the white line. We buy from the butcher or the baker or the takeaway restaurant, and we trust the owner not to sell us food that is too old to be safe to eat. We buy a drink from a bar, trusting that it has not been adulterated with water, or indeed pepped up with industrial alcohol. We work for weeks at a time before being paid – and then trust that our reward of bits of nicely patterned paper are exchangeable for more tangibly useful goods. We trust our spouses to keep their hands off our best friends, our teachers to improve our children, and our doctors to try to keep us well. When we get on a bus, we trust that the bus will go where it has advertised, and when we take our seat, we trust that the person next to us will not attack us violently.

Naturally, some of this trust is misplaced; there are bogus callers, dangerous drivers, unfaithful spouses, murderous doctors, criminal policemen and wayward bus services. But – although it may not seem so, sometimes – such betrayals are relatively rare, given the number of times such trust is routinely placed. In fact, we trust some aspect of others' behaviour almost all of the time, and if we didn't, life would be almost unliveable. Perhaps Dante's instincts are sounder than ours; perhaps those who betray trust *are* doing serious and dangerous violence to the foundations of society. Minor betrayals, individually less shocking than the crimes we see in our newspaper headlines, make us less capable of getting on with each other, of living the lives that we want to lead.

Nevertheless, as we have already seen in the Preface, issues of trust can make their way onto those front pages. Tony Blair may have helped drive the unfortunate Dr Kelly to his death, and may have misled parliament and British voters over the dangers from Saddam Hussein's government in Iraq. A previous British government may have placed the interests of agribusiness before those of the public over the dangers of BSE. Accountants Arthur Andersen failed to oversee the accounts of Enron correctly, perhaps because they were also giving Enron advice on how to fill those accounts in. When trust fails, societies are threatened, whether from below or above.

This is a book about trust, about its ubiquity, its history, the forms it takes and the functions it performs. We will look at whether trust is declining, and, if so, what if anything we can do about it. Everyone has something to say about trust, from great authors to sociologists, politicians to computer scientists, philosophers to the person on the Clapham Omnibus or the Yamanote Line. There are a myriad theories, diagnoses, narratives, complaints, complacencies, scaremongerings, prejudices and solutions, and we will try to sift our way through this pile of generally inconsistent analysis to see if there are any lessons we can draw from our experiences as social beings for the last few thousand years. It is a big task, and this is a small book, but we might hope to make a decent start.

The dark matter of the soul

Trust pervades daily life. If we take only a small sample from the bewildering array of occasions where trust plays a role, we can see that, of all social phenomena, it is surely one of the most vital. But this very centrality brings problems for the study of trust – how can one even begin to understand such a protean social force?

What we trust

We can trust all sorts of things, not only people but also animals and inanimate objects, systems and institutions. We trust our physical environment to remain more or less constant and manageable – even devotees of so-called dangerous sports usually survive to bungee another day. Moreover, the extent of our trust depends on who or what we are trusting and why. I would trust a bank clerk with my credit card number, but not the details of my unhappy love affair with a chorus girl; I would trust a counsellor with the story of my affair, but not the keys to my garage; I would trust my next-door neighbour with the keys to my garage, but not my credit card. The twist is that bank clerk, counsellor and neighbour might actually be the same person, unbeknownst to me (if I am very unobservant). Whom I trust, to what extent, and in what field, depends on some very diverse factors indeed.

Trust and morality

Trust can have a moral dimension, or morality may be absent. If my car breaks down, and I take it to a garage, I trust that they have the ability to get it going again. I trust them not to be stymied by any problem that my car can throw up. This isn't a moral claim – I have *expectations* of their ability. On the other hand, if I have paid someone to do something in advance, then they are morally obliged to carry out the task to the best of their ability, and I trust them to do their duty in this regard. It is not that I think they can't perform the task. Indeed, by paying them, I have wittingly given them an incentive *not* to do it.

Trust and predictability

Trust enables us to see the future. We live in a constant state of uncertainty, in a number of respects, most obviously in that we have no idea of what the future holds. Predicting what will happen is a mug's game. But trust helps us in that respect – if we trust someone to do something, and that trust is not misplaced, then that is one less thing to worry about.

Let's take a really trivial example: I walk into my local newsagent's for a newspaper. The transaction is simple, I ask for a newspaper and a bar of chocolate, the newsagent charges me a sum of money, I give him a note, he gives me my change, we wave a cheery goodbye and off I go. Everyday fare, yet so much is taken on trust. I trust the newsagent to calculate the change correctly, to give me the right newspaper, to give me a bar of chocolate that is not past its sell-by date. I trust him to be in the business of selling papers and sweets, I trust him to understand that that is what I wish to buy, as opposed to, say, clothes, drugs or nuclear weapons. In other words, I trust him to behave like a newsagent. And because he does behave like a newsagent, I don't have to think about what to say or do in his shop. It becomes routine. My trust in his playing his role, and his fulfilling that trust, together make the world so much more stable and predictable. This is exactly the sort of socially based predictability that computers find so hard to mimic – no robot, even now, could manage this transaction.[2] The idea of 'self-contained' little vignettes acting as a basis for understanding has intrigued philosophers for some time, including for example Ludwig Wittgenstein.[3]

Because we have this mutual trust in each other's goals and understanding of our interactions, we can order society around such institutions as shops (or families, or postal deliveries, or whatever). Trust makes us more likely to achieve our goals. In the grim jargon of the new century, it is an enabler, a facilitator.

Trust and cooperation

If two people are engaged in any kind of cooperative work they will need to trust each other. When a winger crosses the ball at a nice height into the penalty area, he trusts that the centre forward will be there to head it; when the centre forward makes a run through the middle, he trusts that the winger will get a decent cross in. If either player fails to trust the other, the move will break down. If the centre forward doesn't think the winger is up to it, he won't bother to make the run, and the cross will be wasted, whereas if the winger thinks the centre forward lacks the pace to get in the box on time, he will probably cut inside and go for goal himself (doubtless losing the ball – they always do), and then the forward's run will only have exhausted him. *Any* plan that involves two or more people working together, from cooking Christmas dinner to assembling a bookcase to building an oil rig, demands mutual trust in each other's capacity and inclination to do the job.

Trust and the self

Even in the privacy of our own heads, trust is a crucial part of the psychological account. We may, or may not, trust ourselves. How many people have to put their chocolates or biscuits in relatively inaccessible places to deter themselves, not others, from snaffling them? How many drinkers have to walk their dog the long way round, because if they pass the pub …? There are even classical precedents: the *Odyssey* tells of Odysseus, when he wanted to hear the sirens' song, instructing his crew to lash him to the mast – he didn't trust himself to listen without diverting his ship's course.[4] In cases like these, often in the light of long and sad experience, we try to take our decision objectively, as if we were judging the trustworthiness of a completely separate person.

Well, we all know about that sort of thing. But trust even impinges on the deeper philosophical issues about our selves, and our relationship with the outside world. For example, Freud conceived of psychoanalysis as a kind of trusting distrust. The patient's utterances, writings, etc., are understood as being highly misleading – they need to be studied in depth precisely because their surface meaning is so untrustworthy. But the psychoanalyst still ultimately trusts the patient to the extent that somewhere, buried in the deeper meaning of the patient's utterances, are genuine attempts to 'sneak out' the psychological truth via the unconscious back door. The patient is only misleading if you take him at his word; the savvy psychoanalyst will be prepared to 'decode' the false top level, to find the truthful underneath, disguised as symbols, puns, etc.[5]

Or, still more basic, there is the question raised by René Descartes, which we have all struggled with at three in the morning: whether we are dreaming now, or whether what we consider to be the real world is actually created for us by a malicious demon. We avoid total scepticism about the existence of the external world by trusting the evidence of our eyes, ears and other sensory organs. When philosophy lets us down, trust is all we are left with.

Trust is essential to our identity as individuals and as people in the world; it is also essential for social relations. It is truly the mysterious, barely known entity that holds society and our selves together, the 'dark matter' of the soul.

Trust and knowledge

What does trust buy you? It gets you out of a state of uncertainty. If you need to know that something is the case, and don't, then you can't make plans. But if someone has promised to help you, and you trust her, then you can plan on that basis. The firmer your plans, the stronger your trust, and vice versa.

So let's say, for the purposes of this book, that X trusts Y if X accepts Y's bona fides. X trusts Y (usually to do something in particular, though it can be a generalised trust as well) when he *doesn't bother to investigate further*. If X lends Y £20, and trusts her, then he expects to get the £20 back, and he doesn't bother following Y around making sure she still has the cash. If X only partially trusts Y, then he may make her sign a contract to return the cash; he is not then trusting her with the money, but he is trusting her to abide by her legal obligations (which is a much weaker trust, because there are coercive procedures that he can invoke to get his money back in the worst case).

Not investigating, not entering into legal relations; these are all signs of trust. The truster clearly benefits from trust. Investigating people and initiating legal procedures are expensive and time-consuming, and indeed can undermine trust; sometimes uncertainty combined with trust is better than certain knowledge. Preston Sturges' masterly film of 1949, *Unfaithfully Yours*, shows the problems that can arise when a husband's faith in his wife has to be confirmed by private detectives; 'knowledge puffeth up, but charity edifieth'.[6]

Hence trust gets rather tangled between convenience and morality. One peculiar example of this can be found in some adventure stories of a different age, with the concept of *parole*. If a soldier or policeman has captured an enemy, he could sometimes be making problems for himself; after all, guarding a prisoner is awkward, and stops him doing other important things. In B. Traven's anarchist fable *The Treasure of the Sierra Madre*, prospectors Curtin and Dobbs fall out over their gold; Dobbs pulls a gun, but Curtin wins the fight and takes the gun. However:

> He was no better off than he had been half an hour before. He could not keep a watch over Dobbs for four days and nights. He would have to fall asleep some time and then Dobbs would overpower him. And he would show no mercy, for he was now convinced that his suspicions of Curtin were correct and that if he

put him out of the way it would be in self-defence. There was only room for one of them. Fear and exhaustion would drive them both half-crazy. Whoever first fell asleep would fall a victim to the other.[7]

One solution to this was for the prisoner to give his parole; he would promise not to try to escape. The capturer gained the freedom to continue his investigations, and the prisoner gained some limited freedom, he wasn't tied up, he wasn't watched day and night or covered with a gun. A win-win situation?

Is trusting ever wrong?

Well, it's hard to imagine such an arrangement working nowadays – if indeed it ever worked outside boys' stories. Actually, it didn't always work even then. Some people were just too evil for words.

> Ginger flew flat out with his eyes on the sky, hoping to catch sight of his now hated foe. He could not forget or forgive the foul blow that had struck down the unsuspecting mechanic. Moreover, that the Nazi should escape was bad enough, but that he should take his, Ginger's, Spitfire with him, added insult to injury.
>
> The others had been right, thought Ginger moodily, as he roared on. Biggles should not have accepted a Nazi's parole. It was clear now that Hymann had only given it to obtain the freedom that made escape possible.[8]

And of course, morally, the good guys shouldn't make it any easier for the bad guys.

> 'How about cutting these straps,' suggested Biggles, indicating his bound wrists.

'I will if you'll give me your parole,' offered the other.

'I'm dashed if I do,' replied Biggles through set teeth.[9]

'I am glad to see that you have called on your philosophy,' she said. 'You will need it. Unless you are prepared to face another injection of *F. Katalepsis* you must give me your parole for half an hour … .'

She stood in the open doorway, one slender hand, its polished nails gleaming like gems, resting on her hip. Her eyes were mercilessly hard.

I can't say what it was in her bearing that told me; but I knew, beyond any shadow of doubt, that all was not going smoothly with Madame Ingomar.

'Naturally, I must decline.'

'You mean it?'

'Definitely.'[10]

We should place our trust intelligently, and with an eye to moral rectitude. There are many examples where excessive trusting has led to downfall. As a peculiarly egregious example, consider the unfortunate Native Americans. Faced with an unstoppable flood of European settlers, their representatives negotiated with the US government about the ownership of land and compensation; their representatives were actually well briefed and not under any illusions about government settler policy. But each time, they trusted the government to keep to agreements; the government never did, the settlers pushed their way through to the Pacific and the Native American way of life ended.[11]

Our intuitions

We don't always place our trust rationally or sensibly. We are, for instance, over-trusting of eyewitnesses. Psychologist Elizabeth

17

Loftus performed a dramatic experiment to demonstrate this. People were asked to judge the guilt or innocence of a man accused of robbing a store and killing the shopkeeper, on the basis of a set of evidence. Eighteen per cent of an initial group of subjects pronounced him guilty. To a second group, Loftus presented the same evidence, with the addition of eyewitness testimony identifying the defendant as the killer; 72 per cent of this second group found him guilty. So eyewitness evidence is clearly important. But here's the worrying part: a third group was presented with the initial evidence, the eyewitness testimony, and further testimony proving that the eyewitness could not possibly have seen the killer's face. You would expect, or hope, that the conviction rate of this third group would fall back to something like the 18 per cent of the first group, since in effect they were being presented with the same evidence. Actually, *68 per cent* of the third group found the defendant guilty; there was no significant difference between the two groups presented with the eyewitness evidence, and its proven unreliability had no effect whatsoever.[12]

On the other hand, our intuitions about trust can lead us astray in the opposite direction as well; we can be too untrusting. The technology exists now to fly an aeroplane automatically – this technology is already being exploited heavily for military applications. Most situations that a plane can find itself in are pretty routine, and these are handled perfectly well by on-board computers, maybe with interventions from controllers on the ground. Where the pilot comes into his own is when something unusual happens. But by definition, the unusual doesn't happen very often. It turns out that most deaths during air travel are due to pilot error; the rather wonderful industry jargon for this is CFITs (Controlled Flights Into Terrain – i.e. the pilot flew the plane into the ground). Computers are also immune to hijackings. So we would all be better off if our planes had no pilots, right?

That may be so, but it is hard to imagine anyone getting aboard a plane flying from, say, London to New York if they were told that there was no pilot, and that the only human help the plane would receive would be a couple of mouse clicks from air traffic controllers at Heathrow for takeoff and JFK for landing! Because we *mistrust* computer technology – of course, such technology can and will go wrong, but it will go wrong less often than a pilot will – we actually *increase* the risks our lives are under.

Trust in crisis

Why worry about trust, and why now? On a number of fronts, across the globe, trust has become an issue in politics and public affairs. Politically, the sign of this has been a rapid decline in the number of people voting in mature democracies, and a simultaneous decline in the number strongly identifying with older, class-based political parties. The turnout in the 2001 general election in the United Kingdom was lower than almost all those of the previous century. The choice between George W. Bush and Al Gore in the USA in 2000 also proved a turn-off, at least until the closeness of the race, and the bathos of the arguments about pregnant chads and the like, injected a little life into it. Let us, in passing, take this opportunity to savour once more the immortal election night telephone dialogue between these two giants.

> BUSH: Let me make sure I understand. You're calling me back to retract your concession?
>
> GORE: You don't have to get snippy about it.[13]

Various violent conflicts, deprived of their Cold War importance, have resolved themselves into uneasy peace, leaving statesmen both indigenous and imported to try explicitly to (re-)create trust between former combatants. The South African Trust and Reconciliation Commission was one such heroic effort.[14] But the supply of mistrust seems endless.

Sometimes it can be a very minor matter indeed. Singapore and Malaysia are two highly successful East Asian nations which were once federated. After a rather acrimonious split in the 1960s they went their separate ways, but the manner of their sundering has left a legacy of mistrust. One constant gripe has been the water supply – Singapore is entirely dependent on Malaysia for its fresh water. The contracts governing supply were signed in 1961 and 1962, and Malaysia wants to raise the price, claiming that it loses money under the current arrangement. Singapore retaliated in 2002 by recycling its waste water, under the brand name 'Newater', which apparently is cleaner than tap water, and has an, um, interesting taste. Prime Minister Goh Chok Tong swigged a bottle of it very publicly after a game of tennis shortly after its launch. Locals have rechristened the brew 'loowater', and it remains to be seen whether Newater will catch on, or whether the aim is primarily to place pressure on the Malaysians in the seemingly interminable negotiations about water supply.[15] The Newater incident is a symptom of a common situation; two countries, basically friendly, basically sensible, which can't quite rid themselves of feelings of mistrust – such pairs include Britain and France, England and Scotland, the USA and Canada, Brazil and Argentina.

Investigating trust

Trust can be public or private, undervalued or overvalued, can show a deep moral commitment or be merely an arrangement of convenience. No single volume could ever get to the bottom of such a multifarious topic.

One way of narrowing the scope of a study is to define trust in a particularly narrow way. The problem then is that the phenomenon you define might not fit in with most people's ideas; you might well be addressing a different topic from that which everyone else is interested in. For example, sociologist Adam Seligman defines trust in terms of the roles that people play in society (such as father, teacher, customer, tourist, footballer); the roles determine our actions to a large extent, and the role of trust is to reduce uncertainty when those roles *don't* determine our actions.[16] He creates this definition for perfectly good academic reasons, so that he has a firm definition to write about, and in order to show how trust is different from faith and confidence. Political philosopher Russell Hardin also accepts that there are many interpretations of the word 'trust', and insists that without narrowing down the scope, you can't have a serious discussion; his definition is that X trusts Y if X expects Y to act in X's interests because Y has reasons to do so that are grounded in X's interest.[17]

This is all very well, and quite correct academic practice. However, first of all the definitions are, to say the least, rather forbidding. Second, since the definitions of, say, Seligman and Hardin differ so radically, it is not clear how we could ever compare their work; they are clearly talking about two completely different phenomena. And third, because they have nailed the meaning of 'trust' down so firmly, they end up saying things that seem odd to the layman, as when Seligman says that trust is rare,[18] or when Hardin claims that we can never trust an institution, and hence can never trust government.[19]

I am not singling Seligman and Hardin out as egregiously misguided; they have both done fascinating work on trust and are well worth reading. My point is merely that narrowing the scope of an enquiry might well define a problem out of existence; this is a particular risk for a multi-faceted phenomenon such as trust. Disentangling trust from other related phenomena such as faith and confidence will do way too much violence to the concept.

For that reason, I shall take a different tack. I shall try to address trust in all its various forms and relationships, but I shall focus on a particular context in which it operates. I shall look at trust in public life; I shall not consider why and how we trust inter-personally, even though there is a rich set of questions there. The manifestations of trust with which I will be concerned are those that go beyond personal acquaintance, and which may be in relation to institutions or systems, as well as people. Trusting amazon.com to deliver books, trusting Tony Blair to tell the truth and report faithfully the findings of his intelligence agents, trusting the blood you have been given in a transfusion, trusting the auditors' report about the firms you have invested in, these are all examples of the public operation of trust.

Let me make it even easier on myself. In some parts of the world, public trust is virtually absent. Somalia, Afghanistan, the Democratic Republic of the Congo have hardly any functional state apparatus. Certain groups of people share no trust at all; Israelis and Palestinians, Acehnese and Indonesians, Loyalists and Republicans in Northern Ireland, different racial groups in certain cities of the United States, indigenous populations and those of European descent in many Latin American countries. These are all serious problems, and incredibly hard to deal with; Nobel Prizes await those who can sort that lot out.

Instead, I am going to look specifically at the mature democracies of the developed world, in Europe, North America and the Far East, high-trust societies which nevertheless find themselves feeling that trust is declining and taking social order with it. There are huge gains to be made from trust; the mystery here is why politically mature and tolerant populations seem to be hell-bent on throwing such gains away. Is there a crisis of trust? Many people think so; our perceptions of crisis now affect our actions as voters and consumers, and politicians' perceptions of *our* perceptions now affect the policies they dish up for us.

Trust dominates the news and politics. A quick search through the *Guardian* newspaper, on a day chosen at random (23 January 2003), revealed trust all over the place. Examples include stories about: a con man who is the basis for a Steven Spielberg film; a proposed constitution for the European Union; a new survey finding that public relations people have become less trusted than estate agents; Microsoft's new initiative in open source software;[20] a diplomatic stand-off between the US and North Korea; the confessions of a convicted paedophile; an attempt by two fat children to sue McDonald's; a report from an anti-corruption think tank about the aftermath of the Enron collapse; the lessons learned from the Victoria Climbié enquiry about the persistent failure of the British social services to secure the lives of children in its care.

In short, trust matters in political life now in a way in which it didn't, say, ten years ago. Trust is the big issue of the 21st century. But in the absence of an *understanding* of trust and trustworthiness, the usefulness of trust and the corrosiveness of mistrust, we can't say that this trend has enriched public life.

In this book I want to do three things. I have argued that trust has many forms, and many different interpretations. So in the first part of the book (Chapters 2 to 4), I want briefly and selectively to look at the history, sociology and philosophy of trust, to get a more grounded impression of the variety of its species.

Trust is also ubiquitous; it is very difficult to study it in the abstract, because it intersects with so many other social phenomena. Because of that it is essential to look at it in its context. Therefore Chapters 5 to 8 will take four areas of public life in the developed world to see examples of trust in operation, and of the failure of trust.

Finally, having seen for ourselves what the problems of trust are in the societies in question, we will look, in Chapters 9 and 10, at the question of whether trust is in decline, whether, if so, this counts as a crisis, and, if *that* is so, what we can do about it.

CHAPTER TWO

The Development of Trust in the West

Trust, like all human faculties, has a history which has helped determine its form. No doubt at a deep level, trust originated as some instinctual capacity for accepting certain things at face value. This strategy would have a great deal of evolutionary force behind it, because trust and trustworthy behaviour, enabling cooperation, would help make a species more adaptable. Trust (or, maybe better, 'trust') would enable animals to cease to have to waste time working out what their fellows were going to do, and behaving in a 'trustworthy' way would enable them to cease to have to waste time working out what to do themselves. So, for instance, two stags locking antlers will not attempt to cause serious injury to each other's eyes; furthermore, they 'trust' each other not to, and so do not bother taking evasive action. Hence, instinct probably provides us with the first trust-like phenomena.

But as intellectual and social complexity increases, pre-programmed responses are not good enough. Trust as a social phenomenon has developed differently in different cultures, generally thanks to its presence in different social, political and intellectual histories.[1] The history of trust, then, will affect radically the forms it can take, and the functions it can perform – and hence the structures of the societies it underpins.

In this chapter, I want to spend a little time discussing a few skeins from trust's tangled history, focusing, as advertised above, rather more on the public, social aspects of trust. I certainly don't want to claim that this is an exhaustive account of all the important movements and events. My aim is the more modest one of pointing out that, though trusting is common to all cultures, what gets trusted, and what trusting will sanction, varies; hence we can expect misunderstandings, crossed wires, even overt conflict as a result. There are innovations in trust, some caused by social shifts, some by new technologies, some by clever ideas, some even by stupid ideas, and tracing examples of these in the history of culture may (a) make us alive to the contingencies of our ideas of trust, and (b) help us appreciate the differences between cultures in this respect. I focus on a single instance – Western culture – but we can extrapolate this historical contingency to any culture, and I focus on the West rather than, say, Islam, for no reason other than that European culture is what I can write about most confidently. Western European culture is certainly no richer in this respect than Islam, or Confucianism, or those of African societies, etc.

In the lands of Uz and Moriah

Central to the moral framework of the West is the influence of Christianity, whether we remain practising Christians or not. In the century or so since Nietzsche pronounced that God was dead, Christianity has had mixed fortunes. Forty-seven per cent of Americans go to a religious service once a week, while church membership there is round about 60 per cent (about twice what it was, incidentally, in the mid-19th century). On the other hand, barely one European in five goes regularly to church.[2] But notwithstanding that, Western moral notions, even those which have slipped over into secularity, have a Christian core. To take perhaps the most influential example, it is hard to imagine Marxism taking the form it did without the benefit of Christian ideas of compassion, the nobility of poverty, and indeed the metaphysical ideal of an end point after which suffering and injustice are eliminated (which is not to say that Marxism and Christianity are finally compatible).

Trust plays a major role, it hardly needs saying, in the Bible. The key incidents in Genesis, the episodes which give us a metaphorical idea of the future of Christianity and the ways in which God and man will interact, describe the construction of a trust-based relationship between God and the chosen people. For example, in one well-known tale God repents of His creation of man after seeing the wickedness on Earth, and decides to destroy mankind with a flood; but Noah finds grace in His sight, and so is saved by constructing an ark. The ark, symbolic of the church that will protect believers in the time to come, holds the nucleus of future life on Earth. After the flood, God places a rainbow in the sky as the token of a covenant with man, that He will never again destroy life with a flood.[3]

Man's trust of God in this respect is made concrete by the rainbow, which symbolises God's trustworthiness (it's like a little label attached to a rainstorm saying 'don't worry, I haven't forgotten' – perhaps we might see it as the first logo).[4] This is an important early development in the history of trust – it brings with it a strong implication that, even when the person you are trusting has undoubted authority and power over you, your trust of him or her is dependent on his or her obligations to you being carried out.

And of course, immediately we accept the idea that God Himself has obligations towards us, even obligations that He has voluntarily taken upon Himself, we are confronted with the mystery of human suffering. This leads, almost inevitably, to the greatest poetry in the Bible, the Book of Job.[5] Job is a God-fearing man of substance from the land of Uz. As a result of a petty argument with Satan, God allows Satan first to destroy Job's children, servants and cattle, and then to strike him down with a foul disease. Satan wins the argument, as Job curses the day he was born; he doesn't go as far as cursing God at any time, but he demands to know why man was put on Earth, he denies sinning and denies the justice of his suffering, he demands that God explain Himself, and he laments that he doesn't have the power to bring God to book for His arbitrary rule. Four 'comforters' visit Job, and try to rationalise his suffering – though the reader is fully aware that their analyses are false – and Job replies to them with anguished, driven poetry that expresses violently his sense of injustice: 'He destroyeth the perfect and the wicked'.[6]

Job is ultimately cured, but before the end insult is added to injury when his plaints are finally heard by God, who brushes them aside with a breathtaking account of His own transcendent powers: 'Where wast thou when I laid the foundations of the earth?'[7] Job, says God, is not big enough to contend with Him, and His power will always prevail. Nevertheless, God turns out to be pleased with Job, who has maintained the truth of His arbitrariness throughout his ordeal, and is angry with the comforters who rationalised the injustice away.[8]

Job is a deeply troubling book. It is not alone in the Bible in its depressing message – Ecclesiastes says pretty much the same – but we have to accept that Job's faith, though the root of his ultimate redemption, provides no consolation. The burden of the Book of Job is that there is no consolation, no set of rules to avoid pain, and that God's supreme power renders Him immune from what we might consider traditional limitations of fairness. For sociologist and theologian Adam Seligman, this is trust in its pure form, trust in the 'complete other' whose will is completely opaque to our understanding.[9] Such alienation is hard to take after the story of Noah; the anonymous author's poetic anger is fuelled by the injustice, and readers through the centuries have struggled to understand the confused world of Job in the context of the rest of Christian teaching.

A different aspect of trust is introduced by the story of Abraham and the founding of the Jewish people. God tells Abraham to 'Take now thy son Isaac, whom thou lovest, and get thee into the land of Moriah; and offer him there for a burnt offering upon one of the mountains which I will tell thee of.'[10] Abraham's son Isaac is precious to him; he was born when Abraham was 100 years old, and despairing of ever producing an heir with his elderly wife Sarah. Nevertheless, Abraham goes through with the sacrifice, and is on the point of slaying his son when God calls to him to stay his hand, 'for now I know that thou fearest God, seeing thou hast not withheld thy son, thine only son from me'.[11]

This is a brutal way of proving trust, but the test mirrors the sacrifice that God will ultimately make, the sacrifice of His only son for the wellbeing of mankind. It is important that it is Abraham who is asked to make this sacrifice, rather than another of the patriarchs, for God changed his name from Abram to Abraham precisely to symbolise his centrality as father of many peoples ('Abram' means 'exalted father' – i.e. Greek 'patriarch' – whereas 'Abraham', according to Genesis, means 'father of many nations').[12] Via the father of the chosen people, God is therefore asking mankind as a whole to make the same sacrifice that He will have to make to redeem man, and He is pleased to see that Abraham trusts Him. Intriguingly, Abraham trusts God absolutely, while God requires some proof of faith before He will trust man.

Nevertheless, we see that this extraordinary incident contains the germ of the idea of trust containing reciprocity – if I trust you, then you should trust me – an idea that will help strengthen bonds within peoples and groups. The downside of this reciprocity is that it will be correspondingly harder to reach out to those who are beyond a particular group. It will be more difficult to establish relations of trust with an outsider or a group of outsiders.

The Greeks

The other great pillar of Western civilisation, of course, is Ancient Greece. The Greeks were an intellectually questing people, who thought about anything and everything in extraordinary detail, usually in amazingly acute ways that set the tone for discussions on similar topics for millennia afterwards. They also came to many opposite opinions; consensus was not their long suit. It was inevitable that trust, being the ubiquitous phenomenon it is, would come under their scrutiny, in many different debates and forms. Greek views of trust could take up a library of books; let me restrict myself, with some regret, to just three instances of Greek ideas that remain with us today.

Friendship

Well, the Greeks didn't invent friendship, though they had a (much disputed) word for it.[13] Aristotle, in particular, devoted two of the ten books in his *Nicomachean Ethics* to friendship.[14] The Greeks tended to see physical love as a bodily function best governed by etiquette rather than moral precepts, but other types of affection they studied very closely, and friendship was very important to them.

Friendship, it was thought, contributed to the good life, and since that was what everyone should be striving for, friends should be universally sought.[15] Friendship was highly reciprocal; one wants the best for one's friends, and one wants it for the *friends'* sakes, not one's own. But equally, one wants the best for oneself, for one's own sake.[16] Hence, as Aristotle argued, one loves one's friends as one loves oneself.

Friendships all involve trust, of course. What Aristotle is saying, in effect, is that one's trust in one's friends must be almost unbounded. He does not think that all friendships have this property; we can be friends with people because they are useful, or because they are pleasant to be with (either physically or mentally).[17] But on the highest level of friendship virtue seeks virtue, and people of good character will seek out others. In such a friendship, the selfishness and egoism inherent in the search for the good life will be dispersed, because one comes to regard one's friends' interests as one's own.

It is here that the specifically moral nature of trust begins to show through in Western civilisation. Friendship is good, and friendships require trust; hence without trust one cannot be good. In the basic, raw meaning of 'trust' which we sketched in the opening chapter, trust is a way of saving oneself the time and trouble of finding things out. In the Biblical understanding, trust – of God, rather than anyone else – is a prerequisite for being included in the Jewish (later, Christian) community on Earth and in Heaven. But on this Aristotelian idea, trust becomes part of one's specifically moral visage. Trust in one's fellow man is not only advantageous, it is *good*.

Scepticism

The Greeks had a chaotic tendency to develop each and every possible opinion, and for these to produce a cacophony of debate.

Disagreement was one of the *leitmotifs* of Ancient Greek thought. They even disagreed about disagreement. One of the major schools of Greek philosophy was *scepticism*, the idea that nothing should be trusted at all.

Most of the work of the pioneering sceptics is lost; one early philosopher later claimed as the first sceptic was Pyrrho (*c.*360–*c.*270 BC), hence one branch of scepticism became known as *Pyrrhonism*. It is hard to piece together Pyrrho's own philosophy from the fragmentary evidence.[18] The philosopher from whom much of our knowledge of Greek scepticism is derived is a relatively obscure writer from the 2nd century AD called Sextus Empiricus, who was completely forgotten for 1,000 years after his death, and about whom we know next to nothing, except that he wrote a few works including an extremely useful textbook about scepticism and the sceptical life called *Outlines of Pyrrhonism*.

Scepticism seemed to flourish in the medical profession,[19] and Sextus appears to have been a medical man. The reason for the medics' embrace of scepticism may have been that the plethora of medical theories, based on speculation about what was the real cause of the various symptoms doctors were called upon to treat, did little to cure patients but much to increase doctors' confusion. (Though conversely, the existence of such high-flown theories helped doctors to become respected professionals with esoteric knowledge, *experts*, as opposed to mere healers.)[20]

The sceptics developed quite a subtle idea, which is that if there are two big philosophical theories which basically say two opposite things, and there is no obvious way of choosing between them, then entering into the philosophical debate is pointless. In fact, even having an opinion is pointless; if two great philosophers can't reach a consensus, what can *I* contribute?

For example, Karl Marx believed that the distinction between public and private life began in the 18th century; Hannah Arendt believed the same distinction ended then. Whom should I believe? Well, if I believe Marx, I am in effect saying that Arendt was wrong. But she was a lot cleverer than I am; how can I set myself above her? On the other hand, if I take her arguments as decisive, then I am setting myself up above Marx, who was also cleverer than I am. Either way, I am being presumptive; I should withhold my assent. There is no doubt a truth here, but I am not equipped to see it. As the early poet Xenocrates put it:

> And the clear truth no man has seen, nor will anyone
> Know concerning the gods and about all the things of which I
> speak;
> For even if he should actually manage to say what is the case,
> Nevertheless he himself does not know it; but belief is found over
> all.[21]

If a theory does not refer to observable entities, then even if you happen to be correct – and the sceptics refuse to rule out the possibility that any theory is correct – you can't *show* that you are. If you try to show you are correct, then, says Sextus, you will either come up against rival theories, or your explanations will require more explanations in an infinite chain, or they will have to rely on a hypothesis that is merely asserted.[22] It is not possible to produce an argument for a theory that will prove its case against an opposite theory.

So Sextus advocates withdrawing assent from everything, claiming that then a feeling of wellbeing will follow. Philosophers still argue about the extent of the withdrawal of assent that Sextus prescribes – do we only refuse to judge philosophical, medical or scientific theories, or do we go so far as to reject any matter of fact whatsoever?[23]

The extent of scepticism didn't matter for a Greek medic, who only cared about his patients, and who, according to the sceptics, was now licensed to rely on his common sense and experience rather than what often seemed (and were) remote and uninformed theories about unknowable matters. Doctors of a sceptical bent advocated collecting and remembering their perceptions of particular diseases, and particular reactions to cures. They looked at the evidence, and tried not to go beyond it. Such gathering of the facts and refusing to theorise more than necessary is the beginning of the idea of *empiricism*, the idea that science is based on the evidence of our senses. The name 'Sextus Empiricus' actually means 'Sextus the empiricist'.

What has this got to do with trust? Well, the sceptical philosophers take us to the idea that trust goes beyond faith, and can – in science in particular – be rooted in argument. Trust should be backed with reasons, not merely the authority of the person promoting the idea. They take us to a position that bases action on *mistrust*.

So a sceptic will mistrust until there are good reasons for trusting. The position is *risk averse* – someone sceptical in this way needs to be persuaded very hard to change his view. Such a scepticism, a constructive mistrust, could be brought to bear against theories that claim that particular new systems or ideas will transform everything for the better (theories such as Marxism, or the free market philosophies of the new right). This sort of scepticism declares that such theories of complex things like society are too uncertain to act upon. Alternatively, such a scepticism suggests action (or inaction) when expert opinions conflict, as, for example, in the question of whether BSE can be transferred to humans, or whether the measles, mumps and rubella vaccine can cause autism.[24] In these cases, a risk-averse, mistrusting sceptic would refuse to eat beef, or refuse to give their child the vaccine.

In other words, scepticism and mistrust lead to a form of *conservatism*. We can trace the development of this strain of conservatism through Western political thought quite easily, via Montaigne (1533–92), who was one of the first Renaissance thinkers to rediscover the works of Sextus Empiricus in the 16th century, to Edmund Burke (1729–97), who opposed the French Revolution on grounds that Sextus would certainly have approved of, through to political figures of today.[25]

The Hippocratic Oath

Another interesting innovation in trust that the Greek medical profession gave us is the *Hippocratic Oath*. Hippocrates (460–377 BC) is credited as the author of 76 extant texts, although many were certainly written by other hands.[26] The great achievement of him and his followers was to turn diffuse Greek medical practice into a profession. Medicine was a freelance activity at that time, and there were no professional qualifications. Therefore trust was an important mechanism, and a doctor's *reputation* was what secured – or did not secure – his living.[27]

The Hippocratic corpus of work lays down, in effect, certain guidelines for trustworthy conduct. For example, a doctor should not allow financial considerations to affect treatment, should treat the poor as well as the rich, should not extend or curtail treatment in order to maximise profits, and should not negotiate payment. He must treat the patient's testimony as strictly confidential. He must be gentle and dignified, and should concentrate on correctness of treatment, not on a vulgar display of skill.

The Oath shows us how trust may be made more mechanical. One of the great things about trust, as mentioned in Chapter 1, is that it saves time and energy. When X trusts Y to do A, then X does not need to do A herself, she does not need to watch over Y while Y does it, and she can make decisions quickly, on the assumption that A will be done. If her trust in Y is justified, X will be better off trusting her. What the Hippocratic Oath does is to prescribe a set of actions on the part of the person trusted, which will establish trustworthiness. So while the trusting relationship saves the truster a good deal of time and energy, something like the Hippocratic Oath (in 21st-century managementspeak, a *code of best practice*) saves the trustee the time and energy of working out what to do to be trusted. In our above algebra, Y knows immediately what to do in order to gain the trust of X.

So, a Greek patient looking for a doctor can save time by going directly to one who has taken the Hippocratic Oath. The doctor need not worry about what ethical behaviour is – the Oath lays it out for him. Much time is saved on both sides. The principle of the Hippocratic Oath is used in all professional contexts nowadays, in order to promote trust and preserve standards.

The coming of modernity: Edmund and Cordelia

Dante's 14th-century world, described at the opening of Chapter 1, was a well-ordered and regulated one, with everything in its place in what has been called the great chain of being. Nature was a rational and benevolent arrangement. But this medieval outlook was gradually eroded in favour of a contingent worldview, in which the good did not always prosper and the bad did not always receive punishment. The chief apostle of this view was the Italian politician and thinker, Niccolò Machiavelli (1469–1527).[28]

Machiavelli's works on statecraft, drawing on his own experiences as a leading administrator of the Florentine Republic, are uncompromising in their pragmatism, as he describes how best to achieve and retain power. Ideals, whether Christian or secular, are rejected in favour of a view of power as the ultimate political prize. Once you have power, argues Machiavelli, you can pursue your ideals, if you have any; without power, you cannot. Therefore power is the *prerequisite* of achieving what you want to achieve in the world. Those who are over-scrupulous about obtaining power will be that much less able to transform the world as they want it.

The complex moral relationship between ends and means which this view creates is still being argued over today. Should politicians appeal to their activists, or compromise and move to the mainstream? Should environmentalists work with multinationals, or against them? Should the religious retain their traditions, or should they tailor the language of the Bible and the form of their services to appeal to 'growth constituencies' and to 'young worshippers'? In each case, ideological purity – the medieval view – will more likely than not lead to impotence, while compromise – Machiavellianism – will lead to a certain amount of limited power to push the world in the right direction, though never far enough.

The chief innovation of Machiavelli was to bring mankind out of the thrall of history and tradition; why do something now just because you used to do it before, especially if it is not particularly to your advantage? The debate over the new pragmatism was fierce. A hundred years or so after Machiavelli was writing, William Shakespeare (1564–1616) was still engaged in the debate, with most of his chronicle plays pitting a fixed and proper order of the medieval style against a scheming machiavel (i.e. a representative Machiavellian character); virtually every aspect of this clash between the medieval mind and modernity was portrayed in Shakespeare's plays. The rightful king could be brilliant (Hamlet), weak (Henry VI) or wayward (Lear); the machiavel could be sympathetic (Falconbridge), evil (Richard III), even on the side of right (Antony).[29]

His greatest machiavel, Edmund, bastard son of Gloucester in

King Lear, announces his arrival with a blistering soliloquy aimed at his half-brother Edgar.

> Thou, Nature, art my goddess; to thy law
> My services are bound. Wherefore should I
> Stand in the plague of custom, and permit
> The curiosity of nations to deprive me,
> For that I am some twelve or fourteen moonshines
> Lag of a brother? Why bastard? Wherefore base?
> When my dimensions are as well compact,
> My mind as generous, and my shape as true,
> As honest madam's issue? Why brand they us
> With base? with baseness? bastardy? base, base?
> Who in the lusty stealth of nature take
> More composition and fierce quality
> Than doth, within a dull, stale, tired bed,
> Go to th'creating a whole tribe of fops,
> Got 'tween asleep and wake? Well then,
> Legitimate Edgar, I must have your land:
> Our father's love is to the bastard Edmund
> As to th'legitimate. Fine word, 'legitimate'!
> Well, my legitimate, if this letter speed,
> And my invention thrive, Edmund the base
> Shall top th'legitimate: I grow, I prosper;
> Now, gods, stand up for bastards![30]

For the medieval mind, this speech is pure villainy. However, for us moderns, it is rather harder to appreciate its contemporary impact. Amoral the speech certainly is, but we do not find that hard to deal with. What the modern audience finds very difficult to argue with is Edmund's complaint of injustice. Edmund is the equal of his brother Edgar, yet he is deprived of property and power by his loving but traditionalist father merely because he was created in 'the lusty stealth of nature', and is not 'honest madam's issue'.

For Shakespeare, the problem of the Machiavellian modernity, as compared to the medieval chain of being, was that no one was what he seemed, that people's stations (and therefore deserts) could not be determined in advance, that ambition, drive and, in the end, ruthlessness would inevitably win out. After the removal of the solidity of the medieval hierarchies, nothing is there to take their place except flux. The machiavel is master of the moment, but cannot control the flow of events, and is driven to ever greater cruelties. We see the whole process in Macbeth, who begins the play with a nature 'too full o'th'milk of human kindness'[31] and ends it as a 'bloodier villain than terms can give [him] out'.[32] Even the most evil of them all, Richard III, is overwhelmed; he ends with the prick of conscience after waking from a nightmare in the last night before his death.

> Give me another horse! bind up my wounds!
> Have mercy Jesu! – Soft, I did but dream.
> O coward conscience, how dost thou afflict me!
> The lights burn blue. It is now dead midnight.
> Cold fearful drops stand on my trembling flesh.
> What? do I fear myself? there's none else by.
> Richard loves Richard; that is, I am I.
> Is there a murderer here? No – yes, I am:
> Then fly. What, from myself? Great reason: why?
> Lest I revenge. Myself upon myself?
> Alack, I love my self. For any good
> That I myself have done unto myself?
> O, no! Alas, I rather hate my self,
> For hateful deeds committed by myself.[33]

In such a world, where no one is resigned to his proper place, and where the most amoral behaviour will always win out, trust must be severely restricted. Shakespeare is very alive, in the post-Machiavellian world, to the fact that in such a situation, the honest man is always at a disadvantage. He cannot even trust his own eyes, because the ambitious machiavel may be able and willing to rig appearances to create false impressions. Othello trusts the false evidence with which Iago incriminates Desdemona; Brutus is fooled by Cassius into joining the conspiracy against Julius Caesar. And, equally, when we cannot trust our eyes, we, like Hamlet, may not trust when we should.

Perhaps the most telling example occurs at the beginning of *King Lear*, when Lear upsets the natural order by throwing off his responsibilities in an abdication of the throne in favour of his three daughters. The evil daughters Goneril and Regan fake endless over-the-top gratitude and love: 'Sir, I love you more than word can wield the matter', says Goneril, and Regan goes even further, 'I profess myself an enemy to all other joys.' Cordelia, however, who represents goodness and fidelity to the traditional ways, cannot go along with the flattery and the charade: 'my love's more ponderous than my tongue'. When Lear asks how she can top her sisters' oaths, she replies that she cannot.

> Unhappy that I am, I cannot heave
> My heart into my mouth: I love your Majesty
> According to my bond; no more and no less.[34]

Lear is maddened, and cuts Cordelia out of the spoils. He learns the hard way through the play not to trust smooth flattering tongues.

But the irony is that, on the medieval view of the world, Cordelia's dignified speech tells Lear all he needs to know. She loves him according to her bond, i.e. no more and no less than a daughter should love her father – more than anyone, with the exception of a future husband. Cordelia is merely being honest, and Lear cannot see it. Again, to the modern mind, Cordelia may seem somewhat proud. Why should she not tell the little white lie, flatter the old man, for the sake of remaining a player in the game, preventing Goneril and Regan from carving up the whole kingdom, and keeping the love of her father? The preservation of power is what Machiavelli would recommend, since, powerless, she can do nothing to prevent her sisters driving Lear into madness. It seems a small and correctable sin, and would do so much less harm than her stubborn honesty.[35]

Shakespeare's – and Cordelia's – reply would be that that would continue the evil work of effacing the difference between appearance and reality, still further undermining the foundation of trust. If Lear had simply concentrated on the impossible, outrageous claims of Goneril and Regan, and stopped to think about what Cordelia was *really* saying, he would have realised who was trustworthy, and who was not. But he didn't, and from that moment, Lear and Cordelia were lost. Goneril, Regan and Edmund win the day, but ultimately cannot control their destinies. As they fall, though, neither Lear nor Cordelia can take advantage and regain past glories. Once the old system is destroyed, it cannot return.

What does Shakespeare tell us? In the Machiavellian world, a world we recognise today, of social mobility and meritocracy, the old certainties of the feudal system are swept aside. We have moved, in Marshall McLuhan's phrase, from a world of roles to a world of jobs.[36] The war between the sophisticates of modernity and those who accept their stations in life was to go on for centuries after even Shakespeare – we can see the endgame being played out in Anthony Trollope's Barsetshire novels, for instance –

but in effect, after Machiavelli, trust would have to be created and maintained dynamically, as people move social position, and use others for their ambitious ends. Modernity is characterised by uncertainty.

The Enlightenment and rationality

The overthrow of traditional feudal ways finished the medieval world of Dante for which Shakespeare was already feeling nostalgic. But while the greater freedoms eventually resulted in the creative thinking that brought us the agricultural and industrial revolutions, dramatically increasing wealth and welfare for society as a whole (though, notoriously, not for every individual in it), the new world was seen as harsher and more violent. In particular, a problem arose which, in many ways, is one of the defining questions of modernity: if it is not God-given, why is there social order at all?

In the Shakespearean world, everyone had his proper place, and as long as people kept to their proper place, society functioned well. God sat at the top of the hierarchy, and gave the whole structure legitimacy. But a result of the new freedoms was that even God began to be questioned. After reformation and counter-reformation there were many different ideas of God floating around; holy writ was available in vernacular languages, and did not have to be interpreted from the Latin by a priestly caste. It would be false to say that atheism was rife, but we can say that God's nature was sufficiently disputed that from the 17th century on, people were less confident in imputing particular purposes to God. Without God to legitimise the social hierarchy, the reasons for it looked less impressive. Edmund's plea for his merit to be recognised over his illegitimate birth had found its time.

The hope that gradually developed over the course of the 17th and particularly the 18th centuries was that man could justify social arrangements, not by pointing to contingent traditional practices, which might be extremely unjust and non-optimal, but by *rationality*. Social arrangements should be *engineered* in order to be *just*, *humane* and *sensible*. The movement expressing this hope, known as the *Enlightenment*, was mainly nurtured in France, though other notable centres existed elsewhere, particularly in Edinburgh.[37] The idea uniting the otherwise quite disparate Enlightenment thinkers was that our social arrangements could be worked out by reason. It should be possible to produce a social system that commanded respect by being obviously the *best* system, and it should be the case that the more rational a society is, the better it will be (it will be seen that to a large extent this is the opposite of the Greek scepticism discussed above, though the Enlightenment developed its own brand of scepticism through the work of David Hume, discussed below). The interesting corollary of this for our purposes is that trust should be a rational approach to our interactions with others. It should be possible to show that any sensible rational person should trust his or her fellows, in other words, that there are good reasons, appealing to everybody, for trusting.

The 17th-century political thinker Thomas Hobbes (1588–1679), in his great work *Leviathan* of 1651,[38] developed a theory of the state based precisely on this idea. He wrote at a time when the legitimacy of government in Britain was under severe threat, in the aftermath of a partially successful revolution against despotic, if relatively benign, kings who claimed that their sovereignty derived ultimately from the God who determined their lineage. Increasingly few citizens of Britain were buying that story, which served only to underpin desperate inequalities of wealth and power, and a demonstrably incompetent government (and why would God want to do that?).

Hobbes developed the idea of an authority's having to provide security in return for the legitimation of that authority. This is a very Western interpretation of authority; it is not emphasised in Confucianism, for instance; as we saw above, we see the germ of this idea in the Biblical stories from Genesis. Hence when the Tudor and early Stuart kings of England demanded legitimacy by birthright, because that birthright was God-given, Hobbes was able to give voice to the suspicion that this was ingenuous and self-serving, and ultimately doomed to failure as a political argument in that context.

Hobbes' view was that the state, to be legitimate, must command the support of the governed. But why should people want to be governed at all, why should they support *any* state? To answer this, Hobbes famously examined life without government. In what he called a 'state of nature', with no mediating structures or institutions, we would be stuck in a war of all against all, with massive competition for resources. People would only act as individuals, and cooperation would be impossible.

The reason for this, Hobbes claimed, is that cooperation can never get off the ground. If two people are going to cooperate, then each has to trust the other to do her bit of the work. But how can such trust build? It is possible that if the two people had worked together before, then they could trust each other on the basis of their past experience, but that can't account for the *first* time they worked together. It is possible that certain people – family, friends – might be able to trust each other without prior experience, but these only account for a tiny number of the actual examples of cooperation that we see around us.

Hobbes' answer to the dilemma was that some sort of sanction had to be available for defaulters. Those who betrayed a trust should receive some punishment (not necessarily a formal punishment – it could be a social sanction such as ostracism). One way for this to happen would be for the aggrieved party to carry out the punishment herself. But such a scheme would mean that, although the stronger party could plant one on the weaker party, the weaker would be correspondingly powerless, and so it could not work; true cooperation requires sanctions to be reciprocal, available to *both* parties.

Hence the sanctions would have to be provided by a neutral party, a rudimentary state – which Hobbes called 'Leviathan', after the Biblical sea monster. Leviathan would be the sole legitimate holder of authority and force, which it would use to enforce agreements and contracts even-handedly. Given such a source of sanction, cooperation becomes possible. And now, says Hobbes, people previously in the state of nature would be queueing up to enter the realm of Leviathan. Hence a state gains a sort of *contractual* legitimacy through being the sole authority, underpinning the benefits that flow from mutual trust. Hence the requirements of our private lives produce the beginnings of public life.

Hobbes' fable is not intended as a strict historical account of how the state evolved; it is a thought experiment designed to show us how the state gains legitimacy by doing something that is essential in society, yet impossible for any private citizen to accomplish.[39] And it has not gone unchallenged; many thinkers have taken up Aristotle's thought that man is a political animal to suggest that actually people organise themselves into structures that can support trust. Indeed, people are generally trustworthy. At the other extreme from Hobbes, the anarchists believed not only that people are perfectly capable of organising their lives without the heavy hand of the state upon their shoulders, but that it is the state itself that causes untrustworthiness, by distorting social relations (for example, creating property rights) and so opening up the space for crimes such as theft.[40]

Nevertheless, this is the beginning of the Enlightenment enterprise of demonstrating that trust is rational. In Hobbes' view, people can see that their *advantage* lies in banding together to put themselves under the authority of a state, because that will enable trust, and therefore enable cooperative ventures etc. You can trust me, because I dare not let you down, and vice versa.

But this surely cannot be the whole story of trust. For if it is only fear of punishment from Leviathan that keeps us in line, then it is a pretty attenuated set of dealings we have. First of all, it doesn't *feel* like that when we do actually trust. Trust, from the inside, can feel like a precious and wonderful thing, in some circumstances; when one trusts and is trusted by a lover, for instance, it does not do the feeling justice to say that it is conceived solely out of fear. And secondly, if it were only punishment that we were trying to avoid, we could betray trust whenever we thought we could get away with it, whenever Leviathan wasn't watching. But the whole point about trust (the dark matter of the soul) is that it holds our society together – it cannot merely be something that we ditch when we think we're OK. It is certainly true that people are more likely to behave in reprehensible ways when they think they are unobserved or otherwise untouchable – this truism acts as the premise for many a reality TV show – but if fear of Leviathan was the only reason to be trustworthy, then it would be rational to betray trust almost all the time. The presence of a strong state cannot of itself be enough to create trust.

Added to which, the state itself has its agents, who also have their own interests. Hobbes' picture relies on our keeping our venality in check by agreeing to a strong state – but who keeps the state in check? If people resort, as Hobbes claims, to untrustworthiness whenever they are not restricted by a state, then why should the agents of that state not resort to untrustworthiness themselves? Are they watched over by a Leviathan of their own?

And who keeps an eye on *that*? Conversely, if the agents of a state can be benign in their dealings with others, then why can't ordinary people? As a result of arguments of just this sort, Enlightenment thought developed more sophisticated views of trust and rationality.

David Hume (1711–76) suggested a model that incorporated a more realistic view of human nature.[41] Whereas Hobbes thought man essentially ambitious and self-interested, Hume pointed out that people can be motivated by all sorts of other more pleasant feelings, friendship and sympathy for others, for instance. Accordingly, his *Treatise* was advertised on the original title page as 'BEING An ATTEMPT to introduce the experimental Method of Reasoning INTO MORAL SUBJECTS'. Even if trust can be explained by rationality, as the Enlightenment project insists, one may still feel better when it is one's friends or family who gain. One may create trust out of the pleasure that such sympathetic feelings bring.

This is a more agreeable model of mankind than Hobbes gives us. But fundamentally it still doesn't produce the trusting and trustworthy behaviour that we know we are capable of. We have a complex public life of justice and fairness, and we often act in just ways even when there is little sympathy there to be exploited. Of course, as Hume pointed out, we prefer people closer to us, with whom we have more sympathy. We are more likely to behave well towards our family, our spouses and children, our friends and our townspeople. But actually we also behave well towards complete outsiders. Consider child murderers; despite our revulsion for their crimes, and our lack of sympathy for them, we generally support giving them fair trials, and oppose giving them cruel and unusual punishments. Even in this extreme case, we behave according to principles of justice and fairness that don't seem to be supported by human sympathy.

The end result of Enlightenment argument about trust and our social bonds was the thought of Immanuel Kant (1724–1804), who insisted that we were extremely moral creatures with a strong idea of duty that underpinned such notions as trust.[42] We are capable of being governed by moral precepts, and such precepts should be universal, that is they should apply to everyone equally, to be properly moral. This massively influential and important principle Kant called the *categorical imperative*. Justice depends on this complete neutrality with respect to others, a willingness to treat everybody equally whoever they are, however they are related to us, whatever their history. This explains our trusting behaviour, according to Kant, because the universality of the moral prevents us from interpreting our obligations towards others in ways that favour ourselves. If it is all right for me to rat on a deal, it must be all right for everyone else too. Jean-Jacques Rousseau (1712–78) took this thought, and made it relative to individual societies, by invoking the idea of the general will of a society that provided the moral underpinning, which some have found more plausible than Kantian universalism.[43] Between them, Kant and Rousseau may provide the ideal and the actuality underlying much of our public and political trust.

So the Enlightenment gave us the idea that trust is, in some sense, in our interests, and that we are trustworthy because we benefit from it. It is rational to trust and be trustworthy (though arguments continue about how far and where rationality can take us).[44] We do it not because we are forced to, because we want our place in Heaven, because we have found our correct place in society; indeed some have argued that trust based on fear is hardly trust at all.[45] We do it because, however hard-headed we are, we feel that in some sense we will be better off. It is a foundation for the new capitalist society, where social stability can exist despite the apparent mutual antagonism of competition and free markets, memorably introduced by another Enlightenment thinker, Adam Smith (1723–90).[46] In post-Enlightenment society, people need reasons for doing anything; trusting is no different.[47]

As I say, this has been a partial history of trust in both senses of the word. But the net result is that trust, in the West at least, is now seen as something from which we expect to benefit (both from the general practice of trust throughout society, and from the individual cases when we entrust), inevitably reciprocal, and something that must be earned. It is the basis for our peculiar systems of capitalism and democracy, which in turn have shaped the practice of trusting and concepts of trustworthiness. What may turn out to be the major social change of the last couple of hundred years is that capitalism and democracy have made our trust – in our roles as consumer and voter respectively – much more valuable and sought after than that of the medieval peasant. Put another way, we have become more powerful. In the next chapter, we will look at the ways that thinkers have charted that increase in power.

CHAPTER THREE

Trust and Social Cohesion

Studying trust

Following the new departures of the Enlightenment philosophers, a new question began to seem pressing: as modernity prized rationality, individualism and what Adam Smith called 'enlightened self-interest', how was it that society did not collapse into factions driven by shabby, cold calculation? Why do we stick together at all? Why is there kindness, charity, tolerance? Unsurprisingly, many of the answers focused on the role of trust.

Hence, for the first time, Western society's experience of trust was shaped by thinkers determined to unravel the mysteries of trust itself; trust moved into the foreground, and the discipline of *sociology* emerged. The focus on social cohesion faded as sociology developed;[1] nevertheless, the analytic tools of the early sociologists remained, and the intellectual tradition continued. Trust has been a central topic of investigation through to the present day. As we shall see in this chapter, the major questions about trust remain stubbornly unanswered. What are its forms and functions? How do we reconcile the interests of the individual and his or her society? How can a society keep errant members in line (and when is that justifiable)? How important, relatively, for keeping order are social norms and individuals' interests?

A dream of many sociologists and politicians has been the creation of social institutions that foster and promote trust. It is partly the failure to answer these questions that explains the failure of that dream.

Trust as a consensus of values

Emile Durkheim (1858–1917) was in many ways the father of sociology, pioneering the 'scientific' study of religion and morality. The problem he wrestled with, like many sociologists after him, was the difficult move from tradition to modernity, from the certainties of the primitive life to the complexity and uncertainty that characterise the industrial world.

Trust seems easier to understand in the traditional world, where the circle of one's acquaintances is manageable, and work and technology are severely limited – the main source of one's sustenance is repetitive agriculture, generating such a small surplus if any that disposal of it is straightforward. Strangers are few and far between, and trust can build up via personal knowledge of most of one's interlocutors. Independence is prized, and one's only responsibilities are to a restricted set of people (typically family). Low surpluses mean low education, and so the tendency for differential habits of mind to develop is also flattened.

However, such a set of values is harder to sustain in the modern world – the classic description of the difficulties is Halldór Laxness' epic novel of 1934–5, *Independent People*.[2] Modernity relies on the creation of vast economic surpluses to finance the leisure to support education, art, thought, health care, scientific research and so on. This entails breaking the traditional identification of a person with his or her labour, the division of labour into simpler, more routine steps and the reintegration of these steps to create goods. These routine steps can then be performed either by lower-skilled workers, or often by technology. The integration of the basic tasks is overseen by a managerial class, often based within a single firm; one of the jobs that a firm does is to bring together all the people, doing low-level tasks, needed to produce particular items. The result is that workers by necessity have to interact with a much wider circle of acquaintances; the economics of the situation often require many of the new industrial workers to be brought together in a central spot, which can lead to many of the problems that plagued England in the 19th century, and which still can be found in, for example, Mexico City, Rio or Shanghai – overcrowding, poor sanitation and health, pollution and high crime.

In such situations, economic forces encourage people to think primarily of themselves, and to reduce radically the set of others over whom they have responsibility. Adam Smith in particular emphasised the benefits to all of everyone aiming to improve their own lot. Furthermore, the need to bring workers together meant that people would often be separated from their parents, siblings, or other members of their extended family. They would, gradually, lose touch.

So, for Durkheim and the early sociologists, the problem is quite simple: given that the forces of modernity seem to make trust less likely, while simultaneously destroying the traditional bases of trust, how can society continue to function? And his conception of the purpose of sociology entailed that sociology should be able to help provide mechanisms for keeping society going.

Modernity frees individual judgement from the shackles of collective judgement. This, for Durkheim, was both threat and opportunity. Social solidarity should be nurtured by exploiting the values that people do hold in common. The division of labour encourages individualism and individualistic thinking; hence if social solidarity and trust are to occur, there must be a link between the values of society and the values of its members. Moral conduct in an individualistic world will be mediated by thought and reflection, as opposed to the traditional world in which much moral conduct is unreflective and determined by authorities (such as priests, medicine men, etc.). Hence a society needs to ensure that its collective values are such as to promote moral consensus among reflective moral agents. Where a moral consensus exists, an integrated, cohesive society will be found. As the major central institution, it is the function of a responsible state to try to develop and inculcate this consensus.[3]

To take an illustrative example, many societies display the basis of their moral consensus, and often use explicit symbols. In the USA, the flag, which is displayed in schools, government offices and so on, is very important in uniting that country of disparate incomes and attitudes. France uses the three ideals of the revolution, liberty, equality and fraternity, to bring people together; essential in a centralised nation that nevertheless contains several million people of non-French origin. The UK has gone a different way; the traditional focus on individual liberty and non-interference has meant that it has been able to provide asylum for a multitude of persecuted and hunted people, of whom Karl Marx is only the most famous. However, in the post-September-11th world, many people now believe that the UK is home to too many people whose fundamentalist ideologies are inimical to the 'British way of life', and the idea of citizenship tests (uncontroversial in many other nations) is beginning to be discussed tentatively. Even though many British people find it hard to put their finger on any particular values that the UK stands for, the fear is that moral consensus is breaking down, and that so-called indigenous values are under some sort of threat.[4]

Trust, says Durkheim, develops from shared commitment to consensual norms of moral behaviour. Two people trust each other because they each come from the same moral community. Even if both are individualistic, they can sublimate many of their egoistic demands to the society in which they have a moral stake, and as a result social solidarity can get off the ground (once the basis for solidarity and trust is laid, then an ordered society should be relatively self-sustaining). Relative to society, its members become selfless; the consensus of values promotes a consensus of interests, and the respecting of ties of obligation, mutual sacrifice and even altruism.[5] On the other hand, if there is a lack of consensus about values, then even if one person subscribes to collective values, she cannot be sure that people she interacts with will also subscribe to them.

Durkheim's view is an optimistic and conservative view. He lays an emphasis on social order, and this is prior to any other ideal for society. In particular, order comes before justice for Durkheim; if someone has to endure some unfairness in order to preserve social solidarity, then that is often, if not always, a price worth paying. In his attachment to communities, and his recognition of the importance of duties and obligations alongside liberties, Durkheim is a forerunner of the communitarian movement in American and British politics.[6]

The move to modernity

Durkheim's work set the parameters of our understanding of trust: the fit (or lack of it) between the requirements of society and those of its members, and the methods of bringing over-individualistic people into line. He was optimistic about the possibilities of this, but needless to say this optimism has not often been shared.

Occupying a rather more pessimistic position is the other grand old man of sociology, Max Weber (1864–1920).

Durkheim looked upon the individual and society as more or less of equal status within his theory, although the individual would, in certain circumstances, have to relinquish some rights in order to promote social solidarity. Weber, in contrast, saw society as an agglomeration of distinct individuals and their myriad interactions. Such individuals are largely rational, and perform actions in order to achieve goals.

A society conceived like this is, of course, in danger of disintegration. The goals that Weber's individuals are interested in are personal goals – and they may not happen to coincide with the needs of the collective.

According to Weber, trust will be founded on mutual interest and interdependence. The characteristic relationships of modern life – business dealings, professional contacts, employment relations – will provide a basis for a new type of solidarity in the rationalistic world, and a new basis of identity. Today's commuter, say, in a suburban housing estate will need to develop an identity that is very distinct from that of someone in a traditional society. The bonds that bind him or her to the modern world may be harder to detect than the overt symbols of the traditional. These bonds may be very much less spontaneous or personal, and may focus on material goods. They may be mediated through the market.[7]

These tenuous Weberian bonds are neatly described in the short stories of John Cheever, written at the height of the American phenomenon of the 'company man'.[8] In the fictional suburb of Bullet Park, various souls try to create fragile identities among unforgiving friends/competitors, as they sip their martinis and swap their wives. Neddy Merrill tries to recover from an unnamed disaster by swimming home via his former friends' swimming pools; Cash Bentley relives his youthful successes as a track-and-field star by hurdling the living room furniture.[9]

But, despite the fragility and potential for downfall, Cheever's characters can find happiness and identity with hard work and luck. 'The worm in the apple' describes the Crutchmans, a couple with a perfect marriage, perfect jobs and perfect kids, always considerate of others and prepared to do their social duties uncomplainingly. Their neighbours are desperate to find out what is wrong in their lives, and wait gleefully for them to take a fall. But they are to be disappointed.

> With their own dear children gone away the Crutchmans might be expected to suffer the celebrated spiritual destitution of their age and their kind – the worm in the apple would at last be laid bare – although watching this charming couple as they entertained their friends or read the books they enjoyed one might wonder if the worm was not in the eye of the observer who, through timidity or moral cowardice, could not embrace the broad range of their natural enthusiasms and would not grant that, while Larry played neither Bach nor football very well, his pleasure in both was genuine. You might at least expect to see in them the usual destructiveness of time, but either through luck or as a result of their temperate and healthy lives they had lost neither their teeth nor their hair. The touchstone of their euphoria remained potent, and while Larry gave up the fire truck he could still be seen at the communion rail, the fifty-yard line, the 8.03, and the Chamber Music Club, and through the prudence and shrewdness of Helen's broker they got richer and richer and richer and lived happily, happily, happily, happily.[10]

The narrator of 'The fourth alarm' has misgivings when his wife agrees to appear naked in an amateur dramatic production. When the audience is invited to strip naked on stage too, he does so, embarrassed, but finds he can't bring himself to cast aside his car keys or wallet. Humiliated by the actors for his shallow materialism, he runs from the theatre. But he finds curious and ample consolation in the real world outside.

> It was still snowing. It looked like a blizzard. A cab was stuck in front of the theatre and I remembered then that I had snow tires. This gave me a sense of security and accomplishment that would have disgusted Ozamanides and his naked court; but I seemed not to have exposed my inhibitions but to have hit on some marvelously practical and obdurate part of myself. The wind flung the snow into my face and so, singing and jingling the car keys, I walked to the train.[11]

We often feel guilty about our materialism, and our relative lack of generosity and compassion as we retreat into walled and gated estates. Cheever shows how, sometimes at least, such feelings can be the basis for some kind of trust and community; taken together his stories provide a kaleidoscopic view of a Weberian world.

It is a hard task to construct trust in a Weberian market-oriented society, and there need be no value consensus. A modern secular society throws away many traditional values, and replaces them not with values, but with goal-oriented rationality. As Cheever reminds us, we need to be constantly on the lookout for failures in our humanity, and to balance our interests with those of our fellows. More pessimistic than Durkheim, Weber warns that if the moral basis for institutions is thrown away and instrumental reason over-privileged, we risk destroying the conditions for trust; we risk creating order without trust.[12]

Trust as an integrative force

Trust, then, is ideally based on a consensus, but can function even with only basic agreement and minimal emotional contact between people, or with very few authoritative institutions to foster solidarity. Weber is surely right to say that, in a modern society, we cannot hope to rely on consensus as Durkheim had hoped. The question that now arises, if we take Weber's ideas on board, is what we can expect trust actually to *do* in a society; what functions can it achieve?

One strong theme in social science is that of trust as an integrative force. Talcott Parsons (1902–79) was one of many who tried to pick their way between the atomistic tendencies of modern society, and the individual-crushing force of social solidarity. He agreed with Durkheim that shared values and norms of behaviour were the key, though he didn't go as far as saying that society should be fostered at the expense of the individual. The lack of promotion of such values was the problem in social disintegration, for Parsons; for example, many problems in mid-20th-century America were caused by a lack of support for values by governmental and authoritative institutions.[13]

So, for instance, American values of justice and freedom were reasonably widespread; such values were displayed in a series of depression-era movies such as *My Man Godfrey*, *Fifth Avenue Girl* and a string of sophisticated if sentimental comedies made by Frank Capra. President Franklin D. Roosevelt had begun the process of redistributing wealth from rich to poor with his New Deal. But the institutions that would cement social justice – while protecting freedom and privacy – were not in place, and there was therefore little to restrain self-interest.

We might take another example from Britain today. Britain is a relatively tolerant multicultural country, and most people are prepared to make some commitment to promoting racial harmony. Terms of racial abuse are now more taboo than Anglo-Saxon 'four-letter words'.[14] Such tolerance is one of the shared values that bring us together as Britons. But without institutional support, most obviously from anti-racism legislation, tolerance can easily break down in the face of a few actions from a few racists. In the forgotten corners of Britain, northern industrial towns with little economic hope, racism can be made live once more. Shared values and consensus are easier to achieve when governmental institutions work together to promote them, and to show how they can produce benefits.

It would also be fair to note that such institutionalisation of norms helps produce integration and mutual trust, but often at the expense of justice or prosperity. The Durkheim/Parsons ideas were certainly understood by the Nazi Party in 1930s Germany, or indeed nowadays in the mismanaged and erratic North Korean Republic of Kim Jong Il.

The extent of integration that can be achieved in a society will of course depend on the consistency between the institutions and the values of individuals. Hence the basis of trust, for Parsons, is in the artful choice and crafting of social and institutional roles.[15] As we saw in the previous chapter, the Hippocratic Oath helps foster trust in the medical profession, not because swearing an oath makes a person trustworthy *per se*, but because it describes what we want a doctor to do, and represents a small commitment to that ideal of public service. Its potency is purely symbolic, but it describes a set of values to which doctors and patients can subscribe, and which are constantly being reaffirmed. Doctors who take the Oath will be prepared to set aside their own self-interest for that of the collectivity.

However, trust must go beyond institutionalised roles. After all, if the institutions change, and therefore institutional roles change, that does not entail that a society's morality must change, so there must be more to trust and morality than such roles.[16] Parsons is clear that trust and solidarity depend on relations not only between individuals, but also between institutions themselves. Systems need to interact in order to preserve trust – they have expectations of each other just as much as individuals have. If a particular institution is trusted, then it can be used to achieve social goals. People will 'go along with it'. But if that institution is rendered illegitimate, most usually by other institutions, then our interactions with it will become merely self-interested. We will use it for our own ends, and ignore it otherwise. It will not be trusted and social solidarity will have declined in that institution's area of competence.

For example, many churches have declined in importance in the last century. Scientific discoveries have made their theology look outdated, and increasing cultural heterogeneity has made their pretensions to speak for 'the people' look implausible. As a result, they have been less able to carry out their traditional functions, for example raising and distributing charity, or acting as moral guardians or pressure groups. However, evangelical groups, particularly in America, have usurped governments' traditional role of speaking for the oppressed and downtrodden. Governmental schemes for distributing welfare are perceived as inefficient, iniquitous and bureaucratic, while evangelical charities are seen as much more successful. One result of this is the incorporation of such churches in governmental schemes under 'compassionate conservative' President George W. Bush. This erosion of the constitutional distinction between church and state has gone barely noticed in the States, whereas only a decade ago such a move would have led to an almighty political row.

Even if we don't accept Parsons' ideas in detail, we can borrow from him the idea that trust can bring individuals together, particularly when shared values are embedded in institutions. In this way, the individual and society can be brought into something like harmony without crushing the individual's freedom to dissent. The first function of trust is to help integrate society by helping people accept that they are all 'working towards a common goal'.

Trust, rationality and cooperation

A second key function of trust is to enable people to cooperate. The branch of social thought, very prominent in economics and political science, that is most engaged with this function of trust is *rational choice theory*.[17] Rational choice theory exploits the idea that people will often make decisions on the basis of a consistent set of preferences, and in many ways is the endpoint of much of the Enlightenment thinking that we briefly reviewed in the previous chapter.[18]

Rational choice theory cannot, of course, hope to present a complete picture of human decision-making – for the obvious reasons that people are not always rational, do not always have consistent preferences, and are not always self-interested. But it does have two important advantages.

First, it operates on a minimal set of assumptions about people. Hence it can produce very general predictions and theories. The reason rational choice theory is so associated with economics is that that discipline deals with aggregates of people, and rational choice theory is therefore called upon to explain not so much an individual's actions, as those of a whole population of individuals. So, for example, if the price of something goes up, that tells you very little about whether Abigail or Brian or Chloe will decide to buy it. But over the economy as a whole, the theory predicts, usually successfully, that *fewer* people will buy it. In the context of social solidarity and trust, the minimal set of assumptions means that rational choice theorists can avoid Durkheim's optimism – rational choice accounts tell us how much trust there would be even in the worst case where everyone is selfish. If some people choose to be altruistic, then so much the better.

Second, it connects the individual and the collective. Decisions made by rational self-interested actors in the theory are based only on considerations that the actors themselves can see and appreciate. Yet sometimes at least the individuals' behaviour all comes together to produce cooperation and beneficial results for society as a whole. The actors can see that they will benefit in the longer run from cooperative behaviour, and so the theory can to an extent reconcile the individual and the collective (Hobbes' theory of the creation of Leviathan in the state of nature relies on an early version of this insight).

Rational choices do not always lead to trust. As James Coleman has pointed out, just because everyone realises there is a requirement for a system of norms or voluntary constraint, that does not mean that such a system will appear.[19] Many theorists are candid about the need to understand rational choices alongside or embedded in a system of norms.[20] The norms of society and our individual preferences each influence the other.

Nevertheless, rational choice theory, exploiting the mathematical theory of games,[21] does claim a number of interesting results explaining cooperation in such a way as to dispel the mystery of why individuals should apparently throw aside their self-interest.[22] Sometimes an account involves reinterpreting what counts as self-interest. At the beginning of the 20th century, the anarchist theorist Peter Kropotkin stressed the cases of altruism that occurred in nature, showing how these required some kind of alteration in the theory of evolution, with its slogans of competition and the survival of the fittest. The adjustment was duly provided some decades later by biological theorists such as

Richard Dawkins, who tried to show how people and animals are in many ways hard-wired to produce behaviour that will ensure the transfer of our *genes* to the next generation, rather than selfishly to behave in such a way as to improve our own *individual* chances of life. On such a conception of self-interest, it might be in your interests to help your brother or sister to reproduce; hence you might in some circumstances sacrifice yourself for others.[23]

But there are many cases where the best results are produced by a more thoughtful examination of one's interests. Much social behaviour can thus be explained using only the minimal assumptions of rational choice theory, combined with a sensitive characterisation of interest. As Adam Smith pointed out, the baker gives you your daily bread not out of altruism, but out of self-interest; if he were altruistic, there would be far less bread to go round.

The second major function of trust, then, is to promote cooperation. Cooperation is often in our interests, and on a basic set of assumptions about human nature we can identify situations when it is in other people's interests to cooperate with us. We can also engineer such situations (e.g. when we set up a firm). We can then trust the others, not on moral grounds, but merely because they are rational and self-interested.

Complexity and uncertainty

A third function of trust is the reduction of complexity, as emphasised by sociologist Niklas Luhmann (1927–98). Luhmann noted that the modern world possesses greater complexity than more traditional societies, partly because, as we noted earlier, the division of labour entails that we need many more interactions with many more people. Furthermore, there has been a movement away from danger and towards risk.[24]

In other words, our current actions have many more repercussions in the future. Hence the problem with action in the modern world is not that there is any present danger, and hence a requirement to check for that danger and try to take steps against it. Rather, the difficulty is that, in time, in combination with other circumstances that may be extremely difficult to predict, the conditions are created to produce damaging consequences.[25]

For Luhmann, these circumstances have created a requirement for trust in modern societies. It can reduce the complexity by allowing inference beyond available information, producing generalised expectations of behaviour, and allowing us to discount uncertainty. We don't need to map out the whole truth when we trust.[26]

And similarly, although we may be aware that our actions produce risk, by trusting in risk-amelioration systems we can cease to worry about the risk. For example, we trust the system of money. Notes and coin are intrinsically worth much less than their face value, and so – as we noted in Chapter 1 – if we make an exchange for money, we are taking a risk. But we trust the monetary system, which stops us worrying about the risk. The risk is not negligible; hyperinflation in Germany remains the worst example of a failed money system, while Argentinians rioted when the peso was uncoupled from the US dollar in 2002, and the Burmese found their savings rendered worthless overnight in 1987 when President Ne Win abolished all notes and coins whose value was not divisible by nine, for mad reasons of his own. However, there are systems in place to ameliorate the risk; few of us know anything about them, and if we did not trust them the economy would be in serious trouble – but we do trust them.

It is, therefore, often rational to trust. But Luhmann takes a less schematic view of human nature than many rational choice theorists; just because trust is generally good and useful doesn't mean that it can be conjured from out of a hat. Trust has to be learned slowly, even while increasing complexity means trust is increasingly required. Luhmann is optimistic about the supply of trust, though, because trust is so often the easier option, at least in the peaceful and stable societies which constitute the focus of this book.

Trust, contracts and social capital

Trusting someone is therefore very like having a *contract* with them. Economists see trust as lubricating exchanges in exactly the way that contracts do – the parties to the exchange can worry about the relative values of what is being exchanged, and forget about the risk that they will be defrauded by the other. In the case of a contract, there is some external force that will, in the final analysis, enforce the contract (usually the government). In the case of trust, the parties are assumed to intend to be trustworthy.

The advantage of a contract, then, is that it is enforceable. The advantage of trust is that, although fraud is still possible, the expensive mechanisms of contract enforcement can be dispensed with. Furthermore, trust is flexible in a way that contracts are not. Contracts specify future behaviour in foreseeable contexts. Trust, however, will operate even in unforeseen circumstances. In the event of some weird unpredictable contingency, trusting and trustworthy parties will usually be able to muddle through, whereas contracts simply can't cover all possible contingencies.

We can therefore see why Hobbes and other Enlightenment thinkers attempted to ground trust in contractual or quasi-contractual relationships. Trust and contracts are very analogous, though they operate in different contexts, and have slightly different properties. Indeed, recent studies have shown that the development of trust is actually *inhibited* by binding contracts (not so with non-binding contracts). Where a binding contract governs an exchange, parties tend not to extend trust, leaving the contractual obligations to govern acceptable behaviour in the exchange. The contractarian tradition may well need to adapt to the facts of human behaviour.[27]

Nevertheless, the parallels between trust and legal and economic instruments have been very suggestive to theorists. One especially influential idea is that trust (and related phenomena) constitute a type of social *capital*, capital that works very much the same as economic capital does, as something to be *invested*, that can be *lost* or *squandered*, but which, when invested wisely, can lead to important *gains*.

Social capital theories work on both the individual and the national level. On the micro level, the leading figure is Robert Putnam,[28] whose studies of American local clubs and societies led him to theorise that the experiences people gain from such clubs help them come to behave in trustworthy ways, and to build up their stock of social capital, that then goes to 'fund' their behaviour in wider society. Therefore the problem, as far as Putnam is concerned, is that the decline in the numbers attending such societies is leading to a decline in the amount of social capital being generated, and that therefore many functions of wider society that require social capital will collapse – the amount of trust in society will decline.

Is that bad? Well, yes. The leading theorist of social capital at the macro level is Francis Fukuyama,[29] who argues that the differences in rates of economic expansion between nations can largely be explained in terms of their being high-trust or low-trust countries. Countries such as the US or Japan do well with their high levels of social capital, whereas others such as Italy and China do correspondingly less well. The social capital model, then, sees the function of trust as providing enough social 'glue' to allow advantageous social relations to emerge; a stable, coherent society is what counts.

This is the first theory of trust that feeds on the idea of trust being in decline; to a large extent it was Putnam and Fukuyama that fostered the notion of a crisis of trust in the 1990s. We shall look at their diagnosis of the problem in more critical detail in Chapter 9 when we consider the nature of that crisis. As it is, we should be aware in reading their work of its neoconservative tilt; the aim, apart from fostering the crisis itself, is to describe the crisis in such terms as to make it an axiom that government intervention will inevitably undermine the important spontaneous socialisation that the theory postulates, for more or less the same reasons that contracts undermine trust.[30] Many facts get shoehorned into the theory for the sake of this neoconservatism. For example, Fukuyama's argument, that economic success depends on social capital which depends on shared senses of identity, suddenly requires him to make the, on the face of it, bizarre claim that America, the individualistic country *par excellence*, is not actually individualistic at all.

> Americans typically think of themselves as individualistic, or harking back to their pioneer days, as rugged individualists. But if Americans were traditionally as individualistic as they think they are, it would be hard to account for the rapid rise of giant corporations in the United States in the nineteenth century.[31]

Fukuyama struggles for some pages to make his case. On the way, he makes the correct point that America also has a strongly communitarian streak, no doubt based on its religious heritage. This may be all he needs for his argument about America's economic health, but if America is not an individualistic place I don't know where is.

The interesting point that the social capital theorists make is contained in the name of their theory; trust does function, metaphorically at least, like capital. It is a form of wealth. To explain poverty (Fukuyama) or social breakdown (Putnam) as a result of a lack of social capital may take the metaphor too literally; nevertheless they are surely right that it can provide a partial explanation of social failures.

Trust in public life: reputation

Theories of trust have proliferated during the last century and a half. The parameters of the debate were set by the optimistic, socially minded Durkheim, and the pessimistic, individualistic Weber; ever since it has proved difficult to reconcile the arguments for optimism and pessimism, for individualism and collectivity. Since then, three valuable functions of trust have been identified: social integration, as claimed by Parsons; cooperation, as claimed by various rational choice theorists; and complexity reduction, as claimed by Luhmann.

It seems clear that these different theories are not going to be reconciled very easily. The only alternative to making a choice between these well-argued and entrenched positions is to create a synthesis, a theory that takes all these functions and distinctions into account. An important recent attempt at such a theory has been developed by Barbara A. Misztal,[32] who continues the 20th-century tradition of sociological *description*, rather than the Durkheim/Weber project of attempting to find mechanisms for society's *improvement*. She follows Parsons and Luhmann in producing a *functional* theory of trust; that is, a theory describing trust in terms of its functions, its effects on and contributions to society. This is partly to enable trust to be recognised, and partly to explain why trust flourishes (when it does). However, she parts company from Parsons and Luhmann when she attributes *three* general functions to trust; her predecessors, as we have seen, saw trust as having an individual function (and argued about what that individual function was). Figure 1 illustrates her synthetic theory.

Misztal's work is very useful for our purposes. Recall from Chapter 1 that we are not interested in developing a general account of trust; we are interested in particular in public trust (as opposed to the interpersonal), and in stable, developed societies. Most work on trust has, as we noted in Chapter 1, tried to isolate trust from other social phenomena, to produce a theory applicable to all societies. This is unrealistic. My approach, in contrast, is to isolate the societies we are interested in, and then to produce a theory of trust *and related concepts* applicable to those societies.

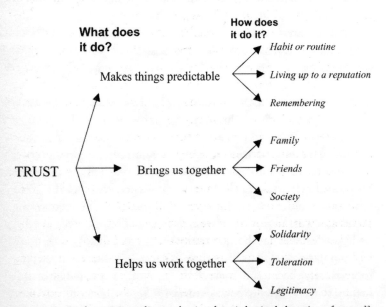

Figure 1. Barbara Misztal's synthesis of sociological theories of trust.[33]

The value of Misztal's work, then, is that, unlike the other sociological theories we have reviewed in this chapter, it brings together various practices and structures that go to make up trust – the components of trust if you like. So, though her theory has more generality than we need, we can select the components in which we are interested. The questions we will be looking at concern how we can interact within different institutions, whether many of the processes that produce value in our liberal-capitalist societies are ultimately trustable. Can we invest after Enron? Is it worth voting after sleaze and corruption are exposed? For questions like these, the key factor that creates and supports trust is *reputation*.[34]

Reputation has its bad side. It can slide easily into stereotype, where people or things are unfairly assumed to possess certain characteristics, based on a general (and often inaccurate) model of their wider social identity. Young black men are stereotypically criminal, for example. But though it may be true that young black men are statistically more likely to have criminal convictions, it is clearly unjust to assume that any particular young black man conforms to the stereotype (even if we ignore the very pressing questions about the ways that the criminal justice system treats black and white youths differentially).

Reputation is a common, and socially held, understanding of a person's standing with respect to trustworthiness. A reputation provides us with information about what that person (or institution) is likely to do in the face of our actions. It therefore helps with our *predictions* about what will happen. The reputation serves as a warrant for trust; we can single out trustworthy people, and also decide what they are trustworthy for. Equally, someone's bad reputation helps us to reduce risk by observing what they do more closely; because it is expensive to watch over someone, it is helpful to have a guide to who should be watched over. It enhances cooperation, via predictability.

A reputation is also something that needs to be invested in, and guarded. We shall see examples of people and institutions trying to create reputations later on; we shall also see the problems that can be fomented by attempts to ruin reputations, for example in the fields of business (Chapter 6) and politics (Chapter 8). Reputations are distillations from a vast number of individual events and actions, and are very creatively managed, both by their bearers and by others with an interest in bringing someone down; the media in particular have a giant job to play, because they are the ones that draw our attention to one set of events that tell 'the interesting story' (Chapters 7 and 8).

Expertise is another aspect of reputation; a group of experts will collectively try to maintain a joint reputation which they can all share, and inherit, by preserving a monopoly of knowledge about the domain of their expertise (Chapter 7). Expertise acts as a reservoir for reputation, upon which experts can all draw down. Because of this, when that expertise is seen to have failed in some way (for example with the BSE crisis, discussed in Chapter 7), reputations of all experts tend to suffer.

Finally, reputation makes a number of presuppositions about identity. The connection of an individual's identity with the group identities he or she might reasonably share in is an intriguing knot of issues. To take one obvious example, left-wing political parties are tacitly understood to be 'against' wars or non-negotiated resolutions of conflict (reality may well be very different from the reputation), and such parties often attract votes on the basis of such reputations; hence much of the anger that accompanied Tony Blair's participation in the Second Gulf War. His fiercely and cogently argued moral case for war counted for little alongside the sense of betrayal of a large cohort of his natural supporters.

What is interesting in that case is how potent group identities are; Blair's attempts over ten years to rid his party of most of its old associations clearly were not sufficient to prepare many of its voters for this. When even individual identities are very fluid, there is a problem in hoisting *any* kind of reputation – and therefore any kind of public life – in such circumstances. The Internet is an example of such a domain, and I shall be discussing it in Chapter 5.

The paradigm case of a reputation is the reputation one can receive in a small community (as a womaniser, a drinker, a gossip), and then have great difficulty shaking off. But for reputations to function in the public sphere, there need to be mechanisms for disseminating and supporting them across space and time. In the next chapter, we will look at how reputations get spread; we will look at the functions of *institutions*.

CHAPTER FOUR

Trusting Strangers

Trust is often based on one's own personal experiences. We use knowledge to inform our trust, to decide who and what is trustworthy, and that knowledge can most easily be gleaned locally. If I go to my local garage, I know that they are trustworthy; if my car breaks down in a strange town, I have no idea whether or not I'll be ripped off.

Yet, obviously, if we are to move beyond the village, if we are to develop – and of course, we *have* developed – extensive, distributed societies where we can easily acquire relationships with people we have never met, will never meet, then trust needs to go beyond personal acquaintance. This chapter will discuss how that happens.

Socrates, speech and writing

We take the extension of trusting relations beyond personal acquaintance for granted; it may be surprising to realise that many thinkers have resisted such an extension, and have tried to develop a conservative vision of restricted communication and trust;

certain strands in radical green thought tend in this direction, for example. One of the earliest attempts to chew on these issues was an early work by Plato (*c*.428–*c*.347 BC), the *Phaedrus*.[1] This piece, like most of Plato's works, is written as a dialogue between Plato's teacher and hero Socrates and an interlocutor after whom the dialogue is named, in this case a young admirer of oratory, Phaedrus (who also appears in Plato's *Symposium*). Much of the dialogue shows Socrates arguing that good oratory requires an understanding of philosophy and psychology, and that such knowledge is essential for great rhetoric. In particular, he argues against views – fashionable then in Athens as much as in today's spin-riddled politics – that rhetoric should be judged by its effects on the audience, as opposed to its fidelity to the facts.

For an encore – which is where we get interested – Socrates goes into a riff about the differences between speaking and writing, specifically the superiority of the former over the latter – superiority which is based on trustworthiness. I think it is reasonable, given what we know of Socrates and Plato, to assume that, though Plato is the author of the piece, and fully responsible for its content, the representation of Socrates in the *Phaedrus* is pretty faithful, and that the argument against writing that Socrates produces in the dialogue is likely to be based on actual arguments that Socrates was wont to deliver.

We moderns find it very difficult to appreciate such views, particularly in a context of almost universal literacy, and when there are clear correlations between literacy and other indicators of social health such as poverty, disease and repression. Writing seems essential to a well-ordered society – and indeed is the source of some of the most profound, and the most trivial, pleasures we know.

Two thousand five hundred years ago, of course, literacy was by no means as widespread as now. And documentation, at that time, was regarded with some suspicion; although classical Greece was of course a literate society, the full implications, the full set of possibilities that literacy could bring, were not realised for some centuries after the Greeks adopted writing. In the Greek comedies, for example, when written documents make an appearance, they are often seen as something new and suspicious, and those that write them as figures of fun. Plato it was who, in his *Republic*, began to sketch the new, literate, way of life as a departure from the old, heroic, oral culture of Homer.[2]

But even though Socrates could not reasonably expect to put the genie of writing back in the bottle, he could imagine living a professional life without committing anything to the page. Indeed, he did just that – despite his reputation as a major philosopher, he never wrote anything. Our main sources for Socrates, ironically, are the writings of two of his friends, Plato and Xenophon.[3]

Plato preserves for us the flavour of Socrates' philosophy in his dialogic representations of his arguments. The *Socratic Method* (or *elenchus*) is a question-and-answer technique that can be used to demonstrate to an interlocutor that his or her assumptions, interpretations and beliefs are inconsistent. To argue in a Socratic way, one has to coax some bold assertions from one's opponent, and – preferably without asserting any concrete opinions of one's own – ask simple questions to expose the points of tension in the opponent's position. The result of the argument will be a greater respect for the complexity and difficulties of the topic under discussion. The modern-day philosophical technique of *deconstruction*, associated with post-structuralists such as Jacques Derrida, has the similar aim of exposing the unexamined assumptions underlying philosophical positions.[4]

Part of the Socratic argument against writing is an extension of an argument against technology of *any* kind. Such an argument trades on the fact that technologies spread skills more *widely*, and allow a task to be performed either by more people, or with less effort (often both). Hence, in some sense, technology reduces the *richness* of experience; it reduces creativity and induces routine. There are many benefits of this process of course – this is why the spread of technology is almost unstoppable in virtually any society – but Socrates takes the romantic view that experience, work and interaction with the world should where possible be *authentic* and *raw*. Writing, for Socrates, reduces the incentives for people to learn, remember and generate wisdom; the great texts become little more than crib sheets.[5]

I won't pursue this argument here, as it is somewhat tangential to our theme – as I say, in our literate (and democratic) times, it is hard for a modern reader to appreciate, although actually the change in consciousness that Socrates forecast has been detected after the fact by later writers.[6] The benefits to an individual of the cultivation of wisdom unaided by writing may be large, but in the nature of the case would be restricted to a very small class of people with the wealth and leisure to do it. Plato was an unreconstructed aristocrat, and would be comfortable with such a restriction. I shall assume – not least because you have bought this book – that you agree with me that the benefits of the written word should be spread as widely as possible. Furthermore, to a very large extent, the constraints of the method of communication used determine what exactly can be said; early written forms vastly increased the capabilities of language and thought (for instance, logic and geometry began to be developed in this period).[7] Western civilisation would surely have been the poorer without them.

What is more germane is the second half of Socrates' case, put with his usual delicate irony.

> SOCRATES: You know, Phaedrus, writing shares a strange feature with painting. The offspring of painting stand there as if they are

alive, but if anyone asks them anything, they remain most solemnly silent. The same is true of written words. You'd think they were speaking as if they had some understanding, but if you question anything that has been said because you want to learn more, it continues to signify just that very same thing forever. When it has once been written down, every discourse roams about everywhere, reaching indiscriminately those with understanding no less than those who have no business with it, and it doesn't know to whom it should speak and to whom it should not. And when it is faulted and attacked unfairly, it always needs its father's support; alone, it can neither defend itself nor come to its own support.[8]

This is a very interesting argument. It has four stages. First, we are invited to consider a painting. It might look like a person, say, but if we try to treat it as a person, we soon discover that it is two-dimensional and static. If we ask Picasso's *Blue Guitarist* for a quick strum, or a gossip about Picasso, or directions to the post office, we will be disappointed. Written words are similar in this respect; they seem to be making sense, to be establishing a point, but if we want to know more, we can't simply ask them. My previous chapter discusses Durkheim, I hope interestingly and adequately, but if you really want to know about Durkheim's view on political legitimacy, then it is no good addressing the question to the relevant page. The page will continue to present the discussion of Durkheim and trust. If that's what you want, then great; if not, then the written word cannot help you. On the other hand, if I were giving a *lecture* on Durkheim and trust, even using the very same words as I wrote earlier, you could stick your hand up and ask me about Durkheim and legitimacy. My answer may or may not be what you want to hear, but you would get a fresh answer to your specific question. Of course, the spoken word does not do this itself, but the circumstances in which words are spoken mean that the hearer is in the presence of the speaker, and can ask for such clarification.

Secondly, the written discourse 'roams about everywhere'. In other words, once the text is written down, the author loses control over the piece. A speaker can decide to whom he should speak, and if he does not want a particular person to hear his words, he merely has to shut up, or whisper. But a piece of writing, once committed to paper (still more if reproduced by professional copiers or printers), could turn up anywhere; it does not select its readers. The written word doesn't even require a physical form to be problematic; in our hi-tech age, many political, business and personal disasters begin with an incriminating email. British readers may remember the incautious email sent by Jo Moore, a bumptious spin doctor, suggesting that the major significance of the horrific terrorist attack on the World Trade Center was that its domination of that day's papers made it a 'good day to bury bad news'. Attempts by her, and her boss, minister Steven Byers, to avoid resignation after this were ultimately fruitless.[9]

Thirdly, there is a moral, political or pragmatic background to this. It is not just the preferences of the author that count. Socrates and Plato think there are people who should not be allowed access to certain propositions, and so writing these things down is irresponsible. An ancient Greek would not, for instance, want slaves to get wind of arguments for egalitarian democracy. This is not as outré a position as it sounds; 20th-century political theorist Leo Strauss defends a similar line.[10]

Fourthly, the written word provides little help for itself. It could spread its ideas much more effectively if it could clarify its arguments when misunderstandings occur. A speaker, when she sees that inimitable glazed-over look in her interlocutor, knows that further discussion is necessary, and as a result is more effective in communication. Similarly, exposure to argument will strengthen a position (an argument that has been properly examined by hostile attack, like a weathered building, is ultimately much more beautiful, even if not quite what its architect intended). Like speech, writing needs its 'father' to explain it – but, unlike a speaker, an author is generally located too far away from his or her writings to be consulted. In Woody Allen's movie *Annie Hall*, Allen and Diane Keaton are standing in a cinema queue arguing about Marshall McLuhan's work. When they cannot agree, Allen summons McLuhan into shot and gets him to decide between them; the joke, of course, is that that is precisely what you can't do with the written.

As an aside, we should bear in mind that the technology of linguistic dissemination means that this distinction between speaking and writing, which was very clear in Plato's day, is much more blurred now. For instance, it is no longer true that the hearer of the spoken word has to be in the presence of the speaker, for she may be listening to a recording or watching the television.[11] Indeed, even in a period of minimal technology, the relationship between the spoken and the written is not as straightforward as Socrates claims. The nature of the relationship varies over time and across cultures.[12]

But however we characterise the distinction, there is an obvious problem with the argument. The *Phaedrus* is a piece of writing that criticises writing! What gives? It is not at all unknown for idealised views of the spoken to be developed and maintained, for political or philosophical reasons, by highly literate people, but there had better be a strong justification behind them![13]

Plato was certainly alive to the incongruity. If not convinced, he was certainly impressed by Socrates' arguments, and showed them being received by an enraptured audience. But – perhaps because of wider ambitions – he was drawn to preserve and disseminate his philosophical work. He found the solution to his dilemma in the dialogue form. By showing Socrates' arguments in the context of real debates – some of them very one-sided, admittedly – we see how the form of discussion changes as people make points and counter-points, how certain issues get blown up out of all proportion under the particular conditions of an argument. And by presenting philosophical ideas in this warring, shifting, uncertain dialogue form, at least partly in response to Socrates' arguments, Plato himself *contributes* to the blurring of the spoken/written distinction.

Additionally, many of Plato's Socratic dialogues are inconclusive. Typically, the discussion may *disprove* many theories, but it often fails to establish the correct one. In that way, Plato's dialogues (particularly the earlier ones) are different from most academic treatises, which are generally concerned to prove a point and amass the arguments in its favour into a static supportive structure. Plato creates a dynamic, dramatic situation where the arguments come from all sides, and are usually inconsistent with each other, with a concomitant failure to establish themselves. Plato's best dialogues give the flash and shock of good debate. They focus on the *process*, not the *outcome*. It is not even the case that Socrates always wins.[14]

Socrates, through Plato, is arguing that the written word cannot be *trusted*. It may say the wrong thing, to the wrong people. It may mislead, and there is little possibility of putting matters right. Socrates lays great store by *presence*. If he is present whenever his philosophy is expounded, then he remains in control; he can present his ideas in the best light, tailor their presentation to the audience, deny certain people access to them, and evolve them in the light of new information or circumstances.

But when ideas get written down, Socrates says they are almost certain to be misinterpreted and misused. When Socrates refers to the author of a text as a father, the metaphor is to be taken seriously; the author has a duty of care that he or she cannot carry out once the text begins to circulate. And conversely, the author, like a father, has a duty to train his or her words so that they fit in with society and don't do it any harm. All linguistic activity must take place in an atmosphere of distrust; all words may be misused, and the only remedy is to stand by on watch.

The implicit model of trust here is a very limited one. One cannot trust what one cannot see. Trust's writ runs as far as the door, no further. Such a strategy of trust may be possible in Greek city-states such as Athens, or other small highly politicised enclaves. C.P. Snow's novel *The Masters* describes the febrile atmosphere in a small Cambridge college during the election of a new master; this is a fascinating and wonderful insider's study of college life where all the political work is done through the spoken word, through after-dinner chat over port or claret, even among the most highly literate people in the world. And witnesses in court cases have to undergo an oral examination controlled by the defence as part of the protection for the accused. Merely submitting a written account of the evidence, even written under some kind of oath, will not do; witnesses have to take part in a conversation in order that their trustworthiness be assessed by the judge or jury. Only very recently have advances in communications technology enabled some witnesses, such as minors or victims of sexual assaults, to give their evidence remotely. And the reasons why courts insist on oral examination are more or less exactly those given by Socrates to Phaedrus 2,500 years ago.

Nevertheless, Snow's college, with its electorate of 13, or Athens, where a few thousand people at most would be involved in decisions, are a very different prospect from larger, or more distributed, societies. There are certainly realistic contexts in which the spoken word assumes a great importance; the world of diplomacy is one, where committing views or strategies to paper can be seen as unwisely limiting future freedom of action. But politicians could not get things done through the spoken word, revealed individually, in a nation of millions. The American electoral system, strongly based around television, is certainly Socratic in its reliance on direct speech to voters, and on firm control by the speaker of the context of the speech. Yet the *reception* of the spoken word even here is outside the speaker's power; he or she cannot control who hears the speech, cannot address individuals, cannot correct misapprehensions, does not edit the news broadcasts. In a larger polity, some move beyond the Socratic linguistic paradigm is required.

Institutions

These difficulties with the spoken, local view of ideal communication have long been thought to be a defining theme in the development of society. The advantages of allowing trust to transcend personal acquaintance, of trusting the written word, of developing a global trust that reaches out beyond the personally known towards the unknown, are immense;[15] given that trust is essential for a functioning society, such written, global trust can support a society that goes beyond the village or the micro-community. It allows the amalgamation of small communities into larger ones, with all the economies of scale that implies. It allows people to specialise, to differentiate themselves via the services they provide; I no longer have to do my own plumbing, because there are enough people around to support a full-time experienced plumber, and because mechanisms can be brought into existence to create trust in his plumbing.[16]

Of course, trust based on acquaintance can spread beyond physical recognition. I trust a decorator because my good friend has vouched for his workmanship and honesty, even though I do not know the decorator from Adam. But there are limits as to how far such a chain of trust-relations can spread, and how reliable it can be beyond two or three links. If trust is to be truly global, something must of necessity support the bonds of trust that transcend the local. The most practical method yet devised is that of the *institution*. An institution is a group of people organised into roles that, in the case of a guarantor of trust, must perform the checks on behaviour that a reasonably suspicious person would ordinarily wish to do on his own account.

So, for example, companies conduct their business according to rules, in order that there be no disparity of information amongst investors; *auditors* are supposed to ensure that those rules are strictly followed. The individual investor need only read the auditor's report of those companies she is thinking of investing in – she does not have to travel to the companies' head offices and demand to inspect the books.[17] An institution does work to establish trustworthiness so that we don't have to. The net result – consider the time, effort and resources saved on the part of each individual – is that we can trust many more people, and much more widely. Institutions globalise trust.

Some kind of personal trust is still required on the part of the individual. And such personal trust is still based on the experiences of the individual. But the institution now acts as a conduit for that trust. The individual trusts the institution, and the institution then decides who, in its zone of competence, is worthy of such trust. Figure 2 shows how such arrangements massively increase the spread of an individual's trust.

If 'trust' is defined narrowly, then it may seem strange to talk of trusting institutions. Political scientist Russell Hardin argues that trust is an interpersonal matter, for example, and that, in effect, trust is always of necessity local.[18] As he points out, even Hobbes' Leviathan, the powerful trust-enforcing state we encountered in

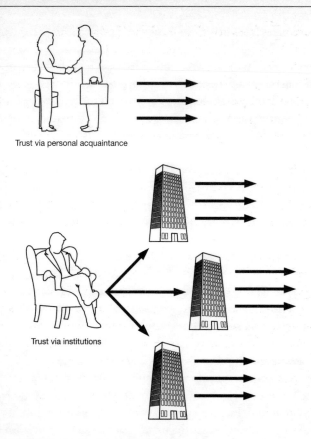

Figure 2. Using institutions to spread trust.

Chapter 2, was designed not to create trust in the state itself, but to promote trust *between* citizens.[19] As we argued in Chapter 1, however, narrowing down the scope of trust, in order to distinguish it from, say, faith or confidence, is not a particularly fruitful strategy. In the case of creating global trust through institutions, the individual still has to have *some* trust-like relation to the institutions, *something* that is depicted by the arrows in the above diagram, and theorists of trust will have to take account of it. Whatever we call it, we will need to include it in our descriptions of the operation of trust; better to save our analytical energies by accepting that the strong analogies between our trust of individuals and our 'trust' of institutions mean that little would be lost were we to remove the inverted commas in this sentence.

The effect of globalising trust with institutions is to increase dramatically the systemic risk. In a world of individual, local trust, suppose I trust ten people, Alf, Bert, Charlie, Dave, Ernie, Fred, Ginger, Harry, Ichabod and Joe. And suppose Ichabod cuts me up – I lend him money and he reneges on the deal. Trust is fragile, so I cease to trust Ichabod, and will probably never trust him again – but I still trust Alf, Bert et al. The loss of trust corresponds exactly to the extent of the betrayal.

Now let us put ourselves in an institutional world, with global trust. I trust an institution, which checks out the financial credentials of several people, let's say 1,000 people. So, because the trusting relation is transferred through institutions of trust, I actually trust 1,000 people. The institution makes the world more trusting, and allows social links to be extended far beyond the local.

However, now suppose that I lend Ichabod money. I do this not because I trust him directly, but because the financial institution tells me that Ichabod is trustworthy, and I trust that institution. Ichabod remains a bad fellow, however, and reneges once more on the deal. I withdraw my trust of Ichabod. But the one ground I had for trusting Ichabod was the assessment of the institution. Trust is just as fragile as it ever was – it is likely that one result of Ichabod's improbity is that I lose trust in the ground of my trust in Ichabod. In other words, I withdraw my trust from the institution as a whole. It has cost me money, and how can I be sure that it won't fail again? But if I withdraw my trust from the institution, thereby I withdraw my trust from all the other 999 people it has certified (unless I have any independent ground for trusting them), Alf, Bert, Charlie et al., and 990 more. The loss of trust is orders of magnitude greater than the extent of the betrayal.

The result of globalising trust through institutions is to increase both trust and risk simultaneously. The potential gains are large, and so are the potential losses. It is essential in such circumstances that the institutions are reliable and efficient, and have effective powers of investigation. These powers typically must exceed those of the individual. It is my lookout if I wish to trust someone because she has a nice smile, or he has a smart suit. Ultimately, the only loser if my trust is misplaced is me. But in the world of institutionalised trust, an institution certifying people as trustworthy had better have proper procedures, because if one of the people it certifies turns out to be untrustworthy, everyone else it certifies falls under a shadow. Uncertainty increases.

Creating trust

When trust is global in this sense, and therefore goes through the institutional intermediary, there are two sets of agents who require trust: the individuals and the institutions. The emphasis for individuals is not so much on trustworthy behaviour, as on meeting important criteria for certification by a trust-bearing institution. This, obviously, can be substantially quicker, in that typically it involves a snapshot of someone's circumstances, as opposed to establishing a history. This need not always be the case, however; a bad credit record can be very hard to discharge.

Another difference for individuals from the requirements of local trust is that the personal qualities of the individuals do not count. The institution that is certifying trustworthiness generally requires that the individual produce the right answers to various questions or criteria. These can sometimes be based on apparently extraneous factors such as race, as in the USA in the years of segregation, but when the institution focuses properly on the factors that are demonstrably relevant to trustworthiness, racism, sexism and other prejudices tend to decline. Globalising trust tends to make such decisions less arbitrary and more rational.

The consequences of individuals' actions matter much more than their motives when trust is globalised. The obvious reason for this is that motives are hard to measure, once we move beyond personal acquaintance, whereas consequences are public and can be inspected by all. The net result is that in a world of globalised trust, individuals are rather more at the mercy of fortune; actions that go wrong can rebound unjustly.[20] Failure to meet a mortgage payment is a failure *tout court*; whether or not the debtor intended to pay it is irrelevant, indeed invisible, to the bank. Theft is theft in the globalised world, whether the thief wanted to pay for designer clothes, drugs or a life-saving operation for their child – despite the obvious differences in terms of morality and personal responsibility. Two schools will appear in the same place in Department of Education league tables, even though they may display very different levels of commitment to their children's education, if the children get the same exam results.

Trust-certifying institutions must also be trusted by their clients. This often means that, like individuals in a world of localised trust, they must demonstrate a track record of reliability. But the basic requirement for an institution in a world of globalised trust is that it has a system in place that can deliver trustworthiness. This means, among other things, that the criteria that it uses to judge individuals can approximate trustworthiness. The criteria are generally inflexible, partly because they have to be shown to be impartial, and partly because it is expensive to tinker with a system once it is in place. Hence they had better be good indicators of the right sort of behaviour.

Unfortunately, when an institution requires particular targets, the incentives for the would-be trustees alter dramatically – trustworthiness is less important, *per se*, than hitting the targets. This leads to what has been called the *performance paradox*,[21] that simple, static measures of performance quickly lose information content, as those being judged learn that hitting the performance targets is more important than the general attempt at 'good performance'. On the other hand, sensitive measures that are changed frequently are expensive to implement, confusing to evaluate, and hard to justify to others. Tony Blair's government's attempts to hold public service to account by performance targets rather than the market mechanisms preferred by his Conservative predecessors have been bedevilled by precisely these problems.[22]

Sanction

So an institution can provide a framework for trust through codes of practice and rules. But this is of little consequence if individuals are likely to revert to either unapproved behaviour, or publicising their heterodox memories of events. In order to be credible as a guarantor of trust, an institution must have decent *sanctions* up its sleeve.

In a sense, the situation is easier with local trust. Although the sanctions available to individuals aren't generally that powerful, in fact peer pressure can be very effective – and peer pressure may be all that an individual can muster. He can also publish any misdemeanours, in order that others may realise the untrustworthiness of a person. Hence untrustworthy behaviour, in a situation of local trust, may lead to someone's risking never being trusted again. This in itself adds weight to local sanctions.

But in the world of global trust, people are more anonymous, and tracing a wrongdoer is trickier in a wider society. Not only that, but, having been 'struck off' one institution's list of trust-worthy individuals, people are able to move on to other institutions with relative ease (consumer programmes on TV, such as the BBC's *That's Life*, often follow the chequered histories of small-time conmen and dodgy repairmen who would register new companies under new names with different professional organisations). And for those untrustworthy individuals handicapped with a conscience, fooling an institution is often less troubling than hoodwinking a person.

Hence an institution that certifies trust must be able to investigate histories, prosecute breaches of trust, and deliver sanctions to the untrustworthy. In short, such institutions must have relatively substantial *power* and *authority*.

Horizontal and vertical

This leads us into a second distinction that will be important in our argument. Some relationships presuppose that their objects are equals; a shopkeeper and a customer have different roles to play, and different responsibilities in the transaction, but there is no possibility of coercion of either by the other (except in very unusual circumstances). On the other hand, a headmaster has authority over his pupils, as does a general over his soldiers or a policewoman over the civilian population (in defined contexts); each can legitimately limit the freedom of action of those over whom they have authority. If we say that the latter relations are *vertical*, because orders can come down from above, then we can call the former relations *horizontal*, implying no imbalance of action between the parties. I will call the parties in a horizontal relation *equals*; this does not mean they are identical. There are obviously asymmetries in such relations; it is just that ultimately, each party preserves his or her freedom of action.

The distinction is not hard and fast; the relation of a bank manager with someone who holds an account with them is often characterised as an authority relation, but can also be seen as a contractual relation between free agents. I am not attempting to set up a distinction with full academic rigour (any more than I was doing with the local/global distinction discussed above), merely to provide some suggestive contrasts for future consideration. The main point to note about the distinction is that when we are in horizontal relations, we preserve the final responsibility for action; in vertical relations we become the object of action (when we're at the bottom). Others do things to us in a vertical relation, we are not fully in control.

The key point about introducing vertical relations is that they change the properties and requirements of trust. If I am in a vertical relation, at the bottom end, I have ceded control of all my actions; I allow (legitimate) authorities to circumscribe my freedom. Sometimes this is done formally, as when I sign a contract, for example with my employers. But this can be informal, for instance if I were the member of a church or a political party. Particularly in the informal case, this introduces the concept of *deference*; I *defer* to the authority, a vicar, a doctor, a politician.

One aspect of a crisis in trust, therefore, could be a decline in deference. In such circumstances, the danger would be that people were either wasting effort by deciding what was the best thing to do (when in the past they would have delegated that decision efficiently to the authority), or getting their decisions wrong (by ignoring good advice). On the other hand, if we have traditionally overestimated the wisdom of our authority figures, then a decline of deference would be rational and timely. It would then be unsurprising that authority figures complain.

Four domains

The horizontal/vertical distinction is independent of the local/global distinction, although it is difficult to sustain global trust without some sort of vertical relations of authority. Hence domains can be roughly characterised as involving trusting relations of four types: local/horizontal (trust in equals via personal acquaintance), global/horizontal (trust in equals via institutions), global/vertical (trust in authorities via institutions), and local/vertical (trust in authorities via personal acquaintance).

In the middle section of this book, I will look at four domains, one for each of these types (see Figure 3). The Internet will be

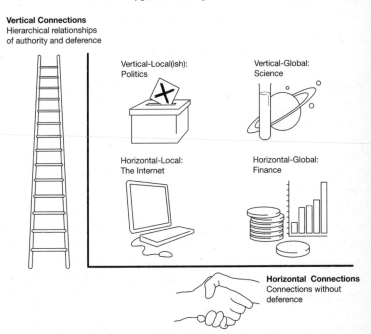

Figure 3. Types of trust relation.

discussed in the next chapter, as an example of a local/horizontal domain (there are few regulatory institutions on the net, and few authority relations). Business is taken as global/horizontal (horizontal relations because I get to decide, ultimately, where I put my money, even if I am very reliant on advice). Science and medicine have enough authority relations, and enough monitoring institutions to be global/vertical. Finally, I take politics, perhaps controversially, as a local/vertical domain; vertical because we delegate powers in democracies to politicians, but local because there are remarkably few institutions between us and them (and controversial because some institutions do have a lot of influence, such as political parties and the media).

I want to do two things in these chapters. First, I wish to show how trust is intended to work, what mechanisms exist to bring people together and reduce risk and uncertainty, and how reputations can spread and act as repositories for trust. However, needless to say, such mechanisms are often fallible. Sometimes they are based on ideal assumptions, which may not obtain in practice. And sometimes the mechanisms have evolved gradually and organically from other practices which may have had other functions, and which may have developed in very different historical contexts. So my second aim is to look at reasons why mechanisms for trust may be failing, perhaps by not providing severe enough sanctions against wrongdoers, perhaps by not reaching people's expectations. In each case I will give a few examples, sometimes in detail, of apparent failures of trust in the domain and try to diagnose the problem. I hope only to be descriptive in these chapters; once we have given ourselves an idea of the scale of the problem, we can start to think about potential solutions to any crisis of trust that we have detected.

CHAPTER FIVE

Cybertrust

Local trust in the global village

Trust in cyberspace has some interesting properties, which are not always replicated in the real world. To begin with, there is very little authority on the Internet; it is a highly decentralised system. There are institutions devoted to maintaining some sort of order, such as the Internet Corporation for Assigned Names and Numbers (ICANN), which manages the system of Internet addresses and domain names (e.g. which ultimately licenses www.iconbooks.co.uk as the homepage of Icon Books), and the World Wide Web Consortium (W3C), which organises inter-operable languages, technologies and specifications for the multimedia bit of the Internet (the World Wide Web).[1]

But the principle of the Internet, like that of life itself, is that a small number of simple building blocks can lead to a dramatic, almost overwhelming, variety of forms. Hence, although there is a requirement to regulate the building blocks themselves via organisations such as ICANN and the W3C, once those are in place any number of online activities and forms can proliferate. In cybermyth if not fact, the creativity and excitement that the

Internet engenders depend on a virtual anarchy. Because people can say pretty much anything they like in cyberspace, ideas – technological, political, artistic – can flourish.[2] People formerly starved of information now have a glut of it, and can hold their masters to rather more effective account. And communications have become instant.

This vision was always unlikely to survive the scrutiny of the authorities, once criminals, terrorists, paedophiles and political subversives discovered the charms of the net. Some countries manage to restrict Internet usage to acceptable sites – in Saudi Arabia, it is the Internet users themselves who suggest sites that should be interdicted (the Internet censors get 500 suggestions a day).[3] The Chinese religious organisation the Falun Gong used to organise effectively in China using the net, but when the government got wise to their use of email and the web, they were forced to back out of the Internet and now they rely on the humble payphone, less convenient but less traceable.[4] Libel laws, and other legal restrictions on free speech, have been used to prosecute websites from different countries, as when a French judge ordered Yahoo! to block French users from seeing Nazi regalia on its pages,[5] thereby giving the lie to the idea that the net could not be brought under local jurisdiction.

But authority is in general a pretty minor presence on the Internet, and the relationships that have developed in cyberspace tend to be what we have called 'horizontal'. In terms of the relations between the denizens of the net, the picture is very flat.

Furthermore, there are few institutions that regulate the net, and so users are reliant on their own resources; cybertrust is local, and based to a surprisingly large extent on personal acquaintance. There are very few independent institutions that can be relied upon to anchor trust or to regulate the Internet space. If you download a document, your choice of whether or not to trust it is pretty well unsupported (other than by finding other sources of the same information, which merely pushes the trust problem a little further back). If you download software, you are in the hands of the publisher.

The question is whether this situation will, or can, continue. As we have seen, trust on the spoken, local model is not generally effective for establishing wide-ranging connections. Given that, we must ask – for example with respect to the burgeoning field of e-commerce – how cybertrust can be globalised with regulations and institutions without crushing the anarchistic tendencies of the Internet that allow creativity and provide all the fun.[6]

The paradox is not only that such localised trust can function even in the global domain *par excellence*. Even stranger, it operates in an area where the notion of identity itself is highly fluid.

The new space

The Internet is often seen as a medium for carrying information. I think this is to underestimate its capabilities; it goes much further than that. In many ways, the Internet can be seen as a *space*.

What do I mean by that? Well, the Internet is an arena in which actions can take place. Unlike other media, the transfer of information is two-way and unlimited. There are connections between actors in the Internet, and indeed the connections may be unsought. There are no monopolies on information sending (unlike media such as television, radio or newspapers, where there are a relatively small number of suppliers and many consumers), and although individuals can exercise some control over whom they encounter on the net,[7] the nature of the space means that there are always unsought interventions, ranging from hacking (rewriting programs without permission), spamming (unsolicited email or newsgroup postings, the electronic equivalent of junk mail) and viruses (programs that can replicate themselves in other computers) through to advertisements and investigations of your websites by others.[8]

The Internet is a space of information, and there are information 'creatures' that roam around it, autonomous software agents that can crawl about looking at websites, doing mundane tasks such as finding cheap air flights, arranging appointments, or bidding in online auctions.[9] Politically, there is obviously a great deal of interest in engaging with people on the net,[10] and its anarchistic, countercultural ethos has encouraged hacking and other informational vandalism as an unofficial tactic in anti-establishment protest, such as anti-globalisation campaigns.[11]

As befits a highly decentralised area, the Internet divides into several subspaces, ranging from newsgroups, to shopping malls, to online games and the quasi-worlds of MUDs and MOOs.[12] These spaces are often partially determined by their own sets of values – very often implicit and not fully thought through – and, equally, the subspaces themselves can determine values. This is not as surprising as one might think; it has long been understood that the architectures that determine our social context can determine our understanding and valuations of the world as a whole,[13] and the virtual infrastructure of the Internet is as restraining and as liberating as any physical architecture.[14]

On the Internet, the architectures define the space. Hence, however trust is created online, the properties of the programs that make the Internet up will be crucial. The nature of the sanctions available to those who are betrayed can be strongly influenced by the structures of the net itself. For example, the very possibility of global trust on the net will depend on whether the programs that create Internet spaces allow any exercise of power at all.

Recall from Chapter 4 that the key aspect of trust with respect to public life is that of reputation. Reputations are generally associated with people or organisations with determinate *identities*, which is what makes the Internet, where identities are fluid, creatable and adjustable, such an interesting case study. More than in most spaces, our online identities are strongly associated with the properties we possess and the roles we play (we might say: *the masks we wear*). Hence the Internet is very open to the difficulties caused by *masquerading*, adopting the properties and roles (the masks) of others. When someone does that, it is very difficult to see through the masquerade online.

Security

If column-inches in newspapers were a measure of importance – which they are not – then computer hacking, viruses, cyber-terrorism would be the most important issues concerning cybertrust.[15] The computing industry, firms, governments, armies and private citizens invest giant quantities of money in computer security: firewalls, cryptographic authentication systems, bio-metrics, access control mechanisms, etc.[16] In 2001, it is estimated that $8 billion worldwide was spent on such security systems, a figure expected to rise to $24 billion by 2006.[17] The idea of all such systems is to prevent attacks on information technology infra-structure. The idea of hacking is not an invention of the Internet age, but of course when computers are routinely hooked up together via telephone lines carrying massive quantities of data from machine to machine, it's made a lot easier – in the same way that, while roads aren't responsible for major crime, they make major crime easier by allowing criminals to get to and from the crime scene quickly.

The war of vested IT interests against hackers will always go on. The interesting point about this struggle is the evolutionary adaptation that it engenders. As a new method of hacking is discovered, the authorities respond with new security measures; these measures are then studied minutely by hackers, who are in competition with each other to hack into new systems; eventually someone cracks the new security system, and the authorities are back at square one. Except that it is not square one, because both security systems and hacking techniques have moved on in the cycle, and something new has to be tried. Because of the malicious nature of the attacks, computer security is an ever-moving target – unlike accidental problems with a system, which, once put right, are fixed for ever.

Hackers tend to have one or more of four motives. Some are filled with the joy of mischief. Some have political motives, perceiving cyberspace as being invaded by big corporations, and wanting to reclaim the net for the individual. Some are fraudsters, wanting access to credit card details, say. And some enjoy the technical challenge. Quite often it is a complex of these motives. For example, the music exchange system Napster enabled people to swap MP3 music files for free. Napster itself was an innovative system design which enabled people to swap files directly between themselves, using only a central search facility. Most of its users were ordinary music fans, whose use of MP3 files was not necessarily a substitute for buying CDs, while some wanted to defraud the music companies out of the returns on their A&R investments, and artists out of the income from their intellectual property. Napster was neither a wholly criminal set-up, nor wholly a neat idea. In the end, it was nobbled by legal action, and it died in spirit if not fact when it was bought by a major company, Bertelsmann.[18]

The problem, then, is rather hydra-headed. And the solutions tend to be techy and dry; they involve an understanding of the nuts and bolts of the infrastructure which would tax the patience of anyone over the age of 17 who has had recent experience of the light of day. So I'm not going to go into details about computer security measures. Suffice it to say that the problem will never be fully controlled, and in general the more money thrown at security, the more hackers will be restrained. The amount of money thrown at the problem will depend on its public profile, and that will depend on publicity, particularly that which follows a major successful attack, or a widely spread virus, or whatever. Hence the problem will seem to get better, and then it will seem to get worse when complacency spreads, and then it will get better again, and so on. There is no halting condition for this, because the authorities can never create the right set of incentives to stop hackers; many if not all of them are uninterested in financial reward, and few if any of them are put off by the time and effort involved in hacking.

However, it is important to realise that technology is far less a part of the problem – and the solution – than economic and human factors. In the column-inch-affirmed version of the security problem, you can spot the guy who is a threat to computer security: he is male, young, unattached, unsociable, wears a black t-shirt, listens to Nine Inch Nails, has the whole of *Star Trek: Deep Space Nine* on DVD, has hair dyed black, lives in his bedroom and is conducting a losing battle with acne. Like most stereotypes, this is way off beam.

The most likely security risk could be of either sex, and will be amusing, witty, well-dressed, informed and extremely pleasant company. Because to penetrate a computer system efficiently, it is much better to corrupt, not the technology, but the people who run it.

Kevin Mitnick, once called the 'world's most wanted cyber-criminal', gave remarkable evidence of this in 2000 to the US Senate Committee on Governmental Affairs.

The most complex element in information security is the people who use the systems in which the information resides. Weaknesses in personnel security negate the effort and cost of ... physical, network and computer system security.

Social engineering, or 'gagging', is defined as gaining intelligence through deception. Employees are trained to be helpful, and to do what they are told in the workplace. The skilled social engineer will use these traits to his or her advantage as they seek to gain information that will enable them to achieve their objectives.

...

In my successful efforts to social engineer my way into Motorola [an American electronics firm], I used a three-level social engineering attack to bypass the information security measures then in use. First I was able to convince Motorola Operations employees to provide me, on repeated occasions, the pass code on their security access device, as well as the static PIN. The reason this was so extraordinary is that the pass code on their access device changed every 60 seconds: every time I wanted to gain unauthorized access, I had to call the Operations Center and ask for the password in effect for that minute.

The second level involved convincing the employees to enable an account for my use on one of their machines, and the third level involved convincing one of the engineers who was already entitled to access one of the computers to give me his password. I overcame that engineer's vigorous reluctance to provide the password by convincing him that I was a Motorola employee, and that I was looking at a form that documented the password that he used to access his personal workstation on Motorola's network – despite the fact that he never filled out any such form! Once I gained access to that machine, I obtained Telnet access to the target machine, access to which I had sought all along.[19]

It is the human element that is so often where the system breaks down, and where serious attempts to breach security will focus. People do daft things with their passwords, like using the name of a pet, or putting it on a Post-It on their computer terminal. Most computer viruses are spread through email, sending the virus as an attachment to an email message activated when the recipient double-clicks on it, so viruses get sent posing as games or nude pictures or other such virtual sweetmeat for the unwary. Merely being careful what we click on would dramatically reduce the incidence of viruses.

In a survey carried out by PentaSafe Security, two-thirds of commuters at London's Victoria Station were willing to reveal their computer password in return for a ballpoint pen. The tightest, most effective security system in the world couldn't deal with that![20]

Even when the human factor is removed, the dodginess of systems will cause more trouble than their vulnerability *per se*. Badly written software ('buggy code') often leaves big holes for attackers to crawl through, yet legal protection against buggy code is minimal, following intense lobbying by software producers. When you buy a piece of software, you generally agree to terms and conditions on a licence, which, though primarily intended to protect the intellectual property of the producer, also takes away virtually all your rights to sue in the event of loss caused by bugs in the code.[21] The rationale for this is that software markets are rapidly-moving, and discovering bugs in code is extremely time-consuming (and not an exact art by any means), so that it would be impossible to produce bug-free code in a timely manner. The net effect of the legal clauses is to remove almost all the incentives for software producers to debug the code, beyond a certain basic level. When bugs are discovered after publication, producers generally distribute 'patches', little bits of extra code that users can add to their software to overcome the effects of the bug, but, like patches on trousers, they make the code rather less reliable, and rather easier to penetrate.

A second problem is closed code. In the ancient history of computing, when you bought a computer program, you bought the program; you could see it, and rewrite it if necessary. One of the innovations of Microsoft and others in the 1970s was to sell, not the program, but an executable file that would carry out the program's instructions – which you were not allowed access to. This enabled the software producers to claim the instructions that made up the programs as their intellectual property. The pre-Microsoft era was analogous to a world where, when you went to a restaurant, the waiter brought not only the meal, but the recipe as well. Then you could take the recipe home, make the meal to your own tastes (reduce the amount of chilli, a bit more salt), and even make the meal for others to buy. In this world, a Microsoft-like innovation would be just to provide the meal, and withhold the recipe. Then if anyone wanted that particular meal, they would have to go back to the *Chez Gates* restaurant.

This restriction did not go down well with anarchic techies, such as Richard Stallman, who initiated the Free Software Foundation in the mid-1980s.[22] But the anti-proprietary software movement really got going with the Internet, which allowed many different people to work together on developing software. The result is *open source* code, where the program is kept publicly accessible, and anyone can work on it. If you develop a clever bit, you publicise the fact, and people will use your bit of the software.

The most famous open-source code is an operating system called Linux, which is a rival to Microsoft's Windows. Windows, theoretically, is superior. But in actual fact, Linux is much more reliable, because so many more people are involved in looking at it, testing it, pulling it to pieces and putting it back together again.

Linux has been much more thoroughly tested. And Linux is more secure than Windows – partly because of this greater public involvement in coding, partly because when security problems are discovered they are publicised more quickly, and partly because there are more people, from a wider range of backgrounds, competing with each other to be first to program the solution. As long as most code is closed to inspection, then security will remain a greater problem than it need be. (In response to worries of this sort, Microsoft has launched a limited initiative on open source software, by which it would provide national governments with access to Windows source code; it hopes thereby to keep those big governmental customers that are tempted by Linux.)[23]

And the third problem is the dominance of the software industry by Microsoft and one or two others. Viruses, for example, tend to live off particular pieces of software, in the same way that real-world viruses pick on particular species of animal. So many virus writers use Microsoft's hegemony as the mechanism for spreading their work. The well-known Microsoft programs, such as Excel (a spreadsheet), Word (a word processor) or Outlook (email), allow users to write special mini-programs called scripts or macros to perform tedious tasks. Viruses are merely special scripts that do destructive or mischievous things. Because the Microsoft programs are tightly connected to the Windows operating system that underlies the function of the computer, it is relatively straight-forward for such a script to get control of the entire computer – and start deleting files, sending millions of email messages, or wreaking whatever havoc the virus is intended to wreak.

Hence when a Windows-based virus gets going, it can infect colossal numbers of computers very quickly – but if there was a smaller proportion of Windows-based computers about, it would be harder for a virus to spread. As with real-world viruses, genetic diversity makes it hard for them, and what they really want is a restricted gene pool with lots of inbreeding – which is what Microsoft provides. In the virtual world, biodiversity is a good thing too.

So it is the way that people use IT systems, and the economic structure of the industry, rather than particular failings of systems, or the evil genius of hackers, that lead to most security problems. Computer security can never be foolproof, though, in the world of the Internet. Being secure involves keeping the wrong people out; being usable means allowing the right people in. This is a trade-off. As long as systems are meant to be accessible to many, often inexperienced, users, it will be easy for a determined and informed hacker to slip in.

It may seem, then, that the key to secure systems is making sure you know who is who. But, as hinted above, the question of identity on the Internet is one of the most fraught in the area.

Identity

On the Internet, as a famous *New Yorker* cartoon once claimed, no one knows you're a dog. In the real world, identity can be altered or changed, but it is not a trivial affair, and most of us do not have the resources to do it. There are so many other signs that follow you around – your face, your family – and so many major assets that would be heartbreaking to junk – your house, your car, your job. All these indicators, and more, are routinely used to trace missing persons. Many features are self-authenticating. For example, I am a white man; I could change my identity, but I could never seriously claim to be a woman, or black. The number of identities I can adopt is limited.

Online, the situation is quite different. The Internet works – is what it *is* – by transferring data around in what are called *packets*. A packet is pretty much like a wrapper around the information, an envelope with the address of the recipient and that of the sender, and when a computer exchanges packets of information with another computer, the only guides to the transaction are these addresses. The addresses are Internet Protocol addresses, or IP addresses, and are represented by four numbers between 0 and 255, in a particular order. IP addresses can be static – the same each time the user logs on – or dynamically assigned, in which case the Internet Service Provider (ISP) holds a range of addresses, and gives you one of them when you log on.[24]

As we noted, the point about the Internet is that it makes much variety out of a small number of simple building blocks. In this case, all notions of Internet identity derive from the IP address you use. You can have multiple identities if you so desire. You can pick and choose the characteristics you want 'yourself' or 'yourselves' to have. The only solid thing in this fluid situation is the IP address.

This immediately gives us a problem of trust on the net, because as we have seen in Chapter 3, stability is vital for allowing many interactions, and identities are not very stable under such conditions. There is very little here to prevent masquerading. Let us take just one aspect of the virtual world where stability of identity is very important for establishing trust relations.

E-commerce – using the Internet to make purchases and other transactions – is big business, even after the crash of the dot.com share boom. In 2002, Americans paid $1.2 billion for Internet content, *excluding* the big earners of gambling and pornography.[25] The last quarter of 2002 saw American consumers buying $25 billion-worth of goods and services online. UK consumers spent over £1 billion in November 2002 alone.[26] Commerce is well suited to going online, because a large proportion of the costs of doing business is made up of the costs of gathering information, about prices and available products (or indeed the costs of *not* gathering information, when typically one will end up paying more). The Internet makes the costs of gathering information negligible.

It hardly needs pointing out how important trust is in an e-commerce relationship. The customer writes his credit card details on an online form, and then expects his books, wine, CDs or whatever to turn up in the post within some stated period of time. He also does not want his credit card details to be made public. Retailers (or e-tailers, as they are distressingly coming to be known), have fewer risks, if they are paid in advance, but any credit card transaction requires an element of trust.

Trust goals include: *confidentiality* – credit card details must remain secret; *authentication* – the retailer must know that the customer is authorised to charge money to a particular account; *integrity* – when a message is received, it must be certain that the message has not been changed after it left the sender; and *non-repudiation* – once an action has been taken, the agent cannot claim not to have taken it.[27]

Essential to all these goals is solidity of identity. Hence the requirement for e-commerce is to build an infrastructure of stable identity on top of the fluidity of the IP address system.[28] This is not just a sneaky capitalist trick to pin everybody down and file them neatly. Though it is true that on the net no one knows you're a dog, it is equally true that on the net it is very difficult to prove that you are *not* a dog, which many people often want to do. There are many good reasons why identity needs to be attestable, and there are plenty of incentives for working out how to do it.

There are a number of ways in which it can be done. First there are geolocation services, which exploit databases connecting IP addresses with particular geographic locations where possible, in some cases even down to the postcode.[29] Second, there are passwords. Third, there are 'cookies', bits of software that the websites you visit pop onto your machine, and which are able to store your preferences. Finally, there are certification systems, where you carry with you a certificate that you are who you say you are, authenticated by an independent certification authority. These act as digital 'signatures'.[30]

None of these systems is generally accepted. The surprise is that despite that online fraud is relatively small beer. In general, it is the retailers and credit card companies that absorb the losses, and in the fourth quarter of 2002, fraud cost retailers in the US $160 million. They lost a further $315 million mistakenly rejecting legitimate sales. In other words, being over-secure actually costs them twice as much as being over-trusting! From 2001 to 2002, incidence of fraud increased more or less in line with the growth in e-commerce, at a rate of about 33 per cent or so.[31]

Privacy

So, it seems that one way to increase trust online, to enable such applications as e-commerce, would be to install some sort of centrally administered system for determining identity. The most nearly foolproof systems, so-called public key infrastructure (PKI), involve encrypting digital signatures with two keys, one private and one public. The public key would then have to be in the custody of a digital certification authority.

The end result of the widespread use of such a system would be, in effect, to move the net in the direction of trust on the global model, with authorities and regulations replacing personal acquaintance. In general, as has been argued in earlier chapters of this book, and in other works,[32] global trust is an improvement. Would it be so for the Internet?

Well, for many purposes such as e-commerce, it clearly would. But there are many other purposes for the Internet. We should also realise that it is precisely the informality, the fluidity of identity, that attracts many users to the net. As it is, there is a creeping reduction in privacy online, as one's IP address gets stored by more and more people. ISPs have to retain IP addresses, and the IP addresses they access, for inspection by various governments if need be. Records need to be kept, and they can undermine the freedom for people to surf the net unhindered. Sometimes, this is no bad thing – credit card transactions at a paedophile site have been traced to their originators by an FBI operation called Operation Candyman, although there appear to be too many transgressors to prosecute successfully.[33] (Legitimate worries about levels of public and newspaper hysteria about paedophilia, and the consequent difficulties in maintaining the presumption of innocence in these cases, do not count against the importance of monitoring illegality of course.) Sometimes, the gain is less obviously wonderful, as when the rock band Metallica found 335,000 Napster users offering their music on MP3 files, and reached for their lawyers.[34] Perhaps they had lost touch with their anti-establishment roots somewhat (this from a band who once made a record called *And Justice for All*!). And, of course, however much liberal democracies may claim that user information, once harvested, will only be used *in extremis*, any techniques developed to monitor Internet use will eventually be copied by less savoury regimes.[35]

The problem, of course, is the development of means of storing colossal quantities of information, together with the means of extracting useful knowledge from that information.[36] As legal theorist Lawrence Lessig has argued, the gathering of information is possible only when the net is configured to allow it.[37] It will be a conscious human decision as to whether to allow the preservation of privacy, or its removal in the name of e-commerce, anti-crime and the war on terrorism.

The danger will be of a lack of debate on the topic, as the infrastructures of global trust are put in place by stealth rather than agreement. For example, most of us find using credit cards very convenient, but they allow the creation of giant quantities of information about us that simply would not have been available in the old days of cash. Using mobile phones leaves a little trail behind us (merely turning them on does this). Electronic toll systems on motorways and in cities add their testimony. The coming thing is RFID, Radio Frequency Identification, microchips broadcasting IP addresses, that are small enough to fit onto the packages of goods (they will ultimately replace barcodes). At the IP address will be found information about the good itself. So, for example, the packaging on your chicken pieces will be able to tell your microwave how to cook them. But that information will be easily updateable, for example, with the credit card details of the person who bought the good. It will be possible to trace a discarded Coke can back to its purchaser.[38]

Each new piece of technology adds another little set of indicators of our movements, our preferences, and the ways in which we use our money. Each little increment in the information gathered about us is no doubt harmless, but the cumulative effect is that it is becoming possible to harvest increasingly complete accounts of people's lives. Improvements in computer memory mean that it is possible to store such quantities of information, and improvements in data mining, and related technologies such as face recognition, mean that the essential patterns can be retrieved from it. The trouble is, there is unlikely to be a major event – comparable with the birth of Dolly the sheep, for example, in the cloning debate – which will cause everyone to stop, think and rethink. Currently, for example, there are movements, slow and halting ones, admittedly, towards using the infrastructure of the Internet to facilitate tax collection.[39] Other initiatives will follow, all conceived for the best. The question is whether trust on the net can be maintained on the global model: that is, can trust be preserved when privacy is not?[40]

Quality

Such are the big political choices that hang over us in the net. They are, indeed, more or less continuous with many of the liberty vs. security issues that face us in wider society, as we try to deal with a stubbornly high (if not actually rising) crime rate and the aftermath of the terrorist attacks of 11 September 2001. There is, however, a further trust-based problem on the net, and one that is much more central to its effective function. The Internet will work reasonably well without global trust mechanisms, as it has for years; it will work just as well with them, although it would be a somewhat more boring place. Commerce is not everything. But quality is.

The Internet is a source of information and services. The information is extremely empowering, for all sorts of people from patients in the medical system to voters and political activists. Information is vital in politics, to hold governments to account. Equally important, of course, is the *publication* of information, getting a point of view across. The Internet reduces the costs of transmitting information dramatically; the costs of entry into other media, such as television or newspapers, are infinitely higher than those of getting yourself a domain name and putting your point of view on a website. Furthermore, because the Internet does not concentrate information dissemination, censorship is made correspondingly more difficult, though certainly not impossible.[41]

Information is also important in more mundane areas. Much of industry relies on timely information. Our universities, and other loci of research, function by sharing knowledge and building on previous discoveries. Furthermore, the Internet enables all sorts of interaction, including receiving research papers pretty well as soon as they are written (which matters in many of the sciences, where cycles of research are no more than a year or two; the lead time to publication in a reputable academic journal is often months). Ad hoc pairings can spring up to create new knowledge; I have written a number of academic papers with people from many countries, and indeed I have written papers with people I have never met. This would be next to impossible without the Internet.

And of course most research is not into the state of the art. It is carried out in the home, where you can find out about the water on your grandfather's knees, your school's position in the league tables, what to do about mildewed petunias, how many books by Malcolm Lowry are in print, how much a beermat autographed by Fats Domino might be expected to fetch at auction, or even just stupid things like who did best in the *Wacky Races* (Penelope Pitstop, since you ask; the worst, apart from Dick Dastardly and Muttley who always conked out on the finish line, was the Army Surplus Special).

Much the same story applies to computing services (which are, after all, merely a special type of information). The paradigm of Internet computing is changing; we are likely to see increasing numbers of 'web services', programs that sit not on your computer, but on the net. Your own computer will call up such programs down telephone lines when it needs the particular services that they provide. Virtually all of this will be invisible to you; it will go on 'behind the scenes', and you will have no idea which things are being done by your computer, and which by a web service on a remote server.[42]

In each case, that of information and that of web services, there is an obvious problem of trust.[43] You, or your computer, need to trust the quality of the information or service being provided. If much of the information available on the web is unreliable, then the great gains afforded by the reduction of cost of information gathering will be chimerical. If the services provided on the web don't work, then the programs running on your computer will break down. In the remainder of this section, I'll focus on information, although pretty much the same story will apply *mutatis mutandis* to web services.

There are a number of problems with ensuring quality. The first is that it is, to an extent, in the eye of the beholder. For instance, in a web page about a medical condition, is it best to be accurate or reassuring? Second, how enforceable should quality be? There are a lot of crazies out there. Are we to deny freedom of speech to people who, for example, hold theories that there is no link between HIV and AIDS? And if we are, what sanctions could we have?

A third problem is that there is so much information on the net that it is just not possible to survey it all. We have to be selective before we even read a webpage, and that means that we have to get someone to select for us. For instance, search engines will narrow down the quantity of pages we have to wade through. Google, currently the market leader,[44] takes in some key words, and gives us back all the pages it can find that contain those words. Figure 4 shows the result of a Google search for me (we all succumb to narcissism at some point).

Now as you will see, there are 804 pages mentioning me (or other impostors with my name). I'd like to think that this made me enormously important, but if you look for Bill Gates (I'm doing these searches in April 2003), you find something of the order of 1,220,000 pages. George Bush gets you 1,020,000, John Lennon 449,000, and Timmy Mallett 1,950. Even John Noakes' dog Shep gets 279. Now, life is too short to go through all these pages, and so Google puts them in order. Typically, you start at the top, and read through them till you get bored or die. The question then is:

Figure 4. A Google search for Kieron O'Hara.

how does the order arise? Because the order is power, here; what we would like to see is the best pages at the top of the order.

Google releases the following information about its ordering system PageRank.

> PageRank relies on the uniquely democratic nature of the web by using its vast link structure as an indicator of an individual page's value. In essence, Google interprets a link from page A to page B as a vote, by page A, for page B. But, Google looks at more than the sheer volume of votes, or links a page receives; it also analyzes the page that casts the vote. Votes cast by pages that are themselves 'important' weigh more heavily and help to make other pages 'important'.
>
> Important, high-quality sites receive a higher PageRank, which

Google remembers each time it conducts a search. Of course, important pages mean nothing to you if they don't match your query. So, Google combines PageRank with sophisticated text-matching techniques to find pages that are both important and relevant to your search. Google goes far beyond the number of times a term appears on a page and examines all aspects of the page's content (and the content of the pages linking to it) to determine if it's a good match for your query.[45]

So Google, it turns out, is trying to mix two sorts of information. It is trying, rightly, to ensure the quality pages are at the top of the list. But it is using potentially unreliable information based on weighted 'votes' (because this information is easy and cheap to collect). This is unreliable, (a) because democracy is not the best way to determine quality, and (b) because the system is no doubt open to abuse from owners of websites (in the same way that pop music charts can be rigged by record companies buying large numbers of their own artists' records). Google does not release the full details of its calculations, partly to stop this rigging of the rankings. I am not in any way impugning Google's system, which is way out in front of its rivals. But there is a clear circularity here: the ranking system relies on democratic input, which then boosts particular pages through the ranks, which then get found more readily by searchers, and then become still more popular, and then get ranked well because of the democratic nature of the system!

There are other ways of ensuring quality. One is to follow particular brands. For example, you could try to make sure that you concentrated on sites run by trusted institutions, such as universities (which generally have the '.edu' suffix in the US, and others in other countries – '.ac.uk' in the UK) or the government, or whatever. But this then limits you to the small number of authors of whom you have personal acquaintance – the big problem with local trust. We will discuss branding in more detail in Chapter 6.

Another way to harness trust is to try to develop networks of trusted testimony about webpages, so that webpages, or documents available online, are constantly annotated by arguments, counter-arguments and recommendations. There are a number of ways of doing this. The Digital Document Discourse Environment (D3E) is an online system which does not alter a document, but provides a forum for discussing it. The page under discussion does not die; it collects accretions of promotion or criticism like barnacles on the bottom of a ship. The arguments – as opposed to straightforward votes – can at least be appreciated and evaluated, and so are less easy to rig.[46] TRELLIS is another interactive computing environment for more or less the same thing.[47]

These and similar systems can be networked to try to create a web of trust, exploiting the increased inferential power of the improved version of the web that should be coming on stream, the semantic web.[48] Some systems neatly try to reconcile trust and privacy by allowing systems to negotiate mutual trust by gradually disclosing their credentials as required.[49] Another approach is to develop mathematical or logical theories of trust. Such theories can only approximate the real thing, naturally. But they are the product of a lot of hard thinking about trust, and can neatly capture many of our intuitions. Some axioms of e-trust that have been produced include:

- You must trust yourself to some extent, but not necessarily 100 per cent (for example if you are subcontracting some tasks).
- Distrust is different from 'trust not to'.
- Trust in an adviser is transferred to the recommended parties.

- Distrust in recommended parties is transferred to the adviser.
- Trust in all subcontractors of an intermediary is transferred into an inclination to trust the intermediary.[50]

Such systems at present are systems of local trust, consistent with the roots of the Internet. But the identity of the giver of testimony matters, and it may be that widespread fraud, or the perceived need to ensure that opinions on some document are really those of the purported author, may ultimately require the shift into a global trust system of identity certification, as discussed above. There would, of course, be gains in security – but there would be losses both of privacy, and of the interesting additions that the occasional weird idea from a free and original thinker can provide. It remains to be seen whether ideas of certification can be grafted painlessly onto unregulated webs of trust.[51]

It's up to us

Local trust worked extremely well on the net when there was a relatively small number of users, and they more or less shared the same set of values (as Durkheim would have predicted; recall from Chapter 3 his theory of trust as the convergence of values). The number of Internet users has increased, and now includes lots of non-techies. The number of activities available has also increased, as the Internet comes to resemble the high street rather than the Comp Sci Dept. Most of the new users are much less committed to the values of freedom and cleverness that built the net (rather as the second wave of immigrants to the US were much less committed than the original settlers to the discourse of rights, liberties, the rule of law and nonconformism upon which America was founded). These newbies will not feel they need to respect the underlying assumptions of the net, even if they know about them;

peer pressure to conform will be that much less powerful. The question is arising – as we might have predicted – as to whether we should move from a local trust model to one of global trust.

It may be that the gains from global trust, and the certification of identity, are just too great to resist. They would allow e-commerce to develop further – which will be to the benefit of most of us, not just the big corporations – help reduce crime both on- and offline, and give us rather more confidence in the quality of knowledge or web services that we receive from the net. If this does happen, we have to hope that the original vision of the net does not get lost in the shuffle.[52]

So, what is it like when trust is globalised? How do institutions work to support trust? What happens when they go wrong? And is local trust compatible with the global variety? In the next chapter, we will look at finance, an area where trust is almost completely globalised, and where regulations dominate performance. Perhaps coincidentally, perhaps not, it is an area where people have been having the odd difficulty of late.

CHAPTER SIX

Crash!

The world according to GAAP

Finance runs according to Generally Accepted Accountancy Principles (GAAP). These vary from country to country, but the basic idea is that such principles ensure that decisions are made in investors' interests, that all relevant information (and as little irrelevant information as possible) is available to investors, and finally – this is the burden of the 'generally accepted' bit – that the principles are such that everyone has confidence in them.

In a nutshell, the system works like this. A firm issues shares in itself. Each share entitles the owner to a share of the profits, and a say in the running of the firm. No one other than shareholders owns the firm. At the end of the year, the firm makes a certain amount of profit; let's say £1,000,000. It will need to invest some of this back in the firm, to buy new capital equipment, rent new buildings, etc.; let's say it reinvests £800,000. That leaves £200,000 as clear profit, which is then redistributed to the shareholders; this is called the *dividend*. If there were, say, half a million shares, the dividend would be 40p per share. If you owned 1,000 shares, you would receive a cheque at the end of the year for £400 (less tax).

The dividend is distinct from the share *price*. Shares in the firm are bought and sold on the *stock market* (for a publicly quoted company – privately if not). When someone buys shares in the firm, we say they *invest* in it. The share price (tends to) rise when the expectations of profits are high, and (tends to) fall when expectations are low. The determinant of the share price is the expected dividend, but actually the bulk of investors buy shares that they expect to go up in price on the stock market. If the price of the shares falls, then that is an indication that the company is badly managed. That should then be corrected, as the low share price means it is easier for a new person to make a takeover bid – that is, he buys as many of the shares as he can, hoping to gain more than 50 per cent of them, in which case he can run the firm as he wishes.

There is a distinction between *owning* and *managing* a firm. The firm's managers are led by the board of directors, and the chairman of the board is the chief manager. She makes the decisions within the firm about what the firm will do. Her duty is to create value for the shareholders. She is appointed by the shareholders, on the basis of a vote. The position of the managers is very difficult, because there are several conflicts of interest. On the one hand, they have to watch the shareholders' interests. But on the other hand, they have interests of their own – for example, they may feel responsibilities to their workforce, and try to preserve employment, even though profits (and therefore shareholders) may best be served by making some people redundant. Other conflicts arise, for example, when the firm has dealings with another firm in which board members have investments (a very common circumstance in the close-knit financial world).

Earlier, we noticed how profits were divided into reinvestment and dividends. *Investments* are expenditures of money now in order to create future profits; an investment involves buying or maintaining an *asset*. If the firm buys a building now, then that helps profits in the future, because it saves on the rent that it would have had to pay to someone else while it uses the building, and when it has finished with the building, it can sell it on and make some money from the property sale. If the firm loans someone some money, then it gains the interest on the loan, which contributes to future profits, and gets the money back at the end of the loan period. If it buys a piece of capital machinery, that contributes to future profits by enabling the firm to produce stuff to sell.

Investments are distinct from *expenses*, which are the ordinary costs of running the firm day-to-day. These expenses are entirely routine, and have to be paid for out of revenue; they include stuff like electricity and other power bills, employees' salaries, the raw materials for the goods the firm produces, stationery and so on. If the firm cannot pay for the day-to-day running of the firm out of the money in its current account – if, in effect, it has to borrow to pay for it – then it will soon go bankrupt.

Global trust comes into the picture with the accountants. The role of accountancy in all this is to make sure that the firm is run for the benefit of shareholders. The firm must produce an annual statement of its accounts which is entirely public – it is sent automatically to existing investors, and can be inspected by anyone thinking of investing. The accounts are checked by accountants called *auditors*, who are independent of the firm, though paid for by the firm (the auditor's fee is another expense). They must ensure, for example, that when profits are reinvested, they are genuinely reinvested, and not used sneakily to pay for expenses. We can see why in Table 1. Both firms are in the same position,

Table 1. Why we need auditors.

Firm	Annual revenue	Annual expenses	Stated expenses	Stated profits	Required reinvestment	Stated reinvestment
Honest John	$10m	$8m	$8m	$2m	$1m	$1m
Black Inc.	$10m	$8m	$7m	$3m	$1m	$2m

making the same revenue, running the same expenses, and reinvesting the same amount – and distributing the same amount of money to their shareholders this year. Honest John tells the truth about this, that the outgoings of $9m are divided between $8m of expenses and $1m of reinvestment. The $8m is for present needs, and contributes only to this year's dividend, but the $1m will contribute to future profits. Black Inc., however, fiddles the books, and pretends that only $7m is used for day-to-day running of the firm, and that $2m is reinvested. That makes Black Inc. look falsely like the better-managed firm for two reasons. First, it appears that it has wrung a profit of $3m out of sales of $10m (30 per cent), as opposed to the 20 per cent profit that Honest John has managed, a better immediate performance. And second, Black Inc. looks better in the long run, because there are apparently $2m of reinvestments that will contribute to future profits, twice as much as stated by Honest John, which will, to a shareholder's eye, lead to a better future performance. These facts will tend to push the share price higher for Black Inc. than for Honest John, thereby rewarding the investors of Black Inc. in the short term, and (not coincidentally) helping ensure the jobs of the directors of Black Inc.

It is the job of the auditor to inspect the books and ensure that firms like Black Inc. account for all of their reinvestments, and show that they are genuine investments. The auditing process conforms to general accountancy rules, and there will also be additional rules that stock markets set as a condition for being allowed to trade within them. The aim of these rules is to make sure that the information that is relevant for decisions to invest in shares is all made public. Investment on the basis of information that is not public is called *insider dealing*, and is illegal.

The fact that accountancy principles have to be generally accepted can cause problems. For example, the assets that get accounted are called *tangible*. Tangible assets are ones that can be easily counted and valued, like cash, shares, buildings, machinery – although the methods for valuing tangible assets (particularly putting a value on their *depreciation*, the rate at which they lose value) can be fairly ad hoc. But they are ad hoc methods that are generally accepted.

However, there are sensible expenditures that contribute to future profits that are hard to account for; these are expenditures on *intangible assets*. Intangibles include knowledge, brands, customer loyalty, staff training, IT systems, and so on. A well-known brand, for example, actually causes people to buy more of a good, or to be prepared to spend more on it, as we will see later in this chapter, so a good brand or logo will contribute to future profits. However, it is hard to evaluate the exact contribution it makes. Intuitively, there is a difference between spending money on intangible assets, like logos, research and development or staff training, and spending money on expenses like decorating, electricity or paper; the former seem to contribute to future profits, while the latter contribute to present profits. But there is no generally accepted way of nailing this distinction down, although there is a burgeoning field of research into how to calculate the value of intangible assets[1] (though the burgeoning has stalled since the collapse of Enron, which we shall discuss below). As it is, if a firm wishes to draw attention to the amount it has spent on intangibles, it can produce a set of footnotes to its annual report, which makes the information available to investors, and there is some evidence that investors respond to information in this form.[2]

The aim, then, of the financial system is to preserve the conditions for investment in shares. If investors thought that they might be at a disadvantage compared to those 'in the know', then they would be less likely to risk their money. And a restriction on investment would be disastrous for society as a whole; it has been argued that something in excess of 80 per cent of the gain of material wealth since the 18th century has been as a result of unintended spillover effects from investments benefiting society in general (i.e. most of the benefits of investments don't go to the individual investors at all, but to everyone).[3] As a result, there is a lot of pressure resting on this system of global trust – of institutions such as stock markets and auditors, and of accounting rules, providing a framework within which everyone must work – to create the conditions of trust that enable people to give their money to someone now, in expectation of future benefits.

There are three difficulties with financial rules which are very hard to get round. First, it is very hard to draft rules that are sensitive to the context of their application. And second, financial forces can be too powerful for rules to govern. In the next section, we will try to give some examples of changes in context, and following that, we will look at stock market bubbles, and the vain attempts of authorities to stop them inflating.

The third difficulty, of course, is criminality. Wherever there is money there are incentives, and wherever there are rules, and a system of global trust, there will be attempts to get around it; this is driven partly by simple greed for extra loot, of course, but also it is invited to some extent, because the remoteness between truster and trustee which is endemic with global trust systems makes it easier to get round rules and easier on the conscience as well. It would be an exaggeration to say that most rule-bending is done for greed alone, or out of sheer criminality – the case of Enron is most instructive on this point, as we shall see in a further section devoted to its unhappy history.

Owing to circumstances beyond our control ...

In the financial world, rules are generally put there to prevent dangerous or risky behaviour. For example, much of banks' profits come from lending money to people (and then charging interest, of course). Lending money is risky, since if the person to whom you lend money goes bust before the loan period is up, or is unable to pay at the end, then you lose the money you lent. Banks always believe that they are able to assess risks, and that, even though they are resigned to losing *some* money to bad debts, the interest they gain from the good debts will more than make up for this. Actually, banks are surprisingly bad at risk assessment, and as a result most countries have banking laws that prevent banks lending more than a certain amount of their capital, and hence exposing themselves to too much risk.

But assessments of risk depend on circumstances. In the boom years, a firm may be sound, but during a downturn, it may not look as sound. There is very little that rules can do here; either they prevent legitimate profits being made in the boom, or they fail to prevent failures in the downturn. For instance, in 1997, a banking crisis hit East Asia, one of the most business-savvy and respectable parts of the world.[4] After a period of high stock market and property values, particularly in Japan, many companies appeared to be very valuable (a) because their share prices indicated as such, and (b) because they owned properties worth a fortune. Banks were happy to lend them pots of money.

Then the Japanese stock market crashed in December 1989, taking the property market with it, and suddenly all those valuable firms weren't valuable any more. In a couple of years, stocks had fallen by 60 per cent and property by 80 per cent[5] (the Japanese government's penchant for spreading largesse using construction programmes hardly helped here). Japan fell into recession, out of which it has never really dragged itself. The Nikkei 225 index is, in 2003, round about 80 per cent *down* on its record high.

The loss of regional trade with Japan was catastrophic for the East Asian region. Governments tried to prevent the flight of capital in the crisis, but in July 1997, the Thais gave up; they let their currency, the baht, float. Panic set in. China has very strict controls on money, and so managed to weather the storm. Malaysia imposed capital controls that helped a little. But everywhere else bombed.[6] An abiding memory of the period is of South Korean housewives queuing to donate their wedding rings to bolster the country's 'save the nation' fund, raising $170 million in three days.[7]

Political turmoil followed economic collapse. The most radical effects were in Indonesia, where long-term strongman President Suharto was driven from office, to be replaced by a string of ineffective presidents. The country began to crack as separatist movements – always potent in that republic of scattered islands – seized the day. East Timor finally got its independence, at the price of a massacre at the hands of pro-Indonesian militias, while the provinces of Aceh and Irian Jaya remain a running sore. Other governments in the region fell. And the wider world suffered; Russia and Brazil were particularly hard hit by the failure of confidence, even though they were blameless for the Asian crisis.

And the root cause was the dangerous level of loans made by East Asian banks. Companies are in trouble, because they have high levels of loans contracted in the days when their assets were worth much more than they are now. Banks are in trouble, because their assets include high levels of bad loans. If banks call in loans, many companies will fold. They will then default on all their loans, and more banks will fold. Bad debt undermined the trust in the region's finances that allowed investment to take place, and is still having an effect. It is hard for foreign investors to invest in the region; neither companies nor banks look safe until the debts of the 1980s are wiped out. The amount of bad debt in these economies is still horrifying (see Figure 5), totalling $2,000 *billion*.

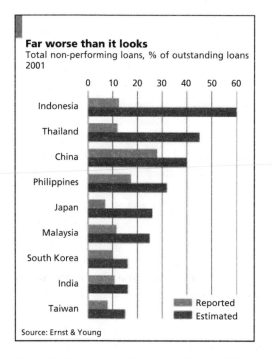

Figure 5. Reported and estimated levels of debt in Asia.[8]

It is not just banks, it should be pointed out, who suffer from incorrect expectations. Businesses of all sorts make many commitments in the future based on their expectations of how much money they will have, and the people on the receiving end of those commitments are forced to trust that these expectations are not unrealistic. As an example of lightning striking in the same place twice, we might take Barings. In 1890, Barings Bank, which had been pushing Argentinian stocks, backed the Buenos Ayres Water Supply and Drainage Company, and tried to issue £2 million of shares. It was a risky venture, and, like many other similar ones of the time, expected to be remunerative. Suddenly, confidence in Argentina dropped, and Barings could only sell £200,000 of the shares. Barings shook. The government, which had interests in Barings, wobbled.[9] It is incredible, but true, that the government of the British Empire was nearly brought down by an Argentinian sewerage company; am I alone in detecting a hint of this episode in Joseph Conrad's great novel *Nostromo*? In the end, it was discovered that Barings had just about enough assets to get through the crisis, and it was wound up, covering its losses, to be replaced by a new firm, Barings Brothers & Co. Ltd.[10]

Which lasted until it was driven out of business by speculations that it could not cover, by a young British trader in its Singapore branch, Nick Leeson, in 1995.[11] *Plus ça change ...*

Bubbles

Another strange phenomenon in business is that of the *bubble*. In most markets, high prices lower demand. But in the stock market, high prices *raise* it. This is because investors make their money from buying shares at a low price and selling them at a higher price, and if they expect the market to climb still further, the sooner they buy the better. Such a situation, if unchecked, becomes a bubble, which is entirely dependent on trust, hope and expectation; when these go, the bubble bursts and prices collapse. Everyone loses out.

So when prices are on the rise, investors get in the mood for risk. Governments may want to introduce regulations to increase trust, but when investors are thirsty for risk, and the money that can be made in risky situations, the government might as well whistle in the wind as try to prevent volumes of money flowing into the overheated markets.

For example, Britain's Bank Charter Act of 1844 was intended to curb speculation; it separated the Bank of England's note issuing function from its banking arm, to prevent the Bank from issuing large quantities of money to fund wild investment sprees.[12] Speculation, it was reasoned, would be curbed if people could not get their hands on sufficient money to do it with, and in the 19th century, speculation terrified people – Dickens' *Little Dorrit* is a magisterial expression of this terror. But events conspired against the 1844 Act.

In 1845, the railway mania reached its zenith, when everyone wanted to pump money into the new railway companies. The Act of 1844 completely failed to prevent it happening. But when other events (in particular, poor harvests following the repeal of the Corn Laws) meant that cash was suddenly needed to keep railway companies, banks and landowners afloat, the limits imposed by the 1844 Act began to bite, and by 1847, bankruptcies were happening with increasing regularity. In the end, the government dropped hints that the 1844 Act would be relaxed, and these hints were all that was required to defuse the crisis. The Act had failed; though based on sound financial principles, it had failed to prevent money pouring into the railway bubble, and had perversely stopped people raising money when they needed it![13]

Bubbles attract money. Rising prices are the sign of a boom, but it is always incredible how few people notice this at the time. There is no difference, except in quantity, between the railway mania and the dot.com boom of the late 1990s. Even at the height of the latter, even after the first signs of collapse of the prices of the dot.coms, one commentator was prepared to write that 'if this is a bubble, it has a pretty thick skin'.[14] And when such sentiments are abroad, it is virtually impossible to stem the flow of money into the speculative market.

The best-known bubble in history was, of course, the 1929 crash, where post-war exuberance escalated until shares were dramatically overvalued.[15] The authorities' response was twofold, to bolster global trust in order to enable a recovery. They set up an institution to act as 'the cop on the corner', the Securities and Exchange Commission (SEC), which carries out the policing of the accountancy practices we discussed at the beginning of this chapter. And an Act of Congress was passed, the Glass-Steagall Act, designed to reduce conflicts of interest. It had been thought that banks had caused the crash (a) by speculating with their customers' money, and (b) by encouraging people to invest in shares in companies to which they had lent money, so Glass-Steagall forbade banks from dealing in insurance and shares. The SEC was quite successful, but Glass-Steagall became the subject of years of sniping and lobbying, and was held responsible for the poor performance of US banks in the next few decades; the banks also found many legitimate ways round it. It was repealed in 1999.[16] No one has ever convincingly shown that the banks were responsible for the crash of 1929. But the conflicts the Act was designed to prevent have returned![17]

In 2000, the stock market crashed again. The authorities' response has been twofold, to bolster global trust. They set up an institution to act as 'the cop on the corner', the Public Company Accounting Oversight Board, which then disastrously became mired in not one, but two messy political arguments, the first over who should chair the board, and the second over what the salaries for board members should be. And an Act of Congress was passed, the Sarbanes-Oxley Act of 2002, designed to reduce conflicts of interest (is this sounding familiar?). The conflicts of 2000 were of auditors' interests; they would audit the accounts of firms while also giving them financial advice (e.g. on tax avoidance), so it could be in their interests to give lax audits. Sarbanes-Oxley is intended to prevent auditors providing other services for the firms they are auditing, to remove the conflict. But the accountancy and legal professions have managed to water down many of the Sarbanes-Oxley provisions as it moved through Congress, so we currently don't know the extent to which it will curb the dangerous behaviour it is aimed at.[18] *Plus ça change ...*

Enron

A certain name has cropped up once or twice in the preceding discussion. Enron conducted a name-recognition survey in 1996, only to discover that people thought it was a Klingon weapon from *Star Trek*.[19] If Enron were to conduct the same survey now, one imagines that name recognition would be the last of its problems.

In some ways, the extent of Enron's notoriety is surprising. When it finally filed for bankruptcy, on 2 December 2001, its $62 billion of assets made it the largest bankruptcy ever at that time, admittedly. But it didn't hold its record for long, only until 22 July 2002, to be precise, when bankrupt telecom operator WorldCom declared over $100 billion of assets.[20] Enron has become a byword for corporate malfeasance, but there have been similar goings on, not only at WorldCom, but also at Xerox and others, and, lest anyone think this is an American problem alone, at the Dutch giant Ahold, the world's third largest food retailer.[21]

Enron has been held responsible for the stock market crash of the first years of the 21st century; the US and UK stock markets have fallen by about half from their peak – a massive fall (Figure 6 shows the UK FTSE 100 index up to the morning of Saddam Hussein's fall in April 2003). And there is no doubt at all that Enron's collapse contributed mightily to the loss in confidence. But there are more plausible causes. Shares were massively over-valued on traditional measures (such as the ratio between share prices and the dividends they generate) during the boom, creating a 1929-type bubble waiting to get burst, as a number of commentators noticed at the time.[22] (Though amazingly, even after the crash had happened, there were still people talking up the bubble.)[23] Even in 2003, some commentators maintain that, on long-term financial and demographic trends, there may be further to fall.[24]

Figure 6. The big crash of the 21st century.[25]

And the September 11th attacks made the rosy picture of a new liberal order[26] seem a little less plausible, as it became clear that there were people who not only did not buy into the liberal capitalist vision, but also were prepared to commit appalling atrocities to make their point. (The number of times I have felt the need to mention the September 11th attacks in this book is in itself an illustration of the way in which their shadow is cast over the whole political and social scene in the West.) The uncertainty that followed the lead-up to the Second Gulf War in 2003 was another aspect of this conflict.

But there is no doubt that corporate wrongdoing has had some effect on the stock markets, that trust in the institutions that supposedly regulate corporate governance has fallen, and that Enron is the most fascinating of the many cases that have combined to undermine that trust. WorldCom, the world's biggest collapse, is comparatively dull. Recall the discussion of accounting practice at the beginning of this chapter; we used the fictitious example of Honest John and Black Inc., where the latter, though performing no better than the former, was made to *look* better by pretending that some of its expenses were investments. It is a very straight-forward fib – and it is exactly what WorldCom did, falsely putting about $4 billion of its expenses in the investments column.[27] Enron, on the other hand, is a case study in the psychology of business.

Even now, few know what Enron actually did for its money. It began life in July 1985 as a merger between Houston Natural Gas and InterNorth, a gas company from Nebraska, intended to pipe gas across states in the US (it became Enron later that year, after Ken Lay became its chairman and chief executive); it diversified all over the place, but energy and natural resources were where its central competence remained.

At the time, gas markets were highly regulated. Enron's strategy was to try to reduce such regulation by political lobbying, and to make money trading gas in unregulated markets. The key to its approach was to allow *hedging*, that is, protecting oneself from uncertainty and fluctuations in prices by making longer-term commitments to buy. In the deregulating markets of the Reagan-Thatcher years, Enron allowed buyers and sellers to hedge energy costs, and so provided mechanisms for reducing uncertainty for energy traders.[28]

This was the first step in the Enron vision of the future. Unregulated markets provide large numbers of opportunities, because people are prepared to pay for hedging against uncertainty – this is what we all do, for example, when we buy insurance. The Enron group became evangelistic, in a terribly American way, about it.

> Rather than fight deregulation ... Lay told the executives, Enron was going to embrace it. Deregulation had opened up an unregulated part of the gas business, which then consisted of just selling natural gas. The company was going to focus on this unregulated business and look for more opportunities in it. And the company was going to move quickly.
>
> Although Lay was anything but flashy, he had absorbed a few lessons from his minister father, and he made it clear that the unregulated market was the new religion at Enron. The executive confab was like a management revival meeting, and executives later dubbed it the 'Come to Jesus' meeting.[29]

Lay was an avuncular-looking Texan, whose management style was relaxed. He set the firm's parameters, and then hired clever people for top dollar to come up with the goods without too much interference. Ironically, this involved a giant quantity of trust on the part of the top management; they never questioned expenses payments, for example, and employees were given an unusual amount of autonomy. Employees were very clever indeed, but they were kept on their toes. Chief Operating Officer Jeffrey Skilling instituted a system where Enron employees would give each other rankings as to who was doing their job best; the bottom 10–20 per cent would be liable to be fired – a system that became known as 'rank and yank'.[30]

Skilling conceived of Enron as a company with few tangible assets, based around intangibles, such as knowledge of the energy markets. It moved out into other types of energy supply, and indeed other resources such as water and bandwidth (i.e. the capacity of telecommunications networks to carry data), and also gained footholds in world energy markets, for example in Teeside in the UK, and, notoriously, in Maharashtra State in India.[31] They owned pipelines and power stations, but they were mainly interested in buying and selling any kind of resource. Their Internet trading arm, EnronOnline, was held up as 'the most successful Internet venture of any company in any industry anywhere'.[32]

The idea was that Enron would be, basically, a universal intermediary. All over the world, there were people wanting to buy, and people wanting to sell. By understanding market conditions better than anyone else, Enron aimed to strike deals that would (a) be better for the buyers and sellers, and (b) still allow Enron to make some money by bringing people together. Enron would create value by making markets happen, and they saw themselves as the ideal company for the 1990s. Innovation, markets, creativity, cleverness: these were the 90s factors that allowed Enron executives to brand themselves 'the world's coolest company'.[33]

Given hindsight, it is easy – indeed fun – to smile at this hubris. The whole idea that there might be a cool company at all is, I happen to think, somewhat chucklesome. But the perceived coolness almost *required* that the company be built on air. Enron needed, beyond all else, a good-looking set of figures to preserve confidence, to keep itself going. Rather like freewheeling downhill on a bicycle, it was fine as long as it didn't slow down.

Because it made money trading, it needed lots of cash. Enron made money by buying gas, selling gas, and buying and selling other commodities, often financial commodities, such as futures. The selling would, of course, ultimately cover the deals, but it needed cash to buy. Also it was doing a lot of investment, in power plants, and in companies that contained the expertise from which it thought it could make money. To get this cash, it borrowed a lot. Nothing wrong with that, but it was therefore essential for the debt not to look too large compared to assets. If that happened, then the three powerful and influential agencies which rate the creditworthiness of companies, Standard & Poor's, Moody's and Fitch, would lower Enron's credit rating. This would mean that Enron would have to pay higher interest on its debt.

This in turn would affect the key parameter of Enron's books – its earnings. In the boom years, a company's earnings were the important measure that financial analysts and investors would look to. Earnings take into account the income that a firm receives, excluding one-off expenses which (in theory) don't affect the long-term health of the firm. Because of this the markets may disregard actually quite serious problems. Loren Fox provides the example of a long-running dispute that Enron had with a number of oil companies over a contract to buy North Sea gas at above-market rates. In 1997, Enron settled the dispute with a lump sum payment of $675 million, which appeared as a one-off problem in that quarter's accounts. Profits, therefore, were disastrous for that quarter, but there was no effect on earnings. But alternatively Enron could have honoured the contract, and lost money steadily over the years, rather than all at once; it may even have lost less money in that time. However, doing it that way would have depressed earnings, and that would never do.[34] There is nothing illegal in this, though to skew the firm away from profits and towards earnings is arguably not always in shareholders' best interests.

Enron's downfall came with its use of dummy companies called Special Purpose Entities (SPEs) to disguise low earnings. Enron used SPEs to make purchases of assets; the SPEs would take on any debt that was required to make the purchase. Hence the debt would not appear on Enron's books, and therefore would not affect its earnings or credit rating.

There were two problems with this. It was essential that Enron control the SPEs. But for accounting purposes, the SPEs had to be independent of Enron. The deal had to look like a temporary partnership between two separate companies. This meant that there had to be outside capital in them, and that they should not act purely in Enron's interest. It was not possible to square this circle.

Many of them were set up by Enron's chief financial officer, Andrew Fastow, a man of large brain but maybe a mild shortage of maturity. Many of the SPEs were named after various popular films and characters: Chewco (after Chewbacca, a character in *Star Wars*), JEDI, Raptor, Hawaii 125-O. The most notorious of these SPEs was called LJM, after the initials of Fastow's wife and two kids. Many Enron employees, including Fastow himself, and their relations, ended up running these companies. The 'outside capital' that was supposed to fund such companies ultimately came from Enron itself.

The second problem was the conflicts of interest – always undermining of trust in the field of finance – that arose. For example, Enron and LJM had a complicated series of relationships, and money frequently passed from one to the other to meet some accountancy requirement. It might be that LJM had to buy some Enron shares; the price to be paid might be more or less than the market price. Fastow the financial officer of Enron would be negotiating with Fastow the chairman of LJM, and the outcome of the negotiation would strongly affect the income of Fastow. On Fastow's own account, he made about $45 million from his SPEs,[35] and there was at least one occasion where Enron employees formed the belief that he was not negotiating as hard as he might for Enron.[36]

D-day arrived when news of these SPEs began to leak out, partly as a result of suspicion by employees within Enron, but largely when many of these dummy deals – which for complex reasons depended on an optimistic view of the stock market – unravelled as the market began to slip. On 8 November 2001, Enron restated its accounts with the SEC, and added $2.59 billion of debt to its books since 1997 – debt that had nominally been shouldered by the SPEs. Investors had not been provided with the right information. Confidence evaporated. That day its share price fell to $8.41.[37] It had, at its high point in August 2000, been $90.56. By 28 November, it was 61¢.

Apologies for the complex tale and the alphabet soup. Actually, I have simplified it drastically! But it is a very interesting and instructive story, for several reasons.

First, the institutions of global trust – the accounting rules and regulations overseen by the SEC – were inadequate to keep track of Enron. And it will always be the case that such institutions are a step behind the most aggressive companies; there is no way round this, however punitive to errant firms you want to be. There was a great deal of debate within Enron itself as to whether the complex sets of deals were legal or not. The spirit of the GAAP rules is that Enron's debt should appear on Enron's books, but the letter of the law is somewhat different, and the whole purpose of Fastow's financial creations was to make sure the debt did not appear. Fastow did not set out to be fraudulent *per se*, he set out to create financial instruments that were not anticipated in the accountancy rules. It may be that most – perhaps all – of the deals that Enron made were legal. And this will always happen in finance – as rules cover one set of shenanigans, more clever people will find ways round them, and so on. This is a never-ending process.

In fact, in this instance, it was less the rules that were at fault than the policing. Enron's auditors, Arthur Andersen, also advised Enron on many of its information-hiding wheezes. Voices within Andersen who raised doubts about the audits were silenced, because Andersen wanted to keep Enron's business.[38] Andersen, which had audited not only Enron, but also WorldCom, and a firm called Global Crossing, and therefore was responsible for the three largest bankruptcies in history, was finished. The 'big five' global accountancy firms became the 'big four'.

But, whether it was the rules themselves or the policing of them, global trust systems alone are not adequate. Rules generally contain loopholes, they separate the spirit from the letter. Rule-following needs to be underpinned by more old-fashioned trustworthiness, the type that will withstand local scrutiny.

Second, many of Enron's operations were innovative and creative. Energy markets have been transformed, and Enron was responsible to a large extent. If shares had not begun to slide – a slide that started in the Internet sector, and spread to telecoms, nothing to do with energy at all – then Enron would eventually have made enough money to cover its back, and it would have continued to prosper without anyone being much the wiser. It's not obvious the world would be a worse place for this.

Third, it may be that criminality is proven in the case. Of the major players, only Fastow faces charges as yet, of fraud, conspiracy and money laundering.[39] Fastow's junior Michael Kopper has made a plea bargain with the US government. Skilling and Lay do not currently face charges. At the time of writing, the

Fastow case has not reached trial, and its outcome is uncertain; Fastow plans to defend himself.

But whether or not criminality is proved, the interesting thing is that personal enrichment is not the central fact of the case. The whole web of SPEs was set up by Fastow, not for Fastow's benefit, but for Enron's. Enron, with its own internal culture of trust, did not object to employees showing initiative, or cutting deals from which they benefited, or being greedy, as long as Enron benefited too. The greed-is-good Enron culture – and this does not pre-suppose that Fastow had received official approval of his actions – was based around people gaining bonuses on top of their salaries for actions that helped Enron. In general, the aim of the project was to create financial instruments that were legal, but that avoided the need for Enron to state its true debts, and from which Fastow and associates might expect to gain hugely on the side. The slippage from bending rules to breaking them is tiny, and happened gradually.

Fourth, a related point is that the aim of the game was not money. These were people who hyped up their company, and who believed the hype. The coolest company in the world. They did what they did because they wanted to be admired in the business world, because they liked seeing their pictures in *Fortune* magazine, because they liked winning polls of great companies. They were showing off, not thieving – and maybe that is more pathetic. Accountancy rules don't take this sort of motivation into account; it is unclear how they would.

And finally, the case throws interesting light on what is important for trusting. *Information* is important; concealment of information is a real trust-destroyer, even when the information concealed is not in itself serious. If Enron had revealed the extent of its debt, it would have had smaller earnings, and would have grown less quickly. But even so it would still have grown at a phenomenal pace. Ultimately, it was reasonable for Enron to borrow, even the billions of dollars that it was borrowing. What was wrong was concealing the facts. The accountancy regime is designed to make all the information available to investors; it does this not for reasons of economics – though markets do thrive on information – but to maximise trust.[40]

Interests are important. The Enron case is overflowing with conflicts of interest. Enron's managers wanted a cool company, whereas its investors presumably wanted profits. Andrew Fastow, an Enron employee, found himself running dummy companies that were negotiating with Enron. Arthur Andersen was auditing Enron, and advising it on financial matters at the same time. Enron's internal audit committee was chaired by Wendy Gramm, wife of Republican senator Phil Gramm, who had taken part in the committee scrutiny of the US Commodity Futures Modernization Act of 2000, which had ended up exempting exchanges such as EnronOnline from regulation, and who had been given $233,000 in political donations by Enron and its employees. Another member of the internal audit committee also had a consultancy contract with Enron, this being famous fixer and former UK energy minister Lord Wakeham.

And, in the world of global trust, *consequences* are much more important than motives. It is Enron's *fall* that has caused the fallout, not the fact of Enron's hiding of information. If it hid information successfully, people would still be drawn to its risky strategies and would invest in it. Surely no one seriously believes that companies voluntarily reveal all the relevant facts about themselves, without spinning them to make them look better than they are. And if the breaking of the rules was, as I have suggested, not primarily to enrich the rulebreakers, but to enhance their image in the business community, then that is irrelevant to the collapse of trust that their rulebreaking has caused.

The *fact* of the rulebreaking is much more important than the reasons why.

Local trust in big business: branding

We have established, at some length, that global trust, founded on institutions and rules, is not by itself a cure-all; it will not establish trustworthy behaviour, it will not eliminate risk-seeking behaviour, and it will certainly not eliminate stupidity. It is true that global trust mechanisms can replace local trust, i.e. that contracts can replace trustworthiness,[41] but some empirical studies have shown that the legalism introduced by contracts tends to dull the sociable instinct for trustworthy behaviour.[42] Unsurprisingly, rules will be got around, and around the next corner will always be another Barings, another Enron, another WorldCom. Some local trust in big business, some trust in reputation that does not rely on institutions, regulation and power as intermediaries will always be vital, even if it cannot do the job on its own.

The problem, then, with a local trust system, is broadcasting your reputation widely enough to get lots of people prepared to trust you. One mechanism that has been remarkably successful over the last couple of centuries is the *brand*, a particular mark or name associated with the goods you sell, which in a weird way holds your reputation for others to see. Rather than trusting a particular vendor, the customer trusts the brand associated with the goods sold, and the vendor merely becomes the salesman for the good. Branding is often associated with advertising, which helps to publish the brand.

So let's take the example of tea. In a brandless world, different vendors would sell different blends of tea, and a consumer would go to the shops which she could trust to serve the tea she liked. This would increase the cost of tea to her, because she would have a very limited number of suppliers which she trusted. If she found herself in a strange town, then her purchases of tea would be risky, because she would have no personal or reported experience of what quality of tea the vendors sold. When brands of tea emerge – Tetley's, PG Tips, Typhoo, Twinings and the rest – our consumer no longer lodges her trust in the vendor; she trusts the product. So what she looks out for in *this* world is the *brand* of tea she likes, which can be sold by anyone, even in a town she does not know.

Branding can also go beyond the individual good or service. Particular retailers use brands, which symbolise their reputation for selling quality goods, for not short-changing the customer, etc.

Branding increases trust by lowering complexity, uncertainty and risk, and increases meaningful choice by making the choice simpler, indicating which teas taste like which. Branding ensures a certain standard of quality, though not necessarily the highest quality. A consumer who buys a meal at a branded restaurant chain is certain of what he will get. In France, where restaurant food is generally wonderful, the consumer, despite gaining certainty, has probably missed a treat, because unbranded restaurants will generally be better than the usual chains; in the UK, where public food is a disgrace, the chain may be a better bet, because the food can be guaranteed to be at a particular standard, and so will be better than the minimum possible (but let's not dwell on British food).

Branding, then, is good for trade. It lowers prices, because it enables larger quantities of a uniform good to be marketed, and it increases demand, because it reduces uncertainty about products (much of the value of trust is that it reduces uncertainty).[43] The brand becomes the repository of consumers' trust: as with any other such reputation-based repository, it can build trust over time – as a customer has more and more cups of that brand of tea – and can lose trust overnight – one rogue tea bag and the consumer can lose trust in the brand and not buy it again.

British readers in particular may remember with some joy the amusing story of the collapse of Ratner's. Ratner's was a chain of jewellery stores specialising in cheap and cheerful jewellery, and the brand was successful, to the extent that most British high streets contained a Ratner's store. But in 1992, the chairman Gerald Ratner made an unfortunate after-dinner speech to the Institute of Directors, joking about the 'total crap' that Ratner's sold. 'We sell a pair of earrings for under £1, which is cheaper than a prawn sandwich from Marks & Spencer, but I have to say the earrings probably won't last as long.' The joke rather backfired, when the Ratner's brand became associated with a reputation for cheap tat; the share price plummeted, wiping £500 million off the value of the company, and Ratner had to depart.[44] The story is amusing only for those who did not lose their jobs as a result of Ratner's indiscretion.

Branding is also, as we mentioned in Chapter 5, one sort of solution for the problem of local trust on the Internet. In e-commerce, one might begin to trust certain well-known branded retailers with one's credit card – Amazon, for example, or e-Bay. And when looking for quality information, one can focus on organisations, such as particular universities, pressure groups, think tanks or other services, whose 'brand' one trusts – i.e. which one trusts to disseminate truthful information.

In her massive global bestseller *No Logo*,[45] Naomi Klein has argued against branding, and the associated creation of logos, as an invasion of public space and an inversion of freedom and diversity. Brands, she argues, have taken over – or sometimes hollowed out – the high street, pushing more interesting retailers out of business. They sell goods for high prices in the developed world, while pushing costs down by producing in third-world sweatshops. And through corporate sponsorship and other intrusions, barely any public gathering is free of their influence. Even the Body Shop, a worldwide brand specifically developed to 'do good', gets many a swipe.

> Similarly, the Body Shop – though it may well be the most progressive multinational on the planet – still has a tendency to display its good deeds in its store windows before getting its corporate house in order. Anita Roddick's company has been the subject of numerous damning investigations in the press, which have challenged the company's use of chemicals, its stand on unions and even its claim that its products have not been tested on animals.[46]

Now, Klein's attack is in many ways well-conceived, and there can be no possible objection to stalking multinational behemoths and exposing them when they exploit labour, distort markets, indulge in corruption or act as bullies. However, from the specific point of view of trust, there are reasons for discounting much of the anti-brand case.

First, as we have noted, branding acts as a repository of trust. The noticeable economic behaviour of individuals is that they will pay a premium in order to reduce uncertainty. In the case of brands, people will pay over the odds to get a branded good, because an unbranded good cannot be trusted to the same extent as its branded counterpart. Companies invest a lot of money in brands and advertising, and they need to ensure that the brand stores their reputations and keeps them spotless.

Beyond that, people will also pay a great deal over the odds for designer goods – by buying the 'right' label, they trust the designers to ensure they are seen to be 'cool'. Most of us have done it sometime. It is stupid, but fun. And no one is *forced* to do it.

People have always done expensive things to mark themselves out from the crowd in some way, and there is nothing intrinsically weirder about wearing Armani jeans than, say, stretching one's earlobes or tattooing one's body. Frivolous it may be, popular it definitely is, but it is debatable whether global corporations have noticeably corrupted society, or that the practice of conspicuous consumption is particularly harmful.

Second, brands have gone beyond particular goods – the brand now connotes a lifestyle.[47] Some people, like Klein, find this worrying. It is, of course, supremely silly to believe that wearing a Nike hat or Calvin Klein underwear will make you any better a person or higher an achiever (though it may contribute at the margin to a slightly greater level of sexual success). But few people actually think such silly things. And – when you look closely – brands and their hype are rather risible than sinister. This is an interview with Tamara Ingram, CEO of advertisers McCann-Erickson-UK.

> She is a bit vague about the number of UK staff made redundant this year, eventually plumping for 10. 'I've got a very simple attitude towards people. Our brand doesn't really exist. We don't sit on a shelf.
>
> 'All we have is the brilliance of our ideas. So the people are the magic and you have to value them and create an environment where you can get the best out of them.' ...
>
> On the table in front of Ingram, are a sheaf of notes to which she refers constantly as she trots out a rather confusing presentation about what her company offers.
>
> 'There's a tool called brand optimisation. It's about connecting what the essence of the brand is, what we need to communicate, and looking at all the barriers and the media opportunities. Then it looks at how you can affect all those boundaries in all the different

markets and, through this black box thing called fusion, you can then plan your money.'

Amid this stream of advertising gobbledegook, she has a moment of clarity: 'In the end, the purpose of all this is to get your thing purchased in preference to something else.'[48]

Er, right.

Most people have a healthy scepticism about all this guff. Some do not. Klein quotes one Carmine Collettion, a 24-year-old Internet entrepreneur (although I have found him hard to trace online – he is even less famous than Shep the dog, never mind me) who apparently had the Nike swoosh tattooed on his navel, as saying 'I wake up every morning, jump in the shower, look down at the symbol, and that pumps me up for the day. It's to remind me every day what I have to do, which is, "Just Do It".'[49] Klein quotes this without comment, but presumably her beef is the Orwellian way in which the Nike slogan has begun to control this unfortunate person's life. I confess I find it hard to get so excited about it. To me, the quote communicates two things: firstly, that Mr Collettion is commendably clean, and secondly, that he is a bit of an idiot.

Third, we shouldn't just assume that the benefits of trade are one-way, and that global trade is a mechanism to transfer money from poor countries to rich ones. In that case, branding *would* be problematic, because – as a local trust mechanism that goes beyond the local – it is an important factor in spreading trade from one country to another. International brands enable the international shopper to buy goods he or she understands, and whose quality he or she can rely on. I recall once in a suburb of Kobe, Japan, trying to find a place to meet up with my wife. Kobe is a wonderful city, but to the non-native speaker it can be deeply confusing, and it is hard to guess what the functions of buildings are: is that a teashop, or a $200 per head restaurant, or a topless bar? How glad we were to see the McDonald's by the subway station! Though we probably got the lousiest culinary experience in Kobe, home of such marvellous beef, we were able to meet there, confident that whoever got there first could spin out half an hour or so of time without spending a fortune or acting inappropriately. Nice for us. But if the global brands are a mechanism for oppression, maybe our gain was not worth the price.

This isn't the case, fortunately. Quite apart from the fact that if a Bushman of the Kalahari wants a can of Coke it seems a little totalitarian to try to prevent him, trade doesn't so much transfer value as create it. The more trades are made, the harder money works, and the more people are enriched by it. Different countries have *comparative advantages* in the production of certain goods, a phenomenon first described by economist David Ricardo (1772–1823).[50] Even a country that is less efficient in producing *everything* can still find a market niche with global trade, because if it produces the goods it is most efficient at producing, its production allows other countries to produce more of other things. It has a *comparative* advantage (*not* an absolute advantage) in the production of those goods.

That some people are underpaid and exploited, and that others are too poor to buy the branded goods on offer, does not mean that no one benefits at all in the developing world from global trade. It turns out that multinationals generally pay higher wages than indigenous firms, and that their investment often brings wider spillover benefits to economies as they open. In Turkey, wages paid by multinationals are 124 per cent of those of Turkish firms,[51] while as China's economy has opened to international trade many of its citizens, in a country often characterised by grinding poverty, are enjoying goods that people in the developed world take for granted.[52] In the immediate post-war period, India and South Korea were more or less equally poor. India, under Nehru, closed its economy and pursued self-sufficiency, while South Korea opened up, with government support for particular groups of companies called *chaebol* – in many ways precursors to the giant corporations that many worry about now. After several decades of contrasting policies, India's gross national product in 1999 was $440 per head, while South Korea's was $8,490.[53] And the costs of restricting a country's exposure to trade can be high; Zimbabwe is plunging into penury at the time of writing as a result less of President Mugabe's political repression, than of his following the prescriptions of anti-globalisation thinkers, and closing his country to the institutions of international trade.

Fourth, most importantly, brands can be used by journalists with the integrity of Naomi Klein to track wrongdoing. As Klein herself puts it:

> 'Ask her what she makes – what it says on the label. You know – label?' I said, reaching behind my head and twisting up the collar of my shirt. By now these Indonesian workers were used to people like me: foreigners who come to talk to them about the abysmal conditions in the factories where they cut, sew and glue for multinational companies like Nike, the Gap and Liz Claiborne. ...
>
> I was sympathetic, of course, but, being the Western foreigner, I wanted to know what *brand* of garments they produced at the Kaho factory – if I was to bring their story home, I would have to have my journalistic hook.[54]

Exactly. One can fight wrongdoing by big multinational brands, because one can complain about it in an effective way *locally* – specifically by boycotting the suspect produce. If I am worried about Nike using sweatshop labour, I just don't buy Nike. Simple. Whereas if the factory Klein wrote about was merely run by the

Jakarta Amalgamated Industries Corp. (or something equally unmemorable) it is hard to see exactly how I could do anything about exploitation, short of going to Jakarta and protesting myself – a noble act no doubt, but ultimately doomed to failure, partly because I have no leverage on the anonymous firm, and partly because obviously it is a course of action that very few people will take.

Klein herself cites a series of cases where big corporations tried to suppress scientific findings – from studies they had sponsored in part – that undermined their products.[55] These are shocking stories – as a scientist myself I can appreciate how such corporate bullying could affect one's career, and how deeply frustrating and unjust it would be. Furthermore, as we shall see in Chapter 7, the principle of such suppression undermines the governing ethic of scientific research. The corporate bullies in question, according to Klein, were Boots, Apotex and an unnamed textile company. But branded corporations make themselves vulnerable by becoming well-known – and when we examine Klein's stories more closely, we discover that Boots backed off and allowed the offending research to be published after exposure in the *Wall Street Journal*, while Apotex ultimately failed either to repress their article or to ensure that the researcher lost her job. In each case, a painful struggle was involved for the researchers, but eventually – because of the prominence that a brand gives a firm – the struggle was successful. The third case, of the unnamed company, does not seem to have ended happily – and one suspects that the problem there was that the textile company's brand was simply not strong enough to be used against it. Strong brands aid protest and enforcement.

Companies can be held to account by their brands. At the 2003 Annual Meeting of the World Economic Forum committee on trust and governance, this point was explicitly made. Kenneth

Roth, Executive Director of Human Rights Watch, USA, noted that:

> ... in the broader discussion on building trust, there has been an evolution in the past decade in the way in which multinational companies have accepted corporate responsibility for their behaviour. 'Today every brand-name corporation has voluntary principles which it seeks to apply.'
>
> Charles O. Holliday Jr, Chairman and Chief Executive Officer, DuPont, USA, praised by [Session chair David Gergen] as one of the business leaders who have been committed to sustainable growth and taking action to reduce global warming, declared: 'We have an obligation to operate to the same standards anywhere in the world and no exceptions.' DuPont sees customers, employees and local communities – not just shareholders – as stakeholders in the company, he said.
>
> Roth suggested the difficulty is in applying rights guidelines: how to apply a policy on gender in Saudi Arabia or on labour rights in China, or how to support human rights in Colombia while protecting industrial equipment and workers. 'We need to move beyond voluntary principles,' he suggested. 'And we are beginning to hear brand-name companies say the same thing.'[56]

Klein, though, is not interested in brands being used to do a little bit of limited good.

> We have heard the same refrain over and over again from Nike, Reebok, the Body Shop, Starbucks, Levi's and the Gap: 'Why are you picking on us? We're the good ones!' The answer is simple. They are singled out because the politics they have associated themselves with, which have made them rich – feminism, ecology, inner-city empowerment – were not just random pieces of effective

ad copy that their brand managers found lying around. They are complex, essential social ideas, for which many people have spent lifetimes fighting. That's what lends righteousness to the rage of activists campaigning against what they see as cynical distortions of those ideas.[57]

For 'righteousness' read 'self-righteousness'. Surely the point is not that big evil companies have distorted the politics of the masses, but the converse: by exploiting the visibility of companies that brands provide for the citizen, relatively small numbers of well-meaning people have forced big companies to proclaim messages about feminism etc. much more loudly than they themselves could manage. No doubt the policies are watered down, and no doubt the companies are guilty of not a little hypocrisy, but can it seriously be argued that this is not a minor victory for the citizen?

And finally, we might cheekily note that Klein herself has become a brand. A counterculture magazine with an interview or article by her would be foolish not to blazon the fact over the front cover.[58] The chic cover of her book features a 'No Logo' logo (nice and ironically postmodern, but somewhat undermining of the argument),[59] and the book itself has become a fashion accessory.[60]

Klein has a whole raft of arguments that go beyond our brief here, about the nature of public space, equality, rights, trade and culture. But from the point of view of trust, branding is the most successful way of spreading local trust through an economy that has been found yet. No institutions are required, and no regulation (though laws of trademark and copyright help firms develop such brands). Brands are essential to promote trust in business (and of course it may be that one of Klein's countercultural aims is precisely to *retard* such trust). Brands hold reputations, and that gives the consumer power within an economy.[61]

It is the anonymous businesses that are the powerful ones.

Figure 7. Naomi Klein's logo.

Horizontal and vertical relations: the emergence of deference

We have until now focused on the distinction between local trust, on the model of speech, based on personal acquaintance, and global trust, on the model of writing, based on institutions and regulations. It is clear from our discussions of the Internet and business that there is a strong tension between them, that global trust can undermine local trust, but on the other hand, for the institutions of global trust to work, they have to be trusted – on the

155

local model! If global trust institutions *could* be themselves trusted on the global model, then we would need institutions to ensure they were trustworthy, which in turn would need more institutions to monitor *them*, and so on *ad infinitum*.

The picture is very complex already. But we have to complicate it still further. Until now, we have been looking at *horizontal* relations in society, relations between equals. However, some essential relationships are hierarchical, and involve authority being passed downwards from on high – these are what we have called *vertical* relationships. Vertical relationships are problematic for trust, because an important element of *reciprocity* is lost. In a vertical relationship, I am affected by decisions I cannot take, by actions of which I have ceded control.

It is time to start to look at domains that contain vertical as well as horizontal relationships, and we will begin with the currently controversial area of science, technology and medicine. Expertise is one area where deference seems to be endemic, and where considerable debate is currently focused.

CHAPTER SEVEN

Virus the Small at Last Shall Inherit the Earth

The nature of expertise: the official story

Who are experts, why do we have them, and what do they have to do with trust? The answer to the first of those questions is pretty obvious; an expert on a topic is someone who knows an awful lot about that topic!

It's not that simple; it never is. Expertise is largely about solving problems, finding answers, diagnosing difficulties, and having a great number of practical skills. Psychologically, it turns out that expertise is less to do with the skills, and more to do with the knowledge – or, rather, that the differences between an expert and the rest of us are that (a) the expert knows more, and (b) the expert has organised her knowledge in clever ways so that she can get at the important stuff quickly.[1] In other words, there are two major psychological aspects of expert knowledge, the *content* of the knowledge, learned, usually, via textbooks, college courses, etc., and the *organisation* of the knowledge, which is what comes with practice. If you don't think organisation of knowledge is important, consider two telephone directories, one with the numbers in alphabetical order, the other in a random order. Both contain the

157

same knowledge, but the second one is completely unfit for its purpose, because it is next to impossible to find the number of the person you want in a randomly ordered directory of any size.

Experts on expertise – yes, there are such things, and I used to try to be one myself! – tend to divide expertise into *deep* and *shallow* knowledge.[2] The deep knowledge is the central theoretical knowledge about the causal and other processes that bring the phenomena of interest about. So, for example, in medicine, the deep knowledge concerns the functioning of the human body, the ways in which the different organs interact, the ways in which the different types of cell contribute to the working of the whole, even down to the body's chemistry. This is all important stuff. But it is useless for problem-solving.

If a problem is brought to an expert (in the case of a doctor, this is likely to be a patient complaining of some symptoms), then the expert doesn't usually have a great deal of time to go back to first principles and deduce what is causing the problem. With a medical patient, it is essential that the diagnosis is produced as soon as possible in order to ease the patient's suffering (*in extremis*, the diagnosis has to appear before the patient dies). Consequently, experts have a lot of shallow knowledge as well, which comes in the form of rules of thumb (such as: if the patient is pale, running a small temperature, complains of discomfort in his stomach, then the chances are the problem is one of diseases A, B or C). These rules of thumb are called *heuristics*, and are more or less uncertain, brittle, open to revision, and dependent on the particular task the expert is performing at the time. Heuristics enable experts to reach decisions quickly enough to be effective; the sacrifice, of course, is that they increase the chances of error.

Put another way, the deep knowledge is what the expert learns at college, the shallow knowledge is what she learns in practice. It is the shallow knowledge that enables her to be *effective*.

Our second question is why we have experts (or why we pay them, more to the point). The issue here is a division of labour. In a social system, rather than everyone trying to know about everything – and of course failing – it makes sense to have specialists who devote themselves to one particular domain. The accumulation of the expertise takes time, and prevents such a person from being productive in other ways. So he will support himself by selling his expertise (on medicine, car mechanics, education, administration or whatever) to the others in the community who have not devoted themselves to that expertise. Societies organise themselves so that there are incentives for people to pursue expertise that is useful; in the case of liberal capitalist economies the laws of supply and demand push up the price of experts who are either sought after or scarce, and push down the price of those who are either not terribly useful, or relatively thick on the ground. Planned economies can organise training for students more directly.

But notice that this requirement on experts takes the idea of expertise (in the sense of a publicly available skill) beyond that of knowledge pure and simple. We have already made the distinction between deep and shallow knowledge to point up the pragmatic requirements of expertise, but there is more. An expert has to be able to transfer her expertise to her customers, because it is ultimately their fees or taxes that will finance her training and provide her income. Expertise is relative, then, to a *constituency* of people, and an expert will need to understand *their* problems, explain them in such a way that *they* can appreciate the important issues, and deliver solutions that *they* can practicably carry out.[3] A doctor, for example, has to be able to meet his patients where they can attend (no point attempting to set up a surgery for a general population away from bus routes or transport systems, or in making the administration so forbidding he gets no patients, or so welcoming that he is swamped), and has to prescribe medicine that his patients might reasonably be able to afford and to take (is it possible for an individual leading a chaotic life to take doses of medicine on a regular basis?). Perhaps the most important ability is to be able to provide clear explanations of actions and diagnoses understandable by his patients.[4]

This is the difference between an expert who needs to solve problems publicly, and one who merely has a hobby (e.g. collecting cigarette cards). For an expert who cannot relate properly to his constituency, there is no better comedic example than Groucho Marx's attempt – as a horse doctor – to treat Margaret Dumont's hypochondria in the movie *A Day at the Races*. Realising some medication is required, he prescribes a horse pill, which is about an inch and a half across. The film's villain sneers: 'Isn't that awfully *large* for a pill?' To which Groucho responds: 'Well, it was too small for a basketball and I didn't know what else to do with it. Say, aren't you awfully large for a pill yourself?' Which is an explanation of sorts, but not a terribly helpful one for his constituency. The expert not only has to imbibe lots of knowledge, but if she is to function in society, she has to be able to interact with and understand her constituency.

Our third question is what all this has to do with trust. The problem with expertise as a division of labour, where the expert undertakes to learn all the knowledge about her domain so that no one else in her constituency has to, is that it is nigh on impossible for the ordinary members of the constituency to hold her accountable for her actions, at least until they have taken effect. There may be redress through the courts if a doctor is shown to be liable for an error, for example, but having that back-up is much less preferable than knowing during treatment that the doctor isn't negligent. And because so much of expertise is actually taken up with social skills it has often been possible for someone to pose as an expert purely by relating to the constituency well. By 'looking the part', many unskilled people have inveigled themselves into positions of trust in hospitals, and performed operations, diagnosed illnesses, and so on.[5] Not only that, but oftentimes it has turned out that some forms of expertise are associated with no usable knowledge at all, as for example with astrology, alchemy or phrenology. People have made similar claims about some sciences popular today, such as psychoanalysis.[6]

Hence, when we encounter an expert, we need to trust that he is who he says he is, that he has undergone the requisite quantity of training, and that his expertise will work. This is not always easy to affirm, so trust is inevitable if we want expert services. We have to trust that the expert possesses the expertise, that he will apply it carefully and rationally, and that – in return for his fee – he will apply the expertise in *our* interests, and not in his. Recall the Hippocratic Oath from Chapter 2; what this oath establishes is that the swearer will put his clients' interests first. It may be in a *doctor's* interests to spin out the illness of a patient, because then he may earn more money from more consultations; it is clearly not in the patient's interests. In the case of such a clash the patient's interests should trump those of the doctor. One problem with performance targets in the British National Health Service has been precisely that hospital administrators are given perverse incentives to fail to address patients' interests (for example, not taking on risky cases that might lower a hospital's survival statistics).[7]

The mechanisms of trust in science

So trust is essential in any relationship between expert and advisee, because the advisee will in general lack the very expertise he needs to evaluate the expert's performance. This is clearly problematic, and very hard to solve, since if the advisee acquires the expertise to evaluate the adviser, then by definition he will not require the services of the adviser! And furthermore, becoming an expert is expensive – the whole point of the expertise system, the division of intellectual labour, was to conserve resources, and those gains will be forfeit if we need to become experts because we don't trust the experts.

On the other hand, being in a position where we *have* to trust the experts can be unsettling. As philosopher Paul Feyerabend puts it:

> Man once possessed complex knowledge concerning his place in nature and was to that extent secure and free. The knowledge has been replaced by abstract theories he does not understand and must take on trust from experts. But should humans not be able to understand the basic constituents of their lives? Should not every group, every tradition be able to influence, revere, preserve such constituents in accordance with its wishes? Is not the present separation of experts and sheep one reason for the much deplored social and psychological imbalance?[8]

One way of steering between the horns of this dilemma is the method of *peer review*. In this traditional method, which began, and is still most prevalent, in the field of science, a scientist is judged by her peers, i.e. similarly qualified persons who, unlike a randomly chosen member of the general public, are able to understand the issues involved in her performance, and therefore properly to assess its quality.

Hence, for example, the publication of a research paper in science is governed by a peer review process. The authors of a paper send it to the editor of a journal, who decides on a couple of people who will understand the paper and who have no obvious connection with the authors (e.g. they don't work in the same university department). These unfortunates then have to review the paper, that is, to read it and decide whether the paper makes an original and interesting contribution to the field, and whether it (the original bit) is the work of the authors themselves as claimed. This reviewing process is extremely dull (and unpaid), but it is a key part of the system, and very few people complain about it. I have reviewed many billions of papers (well, it seems like it), and it is tedious, but obviously essential. I gain more than I lose by the system of peer review, because when my own papers appear I can point to the fact that they have been peer reviewed as evidence of their quality.

Peer review is a particularly elegant way of getting round the dilemma about evaluating expertise. The Internet, as we saw in Chapter 5, has dramatically speeded up the publication process, so that traditional peer-reviewed journals are beginning to look like yesterday's papers. But if something posted on the web is to be taken seriously, some form of peer review is vital in ensuring its claims are trustworthy.[9]

Feyerabend, for example, has argued very strongly that the lay public should retain as much control over scientific research as possible,[10] but one doesn't have to disagree with that proposition to realise that this will be an extremely inefficient and potentially dangerous process if the lay public does not then come to understand the important issues involved. Feyerabend himself conceded as much in a different context, complaining in his usual pithy way about the numbers of uninformed philosophers discussing the work of Thomas Kuhn.

> Kuhn's ideas are interesting but, alas, they are much too vague to give rise to anything but lots of hot air. If you don't believe me, look at the literature. Never before has the literature on the philosophy of science been invaded by so many creeps and incompetents.

> Kuhn encourages people who have no idea why a stone falls to the
> ground to talk with assurance about scientific method.[11]

There should be no limitations on who is able to criticise physics,
say, but if you are going to criticise a physicist you should at least
know some physics.

We noted in the previous chapter that interests are important in
determining trust and trustworthiness. It is of course essential in a
peer-review process that the reviewers are disinterested, that they
do not have any interests in ensuring that the paper gets published
(or indeed suppressed). I was recently asked to review a paper
authored by a group of people from the University of Edinburgh.
Obviously the editor of the journal thought there would be no
connection between me and the authors, because I work at
Southampton, and I have never published anything with any of the
authors. However, some of the paper's authors work on a project
together with me. I informed the editor of this potential clash of
interests, and my name was withdrawn as a reviewer of that paper.
It is not that I would have been unable to review the paper
objectively; but if the process of peer review is even *perceived* as
potentially open to manipulation, then it is that much harder for it
to operate.

Peer review began as a very gentlemanly process; its origins are
in the world of natural philosophers in the early days of science in
the 17th century, when scholarly societies were beginning to
appear and the pursuit of knowledge took its first faltering steps
towards professionalism. The difficulties in determining interests,
and in promoting objectivity, were solved essentially by co-opting
gentlemanly codes of honour, civility and integrity at the centre of
which was trust in one's fellows.[12]

As such, it was a system of local trust. But with the increasing
demonstrations of the efficacy of science as a problem-solving

mechanism, particularly in times of war, science became a means to various different ends. Whereas in the early modern period science was performed by gentlemen who could afford the expense – and more importantly had the leisure time – to indulge their curiosity, nowadays science has three sources of support. Technology that is close to production – near-market, in the jargon – is generally funded by the R&D budgets of the corporations that will exploit the end result.[13] And some highly theoretical work that may, one day, be profitable, such as biotechnology or certain areas of computing, is funded by venture capitalists, who are prepared to make many high-risk investments in the hope of one or two juicy returns in the future.[14] But most 'pure' science is funded by governments, through universities, research councils and research institutes.

It has been persuasively argued that the knowledge created by science is such a benefit to society as a whole that public funding is very defensible.[15] However, it does mean that – since the connections between scientific work and trust are so strong – most governments need mechanisms to ensure that scientific work performed is of high quality. Hence the peer-review process has been transformed, largely in the 20th century, into an institutionalised process providing *global* trust. Scientists now no longer get money unless they can satisfy various objective targets (often to do with publication rates); peer review has ceased to be a gentlemanly occupation.

I have concentrated in this section on peer review of scientific research, because that is the area where peer review began. But so successful has the model been perceived to be that peer-review processes have turned up in most government-funded areas where expertise operates; the processes being suitably amended (a) to adapt them to the particular domain, and (b) to ensure that the trust is global and backed by institutions. In British medicine, for example, one of the functions of the British Medical Association (BMA), the doctors' 'trade union', is to provide a peer-reviewing process of doctors' performance, because most of the few people able to make the technical and ethical judgements about that performance are *ipso facto* members of the BMA.

Expert authority and deference

Expertise is not always accompanied by authority. Account auditors, as we saw in the previous chapter, are not deferred to, though they are experts. They do the books of firms, and make recommendations to investors, and the investors choose whether or not to follow the advice. Philosophers are experts in various specialisms, notably ethics. But, though it has been millennia since Plato mooted the idea of deferring to philosophers over matters of right and wrong, very few people have ever done so.

The worlds of science and medicine, however, seem to carry with them a legacy of deference, hierarchy and authority, giving us *vertical* relationships between the actors. Decisions get taken in science that affect people, and yet those people have little or no say in those decisions. This is, no doubt, partly due to the high rate of government involvement in science. As a consequence, scientists get listened to by those with cash to dispense, and can find themselves quite a long way up the food chain. For example, Ian Gibson, Dean of Biological Sciences at the University of East Anglia, found himself a Labour MP in the landslide election of 1997, and ultimately chair of the Parliamentary Office on Science and Technology, the Parliamentary and Scientific Committee, and the House of Commons Select Committee on Science and Technology.[16]

Another reason is that science has produced success. It is possible to produce philosophical or sociological arguments that science is just one tradition among many, or merely a special type of rhetoric. But irrespective of those, the usefulness of science and technology for certain central purposes of government and society is undeniable. Our comfort is scientifically based; so is our prosperity. Science, alone among competing traditions, is able to alter our environment – dangerous power to have, of course, but power nonetheless. And, depressing as it is to reflect, governments lay great store in defence, security and the ability to wage successful wars. To see what a difference technology makes, we have to cast our minds back only to March and April 2003, when the USA and the UK invaded Iraq, not with a particularly massive preponderance of personnel or equipment, but with a giant technological advantage; as a result a heavily armed military dictatorship, extant for 40-odd years, ingrained in its society, in a country of 24 million people, was snuffed out in three weeks.

Let me be clear; I am saying neither that science can solve every problem, nor that science doesn't cause many new problems, nor that science is only used for good. I am saying only that science, like religion, like magic, like art, is employed by governments, organisations and individuals for particular purposes, and that science, unlike religion, magic and art, usually achieves those purposes. Much of its authority stems from this.

But that can't be the whole story. Scientists, and doctors, have been seen as authority figures to whom we should defer for centuries (long before scientists and doctors were ever able to create the conditions for the successes we have just discussed). Doctors assumed control of their patients long before they ever discovered how to cure them. Plato, for instance, uses a lot of medical metaphors, and mentions doctors in many asides through his work, and together they give us quite an interesting picture of Greek medical practice.

> Doctors provide the clearest parallel. We believe in them whether they cure us with our consent or without it, by cutting or burning or applying some other painful treatment, and whether they do so according to written rules or apart from written rules, and whether as poor men or rich.[17]

The burden of much of Plato's writing about politics is that politicians are like doctors, charged with keeping the body politic well. And to do that, often deception is required.[18]

> And while an inferior doctor is adequate for people who are willing to follow a regimen and don't need drugs, when drugs are needed, we know that a bolder doctor is required.
>
> That's true. But what exactly do you have in mind?
>
> I mean that it looks as though our rulers will have to make considerable use of falsehood and deception for the benefit of those they rule. And we said that all such falsehoods are useful as a form of drug.[19]

> We have an analogy in the sick and ailing; those in charge of feeding them try to administer the proper diet in tasty foods and drinks, and offer them unwholesome items in revolting foods, so that the patients may get into the desirable habit of welcoming the one kind and loathing the other.[20]

In each case, the idea is that a doctor, interested only in objectively removing our pain, can deceive us in the interests of such removal (and in removing illness *only*; obviously the doctor is not allowed to lie to us in order to steal our money). His authority comes dually from his expertise and his disinterestedness; he acts wholly in our interests, and as such exemplifies the idea of the intellectual division of labour. He is our *agent*.

Nowadays, the situation is different – to a degree. Patients' autonomy, their responsibility for their own lives, is respected to a much greater extent, and they are kept informed of treatments and risks. However, there is still an authority situation in place; the switch is that patients are *forced* to be autonomous. Whereas traditionally, doctors would conceal unpleasant facts from patients, because it was not *good for them* to know, now the ethical standard is to insist on confronting patients with the (possibly slightly airbrushed) facts, because autonomy is *good for them*. It is still the medical profession, and *their* ethical codes, that determine the ideal relationship between patients and the knowledge of their condition.[21]

Scientists and doctors have always had this sway over their clients. Perhaps the most bizarre, and disturbing, example of this occurred in experiments performed in the 1960s by Stanley Milgram.[22] The experiments were to test subjects' obedience to authority. Milgram's confederate, posing as the subject of the experiment, was strapped into what looked like an electric chair; it was, in fact, harmless. The volunteer – the *actual* subject – had to press a button to administer what he thought were electric shocks to the fake subject. When the button was pressed, nothing happened, but the confederate in the chair would writhe around in pain. Milgram would observe the results, increase the 'voltage', and ask the subject to 'apply' greater and greater 'shocks'. As this went on, the confederate would appear to be in greater and greater agony, and would scream to be allowed to go free. Ultimately he would collapse, apparently unconscious. Even then Milgram would continue to ask the volunteers to apply greater doses of 'electricity'. He used particular forms of words to get the subject to continue: 'the experiment requires that you continue'; 'you have no choice but to go on'.

Milgram's hypothesis was that 0.1 per cent of the subjects

would continue to the end of the experiment, delivering 'shocks' of 450V (the confederate would feign unconsciousness at 315V). The incredible result was that, contrary to hypothesis, *65 per cent* of the subjects completed the course of torture, often to their own massive mental discomfort.

> I observed a mature and initially poised businessman enter the laboratory smiling and confident. Within 20 minutes he was reduced to a twitching, stuttering wreck, who was rapidly approaching a point of nervous collapse. He constantly pulled at his ear lobe and twisted his hands. At one point he pushed his fist into his forehead and muttered, 'Oh God, let's stop it.'[23]

This extraordinary authority depends to a very large extent on competence and disinterestedness.[24] These are the twin themes that have run through my account of science and medicine in this chapter so far, which has been telling the *official* story of expertise. However, not everyone buys this story. Feyerabend, as usual, has the most extreme set of views.

> But there are some professions which still seem to be exempt from doubt. Many people trust a physician or an educator as they would have trusted a priest in earlier times. But doctors give incorrect diagnoses, prescribe harmful drugs, cut, X-ray, mutilate at the slightest provocation partly because they are incompetent, partly because they don't care and have so far been able to get away with murder, partly because the basic ideology of the medical profession which was formed in the aftermath of the scientific revolution can deal only with certain restricted aspects of the human organism but still tries to cover everything by the same method. Indeed, so large has the scandal of malpractice become that the physicians themselves are now advising their patients not to be content with a

single diagnosis but to shop around and to supervise their treat-ment. Of course, second opinions should not be restricted to the medical profession for the problem may not be the incompetence of a single doctor, or of a group of doctors, the problem may be the *incompetence of scientific medicine as a whole.*[25]

How do science's critics argue their case, and how does this affect both the deference and the trust that scientists have traditionally received?

Experts' interests

Suppose someone is doing something helpful; do we trust her to be always helpful? It depends. If it is in her interests at the moment to be helpful, then it may be that all we can trust her to do is to pursue her own interests; she may not be helpful once her interests change. Hence if Feyerabend is right that scientists and doctors are not (always/usually/sometimes) competent and disinterested, trust will become a serious problem.

In general, there is extraordinary selflessness in the pursuit of scientific progress. The Czech immunologist and poet Miroslav Holub describes the situation of the 'ordinary' scientist rather well.

But what about the technical assistant who is merely thanked at the end of the publication, is not usually personally or existentially interested in the results, has no scientific ambition, and only does his or her technical, ordinary, tedious job? The person puts himself or herself out by sticking to the rules, by admitting the everyday mistakes, and definitively by supplying results in which nine laboratory animals produce values of 90 to 120 and the tenth a value of 600, when you cannot really say the tenth one (technically known as the 'idiot mouse') is different in any way.

> This technical assistant ... really exists in many a laboratory, and we are all dependent on this person, that is, dependent on the categorical imperative by which this person is ruled – nobody knows why. ... As a rule, he or she cannot even expect the revelation of adequate financial compensation ... .
>
> Such a person is the personification of the categorical imperative in conditions difficult to imagine even for a head like Kant's. However, such a person is the *sine qua non* of present-day science.[26]

According to critics of science and the scientific process, this undeniable selflessness – examples are legion – is overridden by other power and interest structures that impose themselves. We have already discussed Naomi Klein's criticisms of the commercial sponsorship of science, and attempts by funding organisations to censor results.[27] There have been many claims that the whole scientific enterprise is actually very much bound up with commercial and military considerations, and that research is pushed in ways that press the interests of these groups within society, not of society as a whole.

Such pressures, it is claimed, mean that scientists' judgements are often value-laden, not the clear, rational, disinterested pronouncements of the official story. In particular, scientific estimates of risk depend to a large extent on which outcomes the funding and controlling forces behind scientists want to happen. There will, for example, be a lot of pressure on scientists to understate the risks from GM foods; the vested interests behind companies like Monsanto, and behind governmental agricultural bodies (hand in glove with commercial interests), are more willing to discount fears of contamination than the people and farmers who might be on the receiving end.[28]

A more measured, less black-and-white version of this criticism is that the narrowly instrumental view that scientists can take –

particularly in commercial or military contexts – of their technologies may be less than adequate for determining all the relevant questions about the introduction of those technologies and the ways these affect society and the requirements of individuals. We can no longer take the stability of the environment, of what scientists call *boundary conditions*, for granted. Scientists and economists often add the Latin phrase *ceteris paribus* to their writings, 'all things being equal'. Actually, all things are not always equal, and sometimes that is a very brave assumption indeed.[29]

The pressure on scientists can come from a number of directions, and at a number of points in the scientific process. Sociologist Edward Shils points out that there are many and various attitudes that scientists themselves can have to pressure, both political and financial.

> Between the extremes of subservient acceptance of responsibility for the purposes of authority and the insistent claim to arrogate responsibility for guiding and counselling if not actually ruling, between the extremes of utter indifference to any responsibility for the wellbeing of society and the rancorous and aggressive rejection of any responsibility and indeed a hatred which would obliterate any sense of responsibility towards the prevailing society, there is a large and various set of attitudes and actions.[30]

Shils' survey of the history of the acceptance or otherwise of responsibility for intellectual work from Plato to the former Soviet Union certainly demonstrates the massive politicisation – the use of technical work to justify political actions – of the sciences, particularly the social sciences.[31] Indeed, in the 1980s, the United Kingdom's Education Secretary Sir Keith Joseph went so far as to launch an attack, from his Thatcherite position, on the main funding body for research into social science, the Social Science Research Council (SSRC), on the ground that the social sciences were packed with people of the left. After cutting budgets, and setting up an enquiry to determine whether social science projects could or should be funded from the private sector (and therefore whether the SSRC could be safely abolished), in the end the best he managed to do was to change the name of the organisation to the Economic and Social Research Council (ESRC), hoping to undermine the idea that social studies might be 'scientific' at all.[32] Governments elsewhere have been, on occasion, more effective at controlling the milieux of scientific research.[33] Research is so strongly associated nowadays with political authority that scientists, particularly social and environmental scientists, are going to have to get used to it.[34]

Influence on research can also happen in a more direct way. Rather than creating the environment in which research is performed, and appropriating helpful results that may have been achieved more or less independently, it is also possible to set up research that is guaranteed to produce the right result. The creation of research institutes funded by industry at times threatens to merge the professions of scientific research and public relations. If a company puts forward a defence of its own products, then no one believes it. But a third party can say much that the company itself can't say in its own defence. Hence there are very obvious incentives for firms to set up third parties to act in their own interests.

For example, a women's environmental group called Mothers Opposing Pollution (MOP) campaigned in the 1990s against plastic milk bottles, on the grounds of waste disposal problems, potential carcinogenic reaction between plastic and milk, and the reduction of the quality of milk after exposure to light. Their spokeswoman, Alana Moloney, was very prominent, yet strangely mysterious, as were the finances of the organisation. Alana Moloney turned out, as a newspaper revealed, to be really one Janet Rundle, head of a public relations company called J.R. and Associates. One of her partners was a Trevor Munnery, who also ran a PR firm called Unlimited Public Relations, one of the clients of which was the Association of Liquidpaperboard Carton Manufacturers, who made paper milk cartons instead of plastic ones.[35]

And scientists have interests even in the absence of research money. The high status of expertise in society gives scientists incentives to preserve the exclusivity of expertise, for example by restricting entry to professional bodies. Expertise relies on a monopoly of knowledge by experts, and to that end we can find experts deliberately obfuscating issues to deny the lay public a reasonable perspective on their actions.[36]

Scientists' interests matter. But equally we should beware of simply assuming that total public control is a panacea, and that it is the establishment that always wields the pressure.

First, it is often the case that trust mechanisms are exploitable in science to *evade* responsibility. When a discipline bows to the pressure from thinkers (and organisations) who wish to prevent scientists from taking decisions that affect the rest of us without consultation, procedures are often set up that include affected people in decision-making. For example, since the 1960s the medical profession has been much less tolerant of doctors using lies or deception to get consent for treatment from patients, even when that consent is 'for their own good'.[37] However, sometimes it may be that the doctor/scientist actually is the only person who can make a genuinely informed decision here (*pace* Feyerabend). And in that case, it may be that processes of 'keeping patients informed' become methods for *avoiding* responsibility, in today's litigious times, for decisions taken.[38]

If we tell patients about bad outcomes and they consent, then they
are responsible, not us. Rather than a way of sharing power, truth
telling and the process of seeking consent has become a way of
evading accountability.[39]

And second, do not think that the complex of interests that, for
example, Shils describes is only a matter of evil governments and
the military-industrial complex leaning on scientists in order to
pollute and arm our world without let or hindrance. The good
guys can bite back as well, and quite hard too. In 2001, a
statistician, Bjorn Lomborg, published an extensive study of the
data behind many scientific works in environmental science.[40] The
results were startling; according to Lomborg, environmental
scientists had dramatically overplayed the significance of their
data, which proved very little beyond the obvious fact that
humanity affects its environment. The facts, Lomborg claimed,
were often distorted, and many solutions to problems were more
suited to easing Western consciences than actually achieving much
(paying extra for organic lemon grass makes no difference; paying
a dollar towards providing clean water or diarrhoea treatment in
Africa goes a long way). There are environmental problems which
need our attention, but they are not insoluble, and the situation is
not dire.

The reaction has been impressive from the environmental
science lobby. The Danish Committee on Scientific Dishonesty has
judged the book dishonest.[41] *Scientific American* ran an editorial
to 'defend science'[42] – which is mildly bizarre given that actually
Lomborg, as a statistician, *relies* on scientific data to make his
case, and far from criticising science, is supporting it. He is
criticising those who extrapolate (as he sees it) too far from the
data, those who make a public case. Much of the counterattack on
Lomborg ignores the arguments he makes. Like any whistleblower,

he has trodden on toes; it just so happens he has not trodden on the usual toes. What the Lomborg case shows is that heretical scientists will always find themselves marginalised, whether they are pro- or anti-establishment (other marginalised anti-establishment work includes research that is pro-smoking[43] or anti-vaccination).[44] Just as with industry-sponsored 'research institutes', many environmental scientists see their brief explicitly *not* as creating objective and disinterested science on the model of the official view outlined in the first sections of this chapter. Stephen Schneider, Professor of Environmental Biology and Global Change at Stanford University, has argued as follows.

> On the one hand, as scientists we are ethically bound to the scientific method, in effect promising to tell the truth, the whole truth and nothing but – which means that we must include all the doubts, the caveats, the ifs, ands and buts. On the other hand, we are not just scientists but human beings as well. And like most people we'd like to see the world a better place, which in this context translates into our working to reduce the risk of potentially disastrous climatic change. To do that we need to get some broad-based support, to capture the public's imagination. That, of course, entails getting loads of media coverage. So we have to offer up scary scenarios, make simplified, dramatic statements, and make little mention of any doubts we may have. This 'double ethical bind' we frequently find ourselves in cannot be solved by any formula. Each of us has to decide what the right balance is between being effective and being honest. I hope that means being both.[45]

This quote has been widely used against Professor Schneider, often unfairly. But it certainly should put to rest the idea that it is only rapacious capitalists who use science to promote their views and interests. Though scientists have interests, and though any attempt to understand a scientific situation should be informed with an appreciation of where those interests lie, it equally should not escape our notice that those who study and comment on scientific work also have interests. Academic reputations developed through years of criticising scientific method, or scientific myth, are important to the critics, and it should not be assumed that only scientists, companies and governments have interests. It would be foolish to assume that scientific critics have nothing at stake.

Failures of the system

Given that science relies on various processes carried out by fallible people, it is unsurprising that on many occasions its course can go awry. When interests conflict, then scientists can often find themselves interpreting evidence over-optimistically or over-pessimistically, providing misleading advice to administrators, or otherwise failing to see the world as objectively as the official story would have it. Specialists have often found themselves as key figures in power struggles, and objectivity is extremely difficult to retain under such circumstances.[46]

Failures of this kind are generally unconscious. But of course fraud can also occur. In a particularly prominent recent example, a physicist called Jan Hendrik Schön was exposed as having lied about some potentially marvellous results in physics and electronics. The peer review system had broken down. Schön actually co-authored all his papers, but none of his co-authors noticed the fraud. The papers' reviewers seem to have suspended their critical faculties, so exciting were the results (to a physicist, I hasten to add). And his employers, Bell Laboratories, poured a lot of money into useless investments.[47]

All the same, this incident, and others like it, are not too worrying. Schön's results, if verified, would certainly have put him in line for a Nobel Prize, but in the nature of the case they were unlikely to be verifiable. He seems to have gained little beyond his salary, and in the long term to have lost his career and credibility. He appears still to believe that the results are correct, but that mistakes in method have discredited them.[48] Outright fraud is unusual, and the peer-review system – though there is nothing wrong with a shake-up now and again – functions reasonably well.

Failures of scientific procedure tend rather to have multiple causes and to happen in areas that for some reason are not very amenable to scientific study. Perhaps the most publicised event where scientific ignorance led to human, political and commercial catastrophe is the BSE crisis in the United Kingdom (and else-where) from the mid-1980s on, and it is worth rehearsing the unfortunate story to pick out a few issues that confront scientists when working on such difficult problems.

Bovine spongiform encephalopathy (BSE), scrapie and Creutzfeldt-Jakob disease (CJD) are three examples of a mysterious group of diseases called transmissible subacute spongiform encephalopathies (TSSEs), which cause lesions in the brain and nervous system (giving tissue a spongy texture), and so gradually inhibit sufferers' motor coordination, alter personality and behaviour, and ultimately lead to dementia and death; they are not romantic or pretty afflictions. Scrapie, a disease of sheep, has been known for a couple of hundred years; it is not transmissible to humans. CJD is a rare TSSE that appears in humans, first described in 1913.

In 1985 a new TSSE, BSE, began to afflict cattle in Britain. A theory began that consumption of beef might lead to the spread of this disease to humans. Governments and scientists insisted there was no identifiable risk. Nevertheless, in 1993, a British farmer, one of whose cattle had contracted BSE in 1989, was diagnosed with CJD; this was worrying, although actually his CJD seems not to have been related.[49] More people began to be diagnosed with CJD, however, and by 1996, an article in the medical journal, the *Lancet*, put forward the theory that a new variant of CJD (vCJD, sometimes nvCJD), possibly connected with BSE, had been identified.[50] There *was* a risk from eating beef, and of course the results were catastrophic for the beef industry. When the findings were announced by Health Minister Stephen Dorrell, confidence collapsed, and British beef was off the menu.

Science, it has been said, has never recovered the trust of people after this farrago.

> [Mistrust in science] has been crystallized by ... BSE and its associated human form nvCJD. ... As researchers from the University of Lancaster have argued, BSE was a watershed point in collective understanding about the fallibility of science and about the possibility of long-term unknown consequences. Institutional government and corporate science seemed blind to these consequences.[51]

Well, science is not infallible, and no one worth a candle has ever claimed it was. But in this case, medical science for a long time failed to spot any risks at all, and when a risk was suspected (the risk of a risk, one might say) scientists were still slow to find any evidence for it. Why were the risks from BSE overlooked for so long?

The first point to note is that TSSEs are deeply unusual and mysterious diseases. They are caused by viruses, but very unusual ones. Viruses generally need some material to help them reproduce; like animals and plants they use a nucleic acid (DNA, which carries human genes, is a nucleic acid). A TSSE virus does not carry nucleic acid;[52] it is actually a virulent form of a generally harmless protein that is carried in all our bodies (called a *prion*), and it reproduces by causing the body to produce, not the harmless version, but the virulent version.[53] This is an extremely unusual form of transmission, the theory of which was only developed in 1982.[54] Though it is infectious, it triggers no immune reaction in the human body;[55] it is after all a protein ordinarily found in the body. It is resistant to all usual decontamination procedures, and so has often been spread by apparently sterile implements and instruments.[56] And its incubation period is colossal by viral standards, being several years rather than a few days.[57] Hence scientists often began investigations by looking in the wrong places and for the wrong results.

Second, science itself, as has already been pointed out, alters the background conditions of its investigations. Quite often scientific procedures actually contributed to the spread of TSSEs. For example, in 1935, an attempt to vaccinate sheep against a tick-spread disease of the nervous system called louping ill used an inactivated louping ill virus as vaccine; the formaldehyde in the suspension deactivated the louping ill virus, but not the scrapie virus, which was present in at least one and perhaps as many as eight of the 300 sheep used to create the vaccine. The louping ill vaccine – which worked excellently – spread scrapie to blackface sheep for the first time.[58] CJD (*not* the vCJD that developed from BSE) has been spread in France by the injection of human growth hormone extracted from the pituitary glands of CJD sufferers into sufferers from dwarfism,[59] in Japan by the use of dura mater (a membrane that protects the brain) taken from cadavers to protect exposed areas of brain in neurosurgery,[60] and in America by corneal transplants.[61] People have been affected by surgical instruments, for example by electrodes inserted into the brain for taking EEG readings, which had been used a few weeks earlier on a sufferer. They had been sterilised as usual with alcohol and formaldehyde – but the CJD virus is not destroyed by such measures.[62] All of these accidental incidents were down to ignorance, not negligence; scientists cannot know the facts in advance of their discovery.

Third, science produces enormous quantities of information, and it is impossible for people in disparate fields to comprehend all of it. Hence when it comes to making connections between topics – for example, between the veterinary literature on scrapie and the medical literature on CJD – it is not unusual for there to be gaps of several years. *They* knew all the time, goes the impatient refrain, but *they* might be a highly focused and distributed group of people who rarely communicate. The Internet will help cross-fertilise knowledge,[63] but even so it is unrealistic to expect anyone to know everything. For instance, the knowledge that scrapie could be spread via products of the pituitary gland existed, but the people working on growth hormones taken from human pituitary glands simply were unaware of that research.[64] Indeed, it was barely understood at all that scrapie and CJD were both examples of TSSEs.

Fourth, science generally consists in dominant theories that are more or less taken as read, and all other work is done within their limits; such dominant theories are called 'paradigms' in the literature.[65] Evidence against such paradigms needs to be unusually strong, and the fact that prions can take several different forms contradicted some well-founded theory in molecular biology that proteins have a single form determined by the amino acids that make them up.[66] Hence understanding TSSEs involved a large leap of the scientific imagination (which gained a Nobel Prize for scientist Stanley Prusiner).

Fifth, science tries to produce generalisations. But TSSEs are very rare, and the virus that causes them is very singular. So it was extremely difficult to get information on them at all, because the phenomena are very hard to isolate and observe. When a victim of a TSSE *is* isolated, it is hard to determine what causal factors were involved in his contracting it, and hence hard to generalise to a wider population. It is still unknown whether the farmer who contracted CJD in 1993 had vCJD or was one of the rare cases of standard CJD; it is still unknown whether BSE was first transmitted to cows from the use of sheep offal in meat and bone meal fed to them. This may be the obvious theory, but there is very little evidence for it;[67] one question is why recycling herbivores in this way should have caused BSE only in 1985, since the practice goes back to the 19th century. Indeed, it is possible that the original epidemic was caused by the use of tigers from Bristol Zoo which had died from a feline TSSE, in meat and bone meal.[68] This is extremely hard to generalise from: how often does a cow eat a tiger?

Sixth, fraud cannot be ruled out in the spread of diseases. Science can isolate risks, and suggest ways to mitigate them, but if people do not follow correct procedures, then there is little that scientists can do. In the case of vCJD, British measures for preventing the spread of BSE implemented in 1988 failed to eradicate the feeding of meat and bone meal to cattle, and only in 1996, at the time of the deepest crisis, was possession of such meal made a criminal offence.[69] In France, extremely rigorous measures included the forcible destruction of the entire herd once a case of BSE had been detected; without a doubt this meant that not all cases were reported.[70]

Seventh, risk is inevitable, and science cannot remove risks, except by causing a great deal of harm in other ways. For example, human growth hormone could have become risk-free only by not using it at all – in which case childhood dwarfism would have had to go untreated.[71] We will discuss the implications of the so-called *precautionary principle* below.

And eighth, science is a complex and slow business. Assiduous readers of footnotes will see that I have relied heavily in this section on Maxime Schwartz's book, *How the Cows Turned Mad*. As well as being the foremost source for the general reader on TSSEs, it is a narrative of the scientific investigations into their various forms, beginning with scrapie and ending up with vCJD. Rarely have the twists, turns and luck involved in scientific investigation been so brilliantly revealed by an author. Thinkers about science are divided about how methodical science can be: some claim that the gathering of knowledge can be regimented,[72] others that pretty well anything goes;[73] most assume it is something of a middle way.[74] But such thinkers tend inevitably to think about single scientific enterprises, perhaps performed by one person or one laboratory; the TSSE case shows that investigations can cross centuries and disciplines, and that coincidence and luck inevitably play a massive part. Schwartz, in a moment of splendid Frenchness, even ascribes a misplaced experiment by an Edwardian veterinarian to his working in English, not French![75]

Science is certainly fallible. The vCJD crisis is clearly a terrible combination of factors, risks, ignorance and indeed blunders and fraud. Scientists have found it extremely difficult to keep politicians and the public fully informed, and have struggled to balance the reduction of risk with the prevention of the collapse of the beef industry, on which so many jobs depend. Tabloid news reporting, as ever, has not helped matters. But despite the uncertainty, in fact the evidence is relatively optimistic. Up until May 2003, 129 people had died from the disease, and the rate of death is not increasing exponentially (at the moment, numbers are even declining, with 17 deaths in 2002, contrasting with 28 deaths in the worst year so far, 2000, though it can't be automatically assumed that that decline will continue). Estimating the full extent of the disease's toll is next to impossible, because the incubation period of vCJD is unknown – the latest study at the time of writing placed the range of future deaths between 10 and 540. There is clearly great uncertainty here, but the final figure is unlikely to reach the hundreds of thousands, as was initially feared.[76] One does not want to minimise the appalling nature of the disease, or the distress caused to relatives of sufferers, but as a public health problem, it is reasonable to hope that the most pessimistic pictures were false. If, as claimed earlier, the BSE crisis was a watershed, and trust in science has been significantly undermined, then this loss of trust has happened as a result of a public health crisis that seems mercifully to have been extremely minor.

In other words, scientists initially failed to spot the risks from BSE because knowledge of the disease was slow in coming. Then scientists acknowledged the risk of a risk, but for a while found no evidence for an actual risk. When evidence of a risk was discovered and published in 1996, science suggested extremely zealous measures for reducing the risk (measures that appear, with hind-sight, to have been over-zealous). So far, all the evidence is that the risk is fairly minor – certainly compared with risks we don't think twice about, like those associated with driving a car or eating chocolate. Despite what the critics of science seem to be saying, the performance of science in investigating this terrible illness, in the almost total absence of usable data, has actually been pretty good. The UK Parliament's Phillips Report concluded that 'most of those responsible for responding to the challenge posed by BSE emerge with credit'.[77]

In this section, I have used the phrase 'the risk of a risk' a couple of times. It's an odd phrase when you think about it, and yet it is the centrepiece of the argument of many who wish to withdraw trust from science. The phrase shifts the emphasis from the amassing of evidence to the conceivability of risk; how this affects the trust and mistrust of scientists we will see in the next section.

Stories, narratives and the precautionary principle

Science has always thrived on narratives. When a scientist writes up her research, she will generally put the account in narrative form: I did *this*, then *this*, got *these* results, which suggested *this* theory, which I confirmed with *these* experiments. These narratives actually conceal a great deal of extra material that doesn't get in the report; the dead ends, the mistakes, the dodgy data.

Some of this is dealt with in traditional ways, usually by coded messages that scientists learn to understand. 'Handling difficulties' means 'I sneezed on the petri dish'; 'It has long been known that …' means 'I can't remember who said it'. Such stuff will get ironed out in the course of research.

Scientists' dissembling goes much further than such messages, though. In my own studies of expertise, the aim was to build computer systems that replicated expert performance (*expert systems* or *knowledge-based systems*). The first stage of building such systems – which are widely used in a number of fields – was *knowledge acquisition*, which was in effect asking experts what they did to solve problems.[78] Actually, knowledge acquisition had to be an advanced branch of psychology, because experts would lie through their teeth!

Experts are trained to construct narratives about their work. These narratives appear in scientific papers as we have noted, and also in other contexts such as textbooks or courts of law. They are partly designed to foster the myth of the scientist collecting the data and making sense of it. But for building computer systems, what we wanted to know was *exactly* what experts did, how they *reasoned*, what *mistakes* they made, what dead ends they ended up in, because we wanted the computer systems to make exactly the same mistakes (from which, like the scientists, they could learn).

The gap between narrative and practice was a deeply interesting one (well, it kept me employed for a few years).[79]

So narratives are nothing new in science. But they are coming to play a different role in the discussion of science in wider society. Given the increased interaction between the public and science that everyone seems to be in favour of,[80] issues tend to be dramatised by scenarios that make the problems and benefits clear, and that link the new facts with established understanding, as for example the poet Anne Stevenson does rather well in the work from which this chapter takes its title.

> Nucleic crystals, pursed in the invisible,
> Drift between pyres through pastures emptied of stock.
> If myths were mortal, panic would cull the devil.
> The season's immersed in slaughter and roiled muck.
> What's learned how to fly, propagate, strike
>   and hoard its luck?
>
> Herd's-bane, heart's-bane, clovenhoof's-bane,
> Wandering to and fro among the animals,
> Choosing – to stoke its fires – the human brain
> So that Virus the Small at last shall inherit the earth,
> Outlasting love, the ordeal of it, grief,
>   and the love of gain.[81]

Such scenarios lead fairly naturally to the idea of taking precautions; if it is possible to dream up such a scenario, then surely we should make sure it can't happen. Science, on such an account, is 'interfering' with the delicate balance of nature; such interference, then, creates uncertainty, which must be resolved before any action to disturb the balance is taken. We must make sure our risk-dramatising narratives really can't happen. This leads to what has been called the *precautionary principle*.

The essential idea behind the principle is that, in the face of uncertainty about the possible harm associated with some activity or technology, greater emphasis should be placed on providing evidence that harm will not result. In the absence of such evidence of 'no harm', the principle suggests that an activity or technology should be restricted to protect against possible (potential or theoretical) harm until evidence of safety is reliably established.[82]

It has been claimed that such risk-consciousness is characteristic of modern societies, that the inevitability of risk, its ubiquity and major consequences, and the fact that there is nothing we can do about it mean that our relations with those in authority, our rulers and experts, are characteristically fraught.[83] Like most sweeping generalisations in sociology, this is false; other societies have had similar problems with generalised low-level, high-consequence risk (at least as they perceive it). To take one obvious example, the church or its enemies have often been seen as creating the circumstances for difficult interactions with God. When King John was excommunicated in November 1209, the situation was seen as massively increasing the risks for people in England, and many politicians and churchmen of the day withdrew from court; the country spent an unhappy few years until John was restored to the church.[84]

But even discounting extravagant claims about the massive yet unquantifiable risks we run today, the precautionary principle has a great deal going for it; let's avoid needless risk where we can. Such a principle, it is argued, can restore trust in science by making it clear that needless risks won't be run.[85]

How would such a scheme work in practice? Well, if the idea is to consult scientific accounts of the risk, and then try to shift the onus of proof towards those who wish to take risks, then it is clearly a good idea (if our society is genuinely risk-averse). There seems little doubt that the precautionary principle would have been useful in the management of the BSE/vCJD crisis.

The science that underlay that crisis, as I have argued, was as good as might be expected, given the unusual nature of the virus, the rarity of the phenomena to be studied, and the widespread distribution of the relevant knowledge across veterinarians, doctors, molecular biologists and so on. It is simply unrealistic to expect science to discover more, more quickly.

However, there were risks involved in the treatment of carcasses of cows with BSE, and the fact that there was no evidence in the 1980s that those risks were anything other than negligible does not mean that the risk was handled well. For example, BSE was known immediately to be a TSSE. It had been known for a while that TSSEs could spread across species, albeit with some difficulty. In the laboratory, it had been spread from sheep to goats in the 1930s,[86] and from humans to chimpanzees in 1966.[87] Indeed, virtually all our knowledge about TSSEs is due to its crossing a species barrier, when Richard Chandler succeeded in 1961 in transferring it from goats to mice, so that reliable experiments on the disease could be performed.[88]

Admittedly, such transmission was performed by direct injection, which is much more efficient than oral transmission.[89] But there had been at least one example of a TSSE crossing a species barrier via oral transmission, when scrapie had passed from sheep to mink.[90] And there was evidence of the dangers of oral transmission dating back to the 1950s when a TSSE called kuru, similar to CJD, affected the Fore, a tribe of New Guineans, in epidemic proportions. Children of both genders were susceptible, but among adults, women were much more frequent sufferers than men. To make matters worse, kuru was thought by the Fore to be passed on by sorcery, and so each death led to another as the supposed sorcerer was ritually killed.[91] It turned out that the Fore was a cannibalistic tribe; the men received the best meat from a human carcass – the muscle – while the women and children got the less appetising meat – including the brain and nervous system. Kuru was spread through cannibalism; and just when you thought it was as bad as it could get, it turned out that the Fore used specifically to eat people who had died of kuru in order to protect themselves from it.[92] The Australian government stamped out the tradition, destroying a way of life but preserving the Fore; kuru has pretty well disappeared, though the extended incubation period means that occasionally cases still turn up.[93]

So it would have been reasonable to apply the precautionary principle to the beef industry at an early stage; after all, the first suggestion that BSE could be transferred to people was canvassed in the *British Medical Journal* in 1988.[94] And the first real scare was in 1990, when some domestic cats turned up with TSSEs;[95] many assumed, without proof, that the cats had contracted it via cat food. There was no evidence about this for a long time, but ultimately it turned out that the assumption was indeed correct.

On the other hand, the situation mustn't be judged on the basis of 20/20 hindsight. The pressure on the government to 'deal with the problem' wasn't actually all that great before Mr Dorrell made his ill-fated intervention in 1996. To take one example, Jonathan Coe's witty, immaculately plotted (if ideologically clunking) novel *What a Carve Up!* is a broad attack on all things Thatcherite. In the character of Dorothy Brunwin, Coe creates the sort of monster that characterises much agribusiness; her appalling treatment of animals and employees alike is portrayed in emetic detail. Coe lingers over many of the dreadful things that go on in agriculture, the suffering of the animals, and the colossal and indefensible levels of subsidy that farmers receive. But at no stage does he raise the issue of passing disease from animals to humans (except indirectly, with fatty foods being responsible for heart disease): this in a novel published in 1994 (and certainly written after 1990, dealing as it does with the First Gulf War), well after the initial controversy about the cats.[96]

Indeed, even when the crisis was at its peak in Britain in 1996, much of the ire of voters and commentators alike fell, not on the detail of government advice as such, but upon the unlikely scapegoat of a ridiculous fedora hat that Agriculture Secretary Douglas Hogg insisted on wearing, despite the fact that a flamboyant hat rarely sits happily on the head of a middle-aged man. The Prime Minister of the day later wryly remarked:

> He took to wearing a hat that became a national object of ridicule. 'Douglas, the hat …' I began to say as he left one meeting at Number 10. 'It's a perfectly good hat, Prime Minister,' he replied, plonking it on his head and heading for the cameras waiting outside. The hat did not have a good beef war.[97]

Hogg himself did not have a good beef war, as Major came to think,[98] but the trivial nature of the argument may incline us to the view that some of the furore was connected rather more with frustration on the part of the electorate and the media with a government that was already several years past its sell-by date, and drifting aimlessly towards massacre by Tony Blair in 1997. Voters certainly began by blaming the government for the BSE crisis (51 per cent of them did). But when the European Union banned sales of British beef abroad, the public mood went all patriotic, and foreigners became the target of much of the spleen. Supermarkets had to change their advertising to trumpet that they now *were* selling British beef, and doing it proudly. It was, all in all, a strange episode, and not one in which the complex 'public mood' could be easily read.[99]

When you just have to throw your hands up in the air

There are two major arguments against the precautionary principle being applied *as a matter of routine*. The first is that an important aspect of any particular application of the principle is the status of the risk being posited. *Whose* uncertainty, about *what*, should trigger the application? There is no easy answer to this question. In a democracy, the public should have a major say; so much is uncontroversial. However, the issue is complicated by a number of factors. The first is that 'the public' is actually a very diverse and changeable group of people, and getting the public's 'opinion' is not as easy as it is often made to appear. The second is that 'the public' needs to be informed about the various potentialities and risks being posited, but there aren't that many reliable sources of information – British tabloid newspapers, for example, have an abysmal record of reporting scientific controversies.[100] New 'cures' for diseases are trumpeted, raising hopes even though any actual drug may be years of testing away from the market; health scares are the stuff of front pages, while their solutions, if reported at all, are given a column-inch or two in the middle somewhere. Equally, lazy journalism means that press releases from research agencies get transmitted without investigation into whether the scientists or corporations involved are covering up inconvenient facts. Neither the pro- nor the anti-science lobbies are well served by the media.

The results can be dreadful. In particular, the 'risks' that get mentioned in order to trigger the precautionary principle are often laughable. I mentioned earlier that the notion of 'the risk of a risk' is rather nebulous. It could mean that there is a reasonable scientific hypothesis that deserves investigation about possible deleterious effects of some action or technology – as I argued was definitely the case with the BSE crisis. Personally, I would argue that this is the only plausible interpretation; but the problem with it, for critics of science and technology, is that it still largely leaves scientists in charge of the process.

Or 'the risk of a risk' may simply mean that a risk is conceivable. This is a much better formulation for those who would wish more democracy in science, but it can have unfortunate effects, as for example in an extraordinary public debate over *nanotechnology*.

The prefix 'nano' means 'a billionth'; hence a nanometre (nm) is a billionth of a metre. Nanotechnology is technology that is on the scale of a billionth of a metre. Needless to say this is pretty small; a DNA molecule is about 2 or 3nm. So nanotechnology is technology on the scale of complex molecules. Potentially, there are plenty of interesting things that could be done at that scale.

However, at the moment most nanotechnology is hype. So far, the most impressive creation of nanotechnology is Don Eigler's sculpting of the IBM logo out of xenon atoms in 1990 (see Figure 8). But despite that – and of course as part of the general scientific scramble for research funding – extravagant claims keep coming.

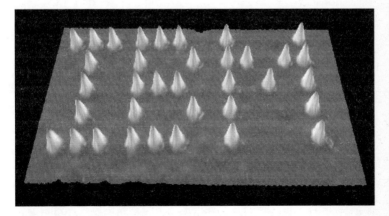

Figure 8. IBM's nanologo.

> We will be able to expand our control of systems from the macro to the micro and beyond. ... Scientists envision creating machines that will be able to travel through the circulatory system, cleaning the arteries as they go; sending out troops to track down and destroy cancer cells and tumours; or repairing injured tissue at the site of the wound, even to the point of missing limbs and damaged organs. ... Nanotechnology is expected to touch almost every aspect of our lives, right down to the water we drink and the air we breathe.[101]

Yeah, right. Actually, the state of the art is rather less exciting. There is a lot of work being done in nanotechnology, and something in excess of 1,000 patents have been granted. But as yet the products are somewhat underwhelming, if useful. Self-cleaning windows use nano-engineering to repel dirt from the glass; you can buy nano-trousers that repel stains.[102] The latter invention, of course, was ironically prefigured in Alexander Mackendrick's great film of 1951, *The Man in the White Suit*, with Alec Guinness as a boffin who invents a dirt-repelling cloth only to cause industrial havoc in Lancashire. However, another British comedy, Val Guest's *Confessions of a Window Cleaner*, may incline one to welcome, rather than worry about, mass redundancies caused by the former invention.

Current nanotechnology makes what little money it does make from this sort of invention, nano-engineered molecules that provide some particular property to a larger object, which is all well and good. But the hype is for nano-*machines*, that is, machines on the nano-scale. Such ideas are fine, of course, and worth exploring. Nevertheless, we should be aware that, as yet, we have no idea, beyond a few ingenious but largely untested theories, about how to get nano-scale objects to interact with each other (i.e. to become nano-machines' working parts). Objects at the nano-scale are subject to the limitations of quantum mechanics; very small objects behave very differently to human-scale objects, so much so that they need a special body of physics to describe their behaviour.[103]

This integration problem is extremely serious, because not only do nano-scale objects need to interact to become the sorts of machines mentioned in the quote above, but they also need to provide information to the outside world about their functioning – they need to be integrated with instruments or computers, other-wise they can't seriously be used. There is a great deal of scientific work still to be done.[104]

Hence hype rather exceeds reality. But even so, *in the absence of any sensible idea of how nanotechnology will work*, the risks are being hyped just as shamelessly. Computer scientist Bill Joy of Sun Microsystems has led the way.

> Accustomed to living with almost routine scientific breakthroughs, we have yet to come to terms with the fact that the most compelling 21st-century technologies – robotics, genetic engineering, and nanotechnology – pose a different threat than the technologies that have come before. Specifically, robots, engineered organisms, and nanobots share a dangerous amplifying factor: They can self-replicate. A bomb is blown up only once – but one bot can become many, and quickly get out of control.
>
> ...
>
> The 21st-century technologies ... are so powerful that they can spawn whole new classes of accidents and abuses. Most danger-ously, for the first time, these accidents and abuses are widely within the reach of individuals or small groups. They will not require large facilities or rare raw materials. Knowledge alone will enable the use of them.
>
> Thus we have the possibility not just of weapons of mass destruction but of knowledge-enabled mass destruction (KMD),

this destructiveness hugely amplified by the power of self-replication.

I think it is no exaggeration to say we are on the cusp of the further perfection of extreme evil, an evil whose possibility spreads well beyond that which weapons of mass destruction bequeathed to the nation-states, on to a surprising and terrible empowerment of extreme individuals.[105]

Hmm.

As this rhetoric spreads, one can certainly agree with Sue Mayer of Genewatch that you 'do not need a crystal ball to predict that the public will be alarmed by the potential for accidents and mistakes as a result of nanotech'.[106] Particularly if respected scientists like Joy and Mayer make weird assumptions on the basis of virtually no data.

With nanotech, the potential horror stories include entirely new disease causing organisms for use in biowarfare and the self-replication process getting out of control, consuming and transforming materials in the natural environment – something which has been dubbed the 'grey goo' problem.[107]

The grey goo problem – which is not a problem, just a narrative – is based on the idea that nano-engineered atom-sized robots could interact with their surroundings to cause everything to turn into undifferentiated grey goo. It is certainly true that there may be interactions that change structures in the environment – something similar happens with the prion proteins in the spread of TSSEs. But a world full of grey goo is a rather bizarre idea, which I can trace back to 1965, not to any scientific work, but to a work of science fiction, Kurt Vonnegut's *Cat's Cradle*, where a substance called Ice-9 turns all water into different chemical substances – fatal to humanity of course, since we are largely water. The 'grey goo' nanotechnology scenario specifically is the work of Eric Drexler, from 1986.[108]

The next stage in dramatising a narrative such as the grey goo narrative is to focus on the outcome, without worrying too much about the preconditions; the results are often risible.

> Cosmetics manufacturers are keen to appear cutting edge, and often blind consumers with scientific jargon. But buzzwords like 'nanocapsules' – currently one of their favourites – could be their undoing.
>
> Scare stories about nanotechnology turning the world to 'grey goo' have led Caroline Lucas, Green Party MEP [Member of the European Parliament] for South East England, to call for new regulations – and one of the targets she has in her sights is the cosmetics industry. Her website claims that 'thousands of women are acting as unwitting guinea pigs for the cosmetics industry ... with many products containing ingredients manufactured by "nanotechnology".'
>
> Famous facial products, such as L'Oréal Plénitude and Lancôme's Flash Bronzer Self Tanning Face Gel, do indeed contain billions of nanoscopic capsules designed to help the skin absorb the cream's active ingredients. Though there's not a goo-making nanobot in sight, Lucas claims to be 'horrified to find nanotech products sitting innocently in my bathroom cabinet'.
>
> We wonder what she expected them to do to her. Drain the colour from her face and make it go all mushy?[109]

It is possible that the products of nanotechnology – for example, drug delivery systems – if ever created, could be problematic. They could be about the right size to cause trouble in the lungs, for example. Naturally, the development of any new technology needs to be monitored. We need to be aware of the dangers. But grey goo?

There is nothing wrong with speculative science fiction about nanotechnology, of which there is a fair amount.[110] But this is just fiction. There is no serious scientific route from the technology we have now to the nightmare scenarios proposed by Bill Joy, which worry environmentalists, including Prince Charles,[111] so much. This all goes to illustrate the first serious problem with the application of the precautionary principle, that the 'risk of a risk' must surely be anchored in serious scientific work – otherwise the result is asinine.

The second serious problem with indiscriminate application of the precautionary principle is that it falsely assumes that doing nothing is not costly. That this is false is obvious; imagine some primitive cavemen who applied the precautionary principle to the development of fire on the (correct) ground that fire can cause serious injury and damage.

Fortunately, our primitive ancestors were not anti-technology. But there have been modern-day instances of problems caused by the precautionary principle. Recall that CJD was spread via the use of human growth hormone to treat dwarfism. When this was discovered, a number of countries including the US and the UK banned the use of such hormone; they could do this knowing that a genetically engineered version of the hormone would soon come on stream. Hence there would be little or no interruption to the treatment of dwarfism. However, the French, suspicious of genetic engineering, continued to use the human version, irrespective of the danger from CJD (although by then, to be fair, much more was known about preventing contamination), until 1988. The genetically engineered hormone proved satisfactory, and eventually France was persuaded to fall into line. What is remarkable here is that the French found the real and proven dangers of CJD much *less* compelling as risk narratives than the *theoretical* dangers of bioengineering.[112]

As a second example, genetically modified (GM) food has been largely rejected by European consumers. This is, of course, their right. Furthermore, the distribution of many GM foods is severely restricted. In democracies, this is also unobjectionable where, as in this case, such measures command majority support, even though it does involve the extra step of denying the choice to those who are not worried. One reason for this rejection is a political argument against control of food supplies by big agribusiness. But the main reason is a classic instance of a narrative suggesting a risk of a risk (a worry that the GM food might contaminate and somehow disrupt the environment) followed by the application of the precautionary principle. There is no evidence that that risk might become fact; the evidence, as far as it goes, is rather dull. GM is a relatively boring and straightforward technology, whose benefits have been somewhat overstated by its supporters. It will neither transform food production nor destroy the environment, and – to an uncommitted reader of the literature – the general level of fuss, both in the green movement and in agribusiness, is inexplicable. But in a democracy, to repeat, there is no problem as long as a majority supports such measures.[113]

However, there have been some unfortunate unintended consequences of the narrative. For example, a food crisis in 2002 in Africa threatened tens of millions of people. Food aid was forthcoming, but Zambia refused to accept American aid, on the ground that Americans use GM food pretty well indiscriminately, that the food aid would most likely be genetically modified and that therefore the stuff would be 'poison', according to President Mwanawasa.[114] To reiterate, there is no evidence that GM food is poisonous; Americans have been chomping on it for years with no discernible effects on public health. So once again we see that a risk that exists *only as narrative* is regarded as *more* pressing than the clear and present danger of malnutrition for millions of people.

As a third example, in the United Kingdom there has been a wrangle over an injection for young children to protect them from measles, mumps and rubella (MMR). A report that the MMR vaccine was associated with autism has provoked a dramatic rebellion against the vaccine. The facts seem clear. There is little evidence for any connection; the initial report was incorrect; the latest major targeted study, of over half a million children, reveals no connection between the vaccine and autism, or indeed any other side effect.[115] Other vaccines about which there is no controversy have much worse potential side effects (e.g. the polio vaccine is actually the only known cause of recent polio in Britain). There are demands to separate out the three vaccines, although in a struggling health service with finite resources, there will be costs to this. Many parents have been leaving the free National Health Service to have the jabs given separately at private clinics; thousands of these vaccines have been reported to have been delivered incompetently, with more risk to the children involved.[116] Measles is on the rise, due to the lack of cover.[117] A further wrinkle to this failure of trust is that those who mistrust the authorities, and do not believe the scientific research (the parents) are not the ones who are suffering directly (the children).

What we are seeing is the interaction between mistrust and harm. The reason that the precautionary principle is being applied in these cases is a lack of trust. The official story about science, which we sketched at the beginning of this chapter, is being undermined by worries about scientists' interests and well-publicised crises and failures. The risks of science are being focused on more closely – which is good. However, the narratives that are being generated to dramatise risks sometimes have little validity. When the precautionary principle is invoked on the strength of such narratives, the result can be harmful; *merely doing nothing about some scientific research is not cost-free.*

Restoring authority

But if that is so, how is it possible to restore the lost authority of experts? How can we create or re-establish trust here? The rhetoric has created a sort of science fiction world of Frankenstein foods and designer babies, a world not unlike Aldous Huxley's dystopian vision of the future *Brave New World*. Scientists seem to be destroying our planet while we are forced to stand idly by and watch. What room for trust here?

We certainly cannot be complacent. We may discount the grey goo problem as being ridiculous, but Huxley's description of the moral choices we will have to make remains essential reading, and people like Paul Feyerabend, Brian Wynne, Sheldon Rampton and John Stauber are absolutely right to remind us how science has its own interests (e.g. in securing funding), and how it often is beholden to the interests of others (most obviously, commercial interests).[118]

Now, there is no doubt at all that science is a social process, it goes on in a social context and is performed by people with interests and social relationships. Any account of science that disregards that will obviously be incomplete to that extent. However, there is a reading of the scientific project that conjoins with the *social* description a *method* for achieving knowledge, the rational scientific method that scientists try to follow, that tells the scientist when a result can tentatively be claimed. Scientific method includes such nostrums as creating falsifiable and testable theories, revising theories when they are inadequate and, all things being equal, preferring simple theories to complex ones, and more explanatory theories to less explanatory ones. This description of the rationality of science entails that scientists can't simply make up results; they must follow a procedure, and their theories will stand or fall by their ability to describe the world and make correct predictions. This sense of being at the mercy of the world, of being discoverers rather than creators, fits in with most scientists' experience of their own practice.

In general, the former reading, that reduces the role of rationality and focuses on the power relations, is the one that fits in with the *zeitgeist* rather more. Fashionable postmodern nostrums dispense with the possibility of knowledge as conceived by the rationalists, and reduce the production of knowledge to a process intermingling rhetoric and power. However, this surely creates a serious dilemma.

If there is no such thing as the method-driven production of knowledge, and rhetoric and power is all there is, then can we really complain when scientists use rhetoric to establish their case? After all, why shouldn't they? If we impale ourselves on this horn of the dilemma, then we can continue to create doom-laden narratives, but hardly represent them as *criticisms* of science. If, on the other hand, we wish to prevent scientists being beholden to special and sinister interests, then we must surely accept that the independent and disinterested pursuit of knowledge is possible, that it can be identified and recognised, and that it is a reliable and repeatable process. Furthermore, if there is such a more or less reliable process, we must, like the scientists, respect its outcome.

If there is no such thing as scientific method, then why do we criticise scientists for not following it? If there *is* such a thing as scientific method, then why do we not accept its outcomes? If we as a society allow ourselves to be swayed by narratives, rather than the outcome of properly conducted scientific processes, then we can hardly be surprised if scientists try to influence or compete by producing narratives of their own. Of course we should be vigilant to ensure that scientists do conduct their science properly, but when they do, we must surely be bound by the outcome as they are.

None of the above actually means that scientists should have the yea or nay about whether some product of technology such as GM foods or mobile phones is allowed into our shops and homes. It is not the choice of scientists, in a democracy, as to what is and isn't allowed. There are many more factors influencing the desirability of the exploitation of some technology than mere scientific feasibility.

The first level of safeguard is the marketplace itself, as long as consumers have a genuine choice. If they exercise their choice against some piece of technology, then that is that; the consumer is sovereign here, and no one can make a reluctant public buy what it doesn't want to. For example, the democratically elected European Parliament voted for tough labelling and traceability rules for GM foods in July 2002, and that seems to be a reasonable reflection of what the European consumer wishes. If Europeans are nervous about GM foods, even if there is no particularly good reason for nervousness, then it is hard to see why they should not be guaranteed access to the information they claim they want. It may well be that survey evidence overestimates the number of people opposed to GM food, in which case more people would buy the labelled food than say they would now (51 per cent of British people say they would never eat it),[119] but if people want the information, of course they should have it.

It may well be that a suitably informed marketplace would provide enough consumers for GM foods to be financially viable. But if a majority of people are still worried about the risks, then it is also an option to ban such foods (though international trade treaties reduce the scope for action here). Again, this is the operation of democracy, and some countries have a ban on GM foods; the EU has a moratorium. Public debate can be carried out responsibly or irresponsibly, it can assume or not assume the precautionary principle, it can be dominated by facts or by rhetoric, but if the majority plump for one side or another, then it can ensure that its views are respected. This is the situation as we have it, and it seems strange for commentators to complain that scientists are riding roughshod over us all. The GM food industry is, after all, in crisis, particularly in Europe; whether the public disquiet is well informed or not, there is no doubt that the crisis is caused by the disquiet. Consumer sovereignty has undermined the GM food industry.[120] Scientists quite clearly do not have the power to bulldoze through opposition; neither should they have that power.

There is a caveat, though. The risk makers are often not the risk takers, says Douglas Parr, correctly.[121] But quite often, those who are doing the complaining are not the beneficiaries of the risks either.

Continuing our GM example, there is a very quantifiable risk to the developing world from GM foods. If an African farmer were to plant some of the seeds from a GM shipment of food aid, then the food grown thereby might find its way, either directly or by pollination, into a shipment of food bound for Europe. Africa gets much hard currency from exporting food to Europe (despite the best efforts of the Common Agricultural Policy to enrich European farmers at the expense of European consumers and farmers from the developing world) and the discovery of GM crops coming from Africa would be a serious threat to this trade.

So we have a situation where European consumers, much more likely to suffer obesity than starvation, have managed, in the teeth of all medical and scientific evidence, to restrict African farming practice, directly by trumpeting a particular unsupported narrative, and indirectly by cutting off certain types of imported food. It is one thing to ignore the facts when it is only oneself that is affected; it is quite another when others are put at definite and immediate risk because one is nurturing a fear of some other quite immeasurable risk.

We are democratically entitled to put others at risk – we always have been. Our acid rain gets exported to Northern Europe, American pollution gets exported everywhere, horrible regimes export millions of refugees. That is what international autonomy is about. There is no solution to this particular crisis of trust, other than paying more attention to the facts, and thinking through the effects of policy on other people as well as ourselves. No one could, or should, force this to happen, but it would perhaps be unfortunate if it did not.

Ultimately, imposing scientific and technological developments on an unwilling public will be counterproductive. The often ludicrous narratives that trigger the precautionary principle might well be merely symptoms of a wider unease about the lack of public control over a larger number of questions – for example the involvement of big corporations, or the defence agencies, in science. If that is so – and the evidence for it is equivocal – then merely insisting on the scientific estimates of the risks will clearly have no effect on public unwillingness to endorse the official story.[122]

There is one potential way through the impasse, and that is to try to alter the balance of incentives in science away from the research aims of big corporations, and towards reassurance of the public. It would have to be clear that such a system was independent of pressure. And yet such a system would still have to employ the methods and language of science in order to assess risks meaningfully. Only a government would have sufficient money, power, clout and democratic legitimacy to support such a scheme.

Wherein lies another problem. People may not trust scientists and technologists very much. But they trust governments even less.

CHAPTER EIGHT

'A Plague on Both Your Houses'[1]

Trust is essential for the smooth running of politics, yet politics is, by necessity, deeply contested. In this book, as we are restricting our view deliberately to relatively mature and peaceful polities, and relatively complex and interdependent societies, a certain baseline of trust can be assumed, along both horizontal and vertical relationships. This is certainly not the standard case in politics; some societies contain ethnic or tribal groups between whom practically no trust exists at all – Israelis and Palestinians, Tutsis and Hutus, even Catholics and Protestants in Northern Ireland. Other societies have deeply dysfunctional governments, and so the vertical relationships do not work, ensuring that the people don't trust those in authority; as a consequence, government becomes either ineffectual or – more usually – repressive, as in Zimbabwe or Chechnya.

Such societies are shaping up as one of the key problems of the 21st century. But even richer, happier societies, the democracies of the developed world, are discovering that the existence of trust to oil the wheels of government cannot be taken for granted. Western democracies are often held up – by themselves – as ideals towards which the developing world should be aiming. In general, it has been roughly true that the countries that do aim towards such ideals tend to do rather better than those that don't; but many people in the developing world find the liberal-capitalist model very unattractive. (Whether it is the model itself, or the hegemonic tendencies of the usual messengers, the USA and the former European colonial powers, that is unattractive is uncertain.) Given that, problems of trust in the mature democracies will impact on the strength of the messages sent to the developing world. They will also undermine the confidence of people 'spreading the word' about liberal capitalism.

So, is trust in politics being undermined? Is the situation getting worse, and if so, how? What is the best system to ensure trust in politics, or trustworthy politicians? How are our views of politicians shaped by the accounts in the media? And is the West particularly prone to problems? These are the questions that will drive our investigations in this chapter; let's start with the first attempts to link trust and politics, in the classical republican cultures of the centuries before the birth of Christ.

'Twas ever thus

It is pretty clear why politics is a focus for deficiencies of trust. Politicians create the conditions for economic and social development and investment, and many of them will be in a position where they can vary those conditions in their own favour. In today's world of high-taxing and high-spending government, politicians have the extra job of disbursing very large quantities of other people's money, from which it is often possible for them, or their friends, to benefit.

This became a problem, historically, when a conceptual distinction was discerned between the interests of the government (the king, or ruler), and the interests of the country. Once the latter were seen to be legitimate, and independent, then there would always be the potential of a clash between what the king did, and what he *ought* to do. It was the Greeks who examined these areas first; the philosophical examination of political action reached an early peak in Ancient Rome with the works of Cicero (106–43 BC), who borrowed heavily from Greek accounts.

The whole problem of trust in politics was set out by Cicero in *On Obligations (De Officiis)*.[2] The structure of *On Obligations* sets out the problems, as Cicero saw them, beautifully clearly: Book 1 examines the honourable; Book 2 examines the useful; Book 3 examines those cases where the honourable and the useful clash, in other words, those times when the politician is presented with the opportunity to do something honourable, but is tempted to do something useful (to himself) instead. The very existence of a code of honour invites the contrast with the expedient.

Cicero's work was a sideswipe at some politicians of the day, whom he conceived as being more concerned with actions useful to themselves than with honourable ones; in particular he was aiming at the recently assassinated Julius Caesar, and Caesar's associate Marc Antony. Within a year or two of Cicero's writing *On Obligations*, Antony had organised his murder (how much spicier politics was in those days – imagine if today the news leaked out that, say, Gordon Brown had murdered Robin Cook). Nevertheless, the work has a universality that kept it relevant for centuries, throughout the Middle Ages, and even up to the time of Kant. For example, Dante was familiar with the work; the structure of Hell with which we began this book, where those who betrayed a trust were given sterner punishments than the violent, was influenced heavily by Cicero's writings.

There are two ways of inflicting injustice, by force or by deceit. Deceit is the way of the humble fox, force that of the lion. Both are utterly alien to human beings, but deceit is the more odious; of all kinds of injustice none is more pernicious than that shown by people who pose as good men at the moment of greatest perfidy.[3]

Trust in politicians follows from the pursuit of justice.

Trust reposed in us can be established by two qualities, that is, if people come to believe that we have acquired prudence allied with justice. We put trust in those whom we regard as more perceptive than ourselves, who we believe can anticipate future events, and who at a critical point in some action we think can cope with the situation by adopting a plan to meet the emergency – for this is the prudence which men account to be useful and genuine. As for men of justice, in other words, 'good men', trust in them depends on their having no suspicion of deceit and injustice in their make-up. So these are the men to whom we believe our safety, our possessions, and our children are most justifiably entrusted. Of the two virtues, justice is more influential in instilling trust, for it carries sufficient authority though unaccompanied by prudence; on the other hand, prudence without justice would be ineffective in inspiring trust, for should belief in a person's integrity be withdrawn, the more crafty and clever he is, the more loathsome and suspect he becomes.[4]

Interestingly, the stern republican Cicero doesn't find it difficult to reconcile the honourable and the useful. This is at least in part because he holds a very different view of reason and rationality than we do. For him, what reason shows is first what is best for society, and second that what is best for society is best for the politician. So if a politician reflects on where his best interests *really* lie, says Cicero, he will automatically do what is best for society.

Accordingly we must all adhere to the principle that what is useful to the individual is identical with what is useful to the community. If we each appropriate such an advantage for selfish purposes, it will spell the end of all human fellowship.[5]

But this account will not do in the modern age; recall from Chapter 3 that our understanding of rationality, rational choice and reason is that it will support enlightened *self*-interest.

For instance, we make more or less the same distinction as Cicero between what he calls 'reason' and 'appetite'.

The thrust and nature of the soul of man have two aspects. The first lies in the appetite ... which pulls a man in different directions; and the second is in the reason, which teaches and expounds what we are to do, and what to avoid. Accordingly the reason commands and the appetite obeys.[6]

The contrast for Cicero is that reason prevents the selfishness of appetite. In the modern account of rationality, however, the appetite is, more or less, the immediate craving for particular sensations, whereas reason supplies (a) an understanding of longer-term goals, and (b) an analysis of the goals to tell you how to reach them. So, suppose you were given £5,000. On the modern account, your appetite would point you in the direction of the nearest pub, or brothel, or Belgian chocolate shop (or whatever lights your candle), but your reason would tell you to put it into a high-interest savings account, because it will be better for you. Better for *you*, not society.

Reason is as inherently selfish, on the modern account, as appetite, and so the contrast that Cicero makes between the honourable and the useful is doubly difficult for us to deal with. According to Cicero, the appetite steers the politician towards selfishness, but his reason points him towards the honourable, and since appetite obeys reason, there should be no serious problem of trust. On the modern account, however, there is no split between reason and selfishness; indeed reason is seen as being inherently selfish. On our account, it is hard to see why any politician should ever be honest at all! This is the stone that Machiavelli dropped into the pond.[7]

Sleaze

And because reason, post-Machiavelli, is supposedly selfish, we have seen the proliferation of corruption and sleaze through democratic politics. In the USA, politics has been awash with money for some years, and the phrase 'pork barrel politics' refers to the specific American practice of voters rewarding their representatives for sending government work in their direction, however useless or contrived. For example, the power of Texan politics is why the first word spoken on the moon was 'Houston',[8] and also why Enron became so successful.[9] In France and Germany, major politicians, from François Mitterand and Helmut Kohl down, have been discovered channelling funds illegally to their parties or other pet causes. The President of France, Jacques Chirac, and the Prime Minister of Italy, Silvio Berlusconi, are both using their offices at the time of writing to impede criminal investigations. There is a strong sense in other countries, such as Belgium and Austria, that the political world, if not corrupt exactly, is self-serving and needs a shake-up.

In the United Kingdom, political sleaze has been relatively minor. The Conservative Party, which held power for a remarkably long period between 1979 and 1997, began to treat power as its right, as a succession of ineffective opposition leaders failed to make any headway against it. Outright criminality was rare, but two senior Conservative figures, Jeffrey Archer[10] and Jonathan

Aitken,[11] were discovered lying under oath, treating the courts as their own personal fiefdom. Archer in particular, an unpleasant yet apparently charming man, had a long history of scandal, suppressed by his deep pockets and willingness to resort to litigation.

Most Conservative sleaze actually consisted of either sexual shenanigans – about which I can't get that excited, frankly – or minor financial wrongdoing. The most colourful story was that of the Hamiltons. Neil Hamilton was a junior government minister who was accused by a newspaper of asking questions in parliament in return for money from Egyptian businessman Mohamed Al Fayed (wrong, but hardly gross moral turpitude). Another minister accused of the same offence in the newspaper resigned immediately and was able to retire into decent obscurity. Hamilton, on the other hand, strongly denied the charges – and still does – and became a household name. He defied the Prime Minister's attempts to get him to resign from his ministerial position, before ultimately getting the sack. He and his supporters managed somehow to get him reselected as the Conservative representative for the Tatton constituency, with the result that he was easily beaten in the 1997 general election by anti-corruption candidate Martin Bell. Indeed, the inability of the Conservative Party to disassociate itself from Hamilton[12] contributed to a fair extent to the landslide defeat to Tony Blair (an unflattering photograph of Hamilton adorned the cover of one bestselling book on Tory sleaze).[13] He took the fight to the courts, ultimately losing a libel battle against Al Fayed, which has meant bankruptcy.[14] Since then, he has been a regular guest on television programmes, even appeared nude with his wife on the cover of a lads' magazine, and has been transformed in the public eye into an avuncular, raffish, slightly idiotic, but rather likeable figure, somewhat like Uncle Giles in Anthony Powell's *A Dance to the Music of Time*. He has clowned his way out of being an icon of corruption.

His wife Christine has had an even more remarkable journey, from her early career as secretary to one of the strangest Conservative MPs ever, Sir Gerald Nabarro.[15] After unwisely berating Mr Bell, and interrupting his press conference outside the Long View Hotel in Knutsford at the beginning of the 1997 general election campaign,[16] she had a claim to be perhaps the most hated woman in Britain. But by playing up to her 'battleaxe' image,[17] she has managed to endear herself to the public so much that in September 2002, she finished third in a bizarre reality TV show called *I'm a Celebrity, Get Me Out of Here!* ahead of assorted spoonbenders, boxers and lesbian comedians, beaten only by a girl who seems to have no role in life at all and the naffest DJ in Christendom.

The perception of sleaze is a problem, and continues to undermine trust in politics and politicians. Tony Blair, as opposition leader, deliberately played up the – in truth, minor – corruption of the Conservative government, but, having made sleaze a big political issue in the UK, has had more or less the same problems since. Senior Labour figures such as Geoffrey Robinson, Keith Vaz and Peter Mandelson (twice) have had to resign, and there have been many suspicions that the Blair government has been too close to certain businessmen, such as Bernie Ecclestone, who runs Formula 1 racing.

The question then is what should be done to stamp sleaze out of politics? What trust-creating practices and institutions are available to us? How can we prevent our politicians choosing the (personally) useful over the honourable?

Local and global trust in politics

The attentive reader will have noticed, in the diagram at the end of Chapter 6, that the trust model for politics is characterised as local(ish). What's that? you may well be asking: that sounds like a cop-out. And of course it is.

Much of the institutional apparatus surrounding politics, defining its efficacy, is global, based on institutions. The British Parliament, for example, is an institution that, in theory at least, restricts the power of the Prime Minister (or actually the power of the monarch, in whose name the Prime Minister acts). We can trust the Prime Minister because there are limits beyond which he or she cannot go, limits described by Parliament. And Parliament is ultimately beholden unto us, the voters, because we vote on who is to represent us in Parliament.

Well, as we know, there are various ways around that – patronage and whipping – but such is the theory. Indeed, to an extent, all democracies are based on global institutions precisely because of a lack of trust, because at some historical point traditional rulers, monarchs, aristocrats, the church, were not trusted enough to exercise their powers in the interests of all; when the people became powerful enough to curb those powers, it was through trust-bearing institutions.[18]

However, to a very large extent, trust in politics remains local. There are media between ourselves and the politicians, usually – most of our access to politicians comes via the television and newspapers. But there are remarkably few intermediate institutions that help us make our judgements about those politicians. We are shown images, and then we make up our own minds (perhaps influenced to some extent by commentaries by journalists and others, but we are usually quite selective about our choice of those).

For example, in the United States, the Presidential election is preceded by the primary season, where each of the two main parties ballots in each state to decide who will be their candidate for the election itself. In 2004, the first primary was in New Hampshire (as it always is, traditionally), on 27 January –

meaning in excess of nine months' electioneering out of a four-year cycle. In days of yore, candidate selection would be stitched up by party bosses; between 1865 and 1900 there were no primaries at all, and it was indeed the bosses who decided the two Presidential candidates, who were, perhaps unsurprisingly, extremely mediocre. Even as recently as 1960, when John F. Kennedy stood for President, only 16 states ran primaries.[19] Yet they were essential to his bid.

> For John F. Kennedy and Hubert Humphrey there was no other than the primary way to the Convention. If they could not at the primaries prove their strength in the hearts of Americans, the Party bosses would cut their hearts out in the back rooms of Los Angeles.[20]

In 1960, the New Hampshire primary was on 8 March, over a month later than in 2004, but now of course the primary season takes place over three times as many states. Not a system you would design. But what other feasible system, continuous with America's democratic traditions, could (a) introduce maybe ten or more candidates (most of whom will barely be known outside of their home state) to the voters, while (b) simultaneously forcing candidates to confront the issues relevant to *all* voters across one of the largest and most diverse countries in the world?

The primary system is a system of local trust; you vote for people unmediated by institutions. Anyone can stand in the primaries. Contrast that with the global system of the party elders choosing the candidates; here the party actually engineers the choice for the voter, and the voters have to trust the choice of the party. The difference is actually one of degree, not kind; in most primaries it is voters registered by the parties that decide (though there are primaries – Louisiana is one example – where all voters can vote). Nevertheless, the main thing is that a large number of people make an unpredictable choice, based solely on their instincts to trust a particular politician.[21] There are no *formal* mediating structures such as were described in Chapter 4, and as we have seen in operation in the fields of finance and science in Chapters 6 and 7.

The power of the press

On the other hand, such a system is highly dependent on the mass media spreading the word, on politicians appearing on radio and television, and in the national press. The nature of that press coverage will to an extent determine the response that candidates get; for a fictional view of how a politician can be made and broken by media coverage, Orson Welles' film *Citizen Kane* is unbeatable. There has been plenty of commentary on the role of the press, and how distorting of politics it can be. Reputation, the holder of trust that is ideal for public life, is created out of a filtered set of a potentially infinite number of events and actions concerning the politician.[22] Clearly the media are a key filtering mechanism.

Print journalism is a major factor in the perception of politics in the United Kingdom, for example. Some British politicians, such as the Labour Party leader from 1983 to 1992 Neil Kinnock, and the Conservative Party leader from 1990 to 1997 John Major, were regularly pilloried in the press; Kinnock never won an election, whereas the only one Major won was against Kinnock! As a popular poet and lyricist from the early 20th century, Humbert Wolfe, put it:

> You cannot hope
> To bribe or twist
> Thank God! the

> British journalist.
> But, seeing what
> The man will do
> Unbribed, there's
> No occasion to.

However, readers are generally aware of the press's reputation, and can be independent; at times it has seemed that some leaders, such as Margaret Thatcher, Tony Blair, Bill Clinton or Ronald Reagan, could have roasted Mother Teresa alive on national television without denting their poll figures too severely. It proved very hard for the oppositional press to land a blow on these figures. After being on the receiving end of a long charm offensive, for example, most newspapers – who don't, after all, like being on the losing side – swung, however reluctantly, behind Mr Blair's Labour Party.

A constant diet of derisive reporting of politics, the creation of standard narratives of politicians 'with their noses in the trough' may well serve to undermine trust. Nevertheless, newspapers aren't the only factor in trusting politicians. For example, in France, the media are much more respectful of their politicians than in the UK, and find British political coverage astounding. But trust in politicians is possibly even lower in France than in the UK, as evinced by the disastrous performance of both major candidates, Chirac and Lionel Jospin, in the 2002 Presidential election. So bored were the French electorate by the choice they were given that in the first round of the election, traditionally the forum to give the main candidates a bit of a kicking, there were no fewer than 16 candidates, of whom no one got more than a fifth of the vote. In the confusion, Jospin – who had so far failed to capture the imagination of the left that he was fighting seven other leftist candidates – received a hopeless 16.2 per cent of the vote, and

Figure 9. The Sun in the process of winning it.[23]

was eliminated in favour of the thuggish racist Jean-Marie Le Pen (thereby presenting Chirac with a trivial shoo-in on the second ballot).

Arguably, one reason for the demonstrable lack of enthusiasm is that the French political elite – still remarkably uniform in background and education,[24] rather like in Britain before Mrs Thatcher's shake-up where politics was dominated by public (i.e. private) school/Oxbridge types – has lost touch with the voters.[25] And a reason for that might well be the *respectful* press; after all, French politics is noticeably more corrupt than Britain's,[26] even though the latter is lumbered with its scurrilous, cretinous, tabloid newspapers. Indeed, there has been a recent kerfuffle in France over the role of stately *Le Monde*, which has been accused of being politically and financially corrupt by two journalists,[27] charges backed up by Roland Dumas, former foreign minister recently acquitted on appeal of charges of bribery.[28] *Le Monde* has retaliated, but the impression is left of a press that is cosily entwined with the politicians, that has failed to prevent corruption spreading through a political culture, and which ultimately hasn't helped the politicians at all (as Cicero would have predicted), as voters continue to regard them poorly.

In other words, it is true that the press does not help foster trust in politicians by constantly poking fun at them. But it is much more serious when trust is lost because politicians do not behave in a trustworthy manner.

Globalising political trust in democracies

The example of the primaries shows the advantages of local trust in democratic politics. Actually, the costs of mistrust in politics, of insisting on strong institutional controls around our politicians, are very high. To see why, let's take a look at arguments for attempting to engineer a political system to exploit *mistrust*.

One problem is that turnouts are low and/or that, as in France, political elites are out of favour. This allows grim populists to gain seats, as with Le Pen, Holland's Pim Fortuyn, or Austria's Jorg Haider. Voting figures could easily be increased by making voting compulsory, as has been suggested.[29] This will obviously ease the symptom of low turnout, but it is not clear exactly how it will increase trust. Another idea mooted is to allow the voter, voting compulsorily, to vote for 'none of the above'. Doubtless several people would take advantage of that possibility, although perhaps not in a close or controversial poll. What would that prove? And what effect could it have on trust? There would naturally be a number of constituencies, perhaps those with rather colourless MPs, where 'none of the above' would be the majority. And would these constituencies be deprived of representation in Parliament? If not, how could the MP function, knowing that his or her mandate could be questioned at any time?

Because politicians are not trusted, goes the argument, they must be taken out of the loop. Return power to the people. There are various methods for this. Citizens' contracts could define the roles, the rights and responsibilities of politicians and voters. Citizens' juries could make all the hard decisions. If politicians are not trusted, let's remove them from the decision-making process entirely. The results, some claim, would be very heaven.

It feels very different to be a citizen in this new political system. ...

The start of the [election] campaign is marked by all political parties emphasising the breadth of their manifesto policies rather than emphasising just five key pledges. Costed manifestos (and a merciless Audit Commission) have radically changed the style of campaigning from a negative attack on the other parties' spending plans to a positive promotion of their own policies. Gone too is the 'beauty contest' between individual party leaders as parties stress instead the broad range of their candidates, especially their women and ethnic minorities candidates. ...

The Alternative AV+ system empowers voters to choose their policy priorities in the sure knowledge that these choices will be reflected in the new parliament. Voters therefore do not mind spending up to fifteen minutes in the voting booth numbering their preferences from the three page ballot paper. Turnout reaches 90% as polling is spread across the Spring Bank Holiday every four years. Increasingly, voters use ICT facilities to examine the manifestos and research the options available before voting electronically during the three day election. ...

The local government elections produce mandates across the country for local hypothecated schemes covering everything from more drop-in centres for the homeless to more pre-school places. Electoral turnouts increase, doubling in local elections, as voters take control of the future of their public services through the proportional voting system. ...

Overall, the liberal emphasis on an individual's freedom permeates every layer of society. Over time, the politics of distrust between citizen and state has a curious effect. In the future, the citizen and the state learn to trust each other as adults for the first time.[30]

This weird, breathless, bizarre vision of the future is one which may send a nerdy policy wonk into paroxysms of ecstasy, but for the rest of us it is the stuff of nightmare. Quite apart from the ghastly idea of spending 15 minutes in a polling booth, what the vision fails to tell us is how and why anyone will trust the political process more as a result of such a transfer of power, and how it will lead to this undiluted joy. If I think my cooker is not working properly, I get no great happiness from fixing it myself. In terms of getting to vote on lots of things, the countries that are most democratic are the USA and Switzerland, which – coincidentally or not – have pipsqueak turnouts for their elections. One is reminded of a minor film from the 1960s, *The Rise and Rise of Michael Rimmer*, starring Peter Cook as a PR man (reminiscent of an ever-smiling Mr Blair *avant la lettre*) who becomes President of Britain by giving people so much power they get fed up with it and transfer it all back to him personally.

Trust can, as we have noted elsewhere in passing, be undermined by formal relationships (such as contracts, which trust resembles).[31] Institutions and democratic methods tend to work best when they take as understood the deep context of custom, habit and interests within which democratic politics takes place, what has been called the 'thick' context of relations.[32] But that may be taken to mean that democracies function best when that 'thick' context is at its richest, i.e. when people have most in common. When people have little in common, when their cultures or interests are most diverse, then the social context will be relatively sparse; this paradox hints at an analogy with Durkheim's idea, explored in Chapter 3, that trust grows from a consensus of values and interests.

Many racial and other problems in the United States, it has been suggested, may be traced to this phenomenon; as the divergence of interests and values becomes clearer in the States, Americans have relied more and more on legal frameworks of rights determined by courts to make decisions in contested areas.[33] Where there is a real split, the lawyers get rich, as for example over abortion, where the focus of all debate is over the landmark Supreme Court decision Roe v. Wade (1972), which decided abortion's legality. Ever since, the right has tried to chip away at this decision, with the result that it has remained a live issue; few issues are as incendiary in American politics. Compare that with the European experience, where in most countries there is a rough consensus of the centre, broken only by the odd fanatic; the actual positions of the consensuses may be different from country to country (e.g. depending on the extent of Catholicism), but debate has stayed generally more polite.[34]

The lesson is that rational or institutionalised planning has a tendency to undermine the informal relations needed to underpin it. For example, the planned capital of Brazil, Brasilia, works only because of tolerance of a much larger unplanned community around it.[35]

Depoliticisation

Another approach to creating consensus (or, more to the point, concealing diversity) is that of *depoliticisation*. In other words, some contentious issue is simply removed from politics altogether. The idea is to represent the issue as a technical matter to be dealt with by experts, not politicians. Argument is stifled, because the decision is made according to clear, bureaucratic principles.

For example, transport issues have been fairly contentious in the UK of late, as traffic congestion grows ever more, while an ever larger acreage of what was once a green and pleasant land gets concreted over. Perhaps the most controversial road scheme was the Newbury bypass; Newbury is a pleasant town in beautiful countryside that unfortunately is on the A34, a major road that runs through the heart of England, connecting Southampton, Oxford, Birmingham, Stoke-on-Trent and Manchester. The congestion in Newbury had to be experienced to be believed – it happens to be a route I travelled a lot at one time – and the disruption to the good burghers of Newbury must have been awful. A plan was developed to run a dual carriageway road around Newbury, thereby making the town somewhat more pleasant and the countryside somewhat less beautiful. The decision became a *cause célèbre* for eco-warriors and the anti-road lobby, and protests went on for years; in the end the bypass was built in the teeth of determined opposition (it cost £74 million to build, and the building operation took £26 million to police).[36]

The dispute uncovered a major faultline in British politics between a particular set of green values and a more mainstream view. There was no consensus to be created. In general what happens at that point in a mature democracy is that procedures are invoked to make the decision automatically – due process of law. One would have to have pretty good reason to go against such procedures, attempting a programme of civil disobedience; such reasons might include that the procedures do not allow some vital set of individual voices to be heard, or that the system is biased in important ways.[37]

But the problem was that the eco-warriors, led by one of their more winsome fellows, a chap named Swampy who gained brief celebrity, believed that the system *was* biased against them – hence there wasn't even a consensus about the fairness of the system. The result was painful for all concerned – a dialogue of the deaf.

The argument over road building turned out to be extremely *political*. The aim of depoliticisation is to turn an issue into a technical matter, one to be worked out by experts, in this case in the Department of Transport, who calculate the costs and benefits of the road-building programme, and of any individual road. The project should go ahead if the gains warrant it. Opposition to such a technical, depoliticised argument is assumed to be similarly technical; it must question the assumptions, or the theories, or the calculations. The problem then – in a political situation that has been depoliticised – is that someone who disputes, not the calculation, but the very fact that a calculation is appropriate at all, is not listened to, because he or she is not saying the sorts of things that technocrats are disposed to hear. In other words, the eco-warriors of Newbury disputed that road building through countryside is the sort of thing that should go ahead at all, even if most people benefit. A cost-benefit analysis of the road is simply not relevant from their point of view. Hence depoliticisation can be an obstacle to consensus; it can cover up divergence about fundamental values, but can end up destroying trust in the 'faceless' bureaucrats that run the country.

A weapon of malign depoliticisation is the euphemistic redescription of unpleasant things, as Orwell's *Nineteen Eighty-four* taught us. When a general tells you that an enemy plane has been prosecuted, he means 'blown to smithereens'. Changing the word doesn't make the death any wronger or righter, of course, but it can anaesthetise the worried mind of the voter. Analysis of politicians' rhetoric often reveals a number of linguistic tricks to depoliticise things. For example, a Labour White Paper on competitiveness says the following.

> In the increasingly global economy of today, we cannot compete in the old way. Capital is mobile, technology can migrate quickly and goods can be made in low cost countries and shipped to developed markets.

In this passage a number of processes – capital movement, technology migration – are referred to without including the agents of the processes, i.e. foreign bankers, investors and multinationals. Such agents, the *bêtes noires* of the Labour Party, are left out of the description to present the situation as an inevitable geopolitical fact, rather than as a consequence of a series of actions taken by Labour's traditional enemies (and therefore something to be stopped).[38]

On the other hand, depoliticisation has advantages too. It

means that more decisions can get taken; as with all delegation to expertise, there is a division of intellectual labour that frees the rest of us to get on with our lives.[39] Some commentators are worried by the possibility that this means a reduction in the *quality* of our democratic engagement,[40] but that surely is a price worth paying to allow those of us not massively interested in politics and resource allocation to mind our own businesses.

It also has the covert advantage that technical evaluation of a proposal may actually be a better way of decision-making, without getting bogged down in ideological or other insoluble arguments. For instance, there has always been a problem deciding where essential but unpleasant facilities, such as incinerators, airports or juvenile offenders' accommodation, should be placed. Everyone is in favour of having such things, but no one wants them in their vicinity. Such arguments will never be resolved, except by a rational, technical case being constructed; someone is bound to be offended, but if the procedure is fair no bias can be claimed. If the procedure is agreed in advance, then tough decisions can be made precisely by depoliticising them.[41]

For example, in democracies, the drawing of constituency boundaries obviously has ramifications about which representatives get elected. In the USA, boundaries are drawn by political figures in a process called 'redistricting'. Republican redistricting committees invent more seats where Republicans will win, Democrats likewise. In Florida – evenly poised as we know from the 2000 election result – there are 17 Republican seats and 8 for the Democrats (surprise, it's a state with a Republican governor). The Illinois 4th district (see Figure 10) takes *two* groups of mainly Hispanic voters and crams them into a virtually *discontinuous* district – so they only elect a *single* Hispanic representative. Worse, in 2003, almost the entire Democratic faction of the Texan House of Representatives went into hiding across the state border,

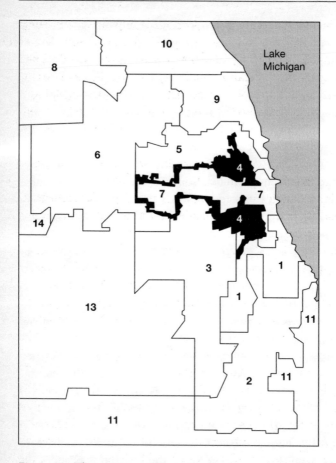

Figure 10. The notorious Illinois 4th district.

pursued by state troopers, in order to avoid having to debate a Republican redistricting plan designed to give the Republicans four to seven more seats in Congress.[42] It is obvious that such events show democracy in a very bad light.

Indeed, the word 'gerrymander', to manipulate a constituency unfairly in order to secure disproportionate influence, has its roots in American politics. Eldridge Gerry (1744–1814), governor of Massachusetts, divided the state into senatorial districts designed to consolidate the Federalist vote in a small number of districts, thereby giving the Democratic-Republicans an unfair advantage. One of the ridiculous districts was popularly thought to be shaped like a salamander, and hence the term 'gerrymander' appeared. The 'g' in Gerry, incidentally, was hard, as in 'good', so the original pronunciation of 'gerrymander' was with a hard 'g', as opposed to its current pronunciation 'jerrymander'.

Iowa is an American exception; it has an independent redistricting bureau that draws the boundaries on agreed demographic principles. It creates fairness, not through a *political*, election-driven process, but through a *depoliticised* bureaucratic operation.[43] The system is clearly fairer; depoliticisation can be a better solution. It can lead to a more trustworthy system. This is not to say that depoliticised processes can't be rigged. For example, the United Kingdom's Boundary Commission is an unpolitical committee that redraws constituency boundaries on demographic grounds, but its pronouncements are often delayed for convenience. As one instance, Harold Wilson's government of 1964–70 realised that as many as 30 Labour seats would disappear as a result of the scheduled 1969 report, and postponed the publication of the report for all but London and the most seriously anachronistic constituencies, until after the publication of *another* report proposing local government reforms (and therefore kicking the whole issue into the long grass until after the 1970 election).[44]

Depoliticisation is a consequence of the inevitable distinction between bureaucracy and democracy, a distinction discussed at length by Weber.[45] The development of democratic government depends on the simultaneous development of a bureaucracy to support it, which then becomes hungry for power (not necessarily in a conscious way). According to Weber, the two forms of government are basically opposed, but the abstract legal decisions that are required to implement the democratic institutions mean that a professional monopoly will automatically have to be created to put them in place.[46] Administration will begin to take over from democratically elected politicians. Such a creeping growth of bureaucracy has always been the bugbear of the right,[47] but to some extent it is going to be inevitable. The Marxist left sees the state as an expression of entrenched and asymmetric class interests, which will disappear as class distinctions are removed;[48] again the Weberian analysis was that this would not happen. If the proletariat seized power, then there would be no structures competing with the existing state mechanism, no alternative; which is exactly what happened in the dreary Soviet Brezhnev years.

To summarise, we have seen, following Cicero, that there is a distinction between what is honourable (good for society) and useful. Cicero solved the problem by contrasting selfish appetite with socially responsible reason, but this get-out isn't possible for modern readers, because we have a tendency to see reason as just as selfish as appetite. Whatever the truth of that, politics certainly isn't as clean as Cicero would have liked (if it ever was). Trust in democratic politics is to a large extent local, as the voters make up their own minds unmediated by institutions; many thinkers have blamed the lack of probity in politics on the inefficient mechanisms of local trust. Consequently, they tend to suggest two ways round the problem: first, more decisions can be devolved directly to voters, reducing the powers of elected representatives (and therefore the need to trust); second, decisions can be taken out of politics altogether, and given to technocrats and civil servants to make. As we have seen, neither of these moves is entirely satisfactory, though each might well be justified in individual cases. Depoliticisation is useful, for example, when politics is very partisan, as with American redistricting. But in general, there is as yet little evidence that the proposed solutions are improvements on the problems. It is not clear at all that conceivable institutional changes to Western individualistic styles of politics will bolster trust as the critics want. Any serious alternative would have to be much more radical and thoroughgoing.

The view from the East

So far, in this chapter, I have focused on the Western, liberal conception of government – as in general through the book I have focused on the problems and advantages of Western societies. But a major debate that followed from the realignment in international relations after the ignominious collapse of the Soviet Union, and the advent of a world dominated by the American hyperpower, arose around a set of moral, political and pragmatic prescriptions for government that collectively went under the name *Asian values*.[49]

Asian values were set up consciously in opposition to Western liberal values, which had been taken as having triumphed in the immediate aftermath of the fall of the Berlin Wall and the unexpectedly simple liberation of Kuwait in the First Gulf War. Francis Fukuyama earned himself some notoriety with the ill-advised publication of the most bullish version of this thesis, which announced nothing less than the end of history; so massively and obviously superior to all other creeds was Western liberal capitalism, said he, that henceforth in general it would be the future philosophical direction of mankind.[50] Now, ten years later, Western liberal capitalism – though still a formidable force, as Saddam Hussein would no doubt testify if he could be found – looks somewhat embattled. Countervailing positions have crystallised in opposition to it; two of the most important are

Islamism, and the anti-globalisation movement (one of whose representatives, Naomi Klein, we have already met in Chapter 6). Furthermore, there are little ad hoc groupings of opponents of America, which include the Axis of Evil, a group of cussed regimes whose opposition to the USA is rooted mainly in their desire to avoid internal interference with their repressive policies, and what academic and commentator Timothy Garton-Ash has called the Axis of Refusal,[51] a group of diverse nations, united only by their neo-Gaullist desire to curb American power, including France and Russia, with Germany as very much a junior partner. None of these groupings, with the exception of Islamism, has anything like a serious or coherent programme of its own to offer, apart from visceral opposition to the United States and to liberal principles of free markets. The problem with Islamism is the parlous state of the regions of the world where Islam holds sway; there are no serious players in world politics that could reasonably put forward an Islamist alternative with any conviction. As it is, the liberal strategy of demonising Islam by association with fundamentalism, egregious illiberality and murderous terrorism is almost guaranteed to work given the lack of any more positive role models.

The Asian values movement, however, does augment proscription with prescription. Indeed, in the early part of the 1990s, Asian values looked like a real winner, as America struggled, with a deadlocked government, to pay off the massive debts it had incurred during Ronald Reagan's unprecedented arms build-up (and which had broken the Soviet Union), and as the Asian 'tigers' (South Korea, Taiwan, Malaysia, Hong Kong and Singapore) plus Japan delivered impressive growth and social cohesion. The unexpected conversion of American deficit to surplus in the later years of Bill Clinton, the giant Japanese recession, and the Asian banking crisis[52] soon evened up the contest, though. But in the arguments following the Second Gulf War of 2003 (and as China continues to grow and put on economic muscle), it may be that the Asian values movement will resurface as the only serious alternative to liberal capitalism.

Asian values are a relatively nebulous bunch of nostrums, many with a Confucian ancestry. Confucianism is based around ideas of authority and responsibility, with many powerful hierarchies, based on the model of the father-figure, who takes responsibility for his charges; in such a situation, trust and trustworthiness are extremely important. The patron must, in return for the trust and power he is given, provide a stable, well-ordered society. The ideas that are most emphasised are attachment to the family as an institution, deference to societal interest, thrift, conservatism in social norms, respect for authority, education and consensus. The free-wheeling individualism of liberal capitalism is rejected as producing too many casualties, too much crime and violence, too much alienation. Fukuyama replies that the Confucian ideals of paternalism actually *restrict* trust, rather than helping it spread.[53] As Confucianism privileges relations of kinship, it becomes hard for societies to develop trust outside families, on the Fukuyama thesis; however, the evidence of surveys doesn't really back that claim up.[54] At its most aggressive, the Asian values movement claims demonstrable superiority over Western liberalism; at its most defensive, it argues only against American cultural hegemony; just because liberalism works in Peoria, Illinois is no reason to think it will work transplanted to Singapore, Kuala Lumpur or Hong Kong.

In the bureaucracy/democracy argument that we alluded to in the previous section, the Asian answer is to downgrade democracy. The argument is made that while America insists on democracy being spread, using the rights-based discourse that it has developed (initially as a way of embarrassing the Soviet Union, later under a momentum of its own), a better way is to provide

233

economic stability and prosperity first, and then democracy will follow. Democracy foisted upon an unready nation will merely cause fissures. Many nations will split along tribal or ideological lines, and the result will be either deadlock, or the domination of the government by a single faction.[55]

Taking the Weberian argument, the Asian values movement equates the interests of the nation with those of its supreme representative, the Prime Minister, who is served by the state; hence the state/nation dichotomy, in which one could trust the nation and not the state, does not arise. The major figures in East Asian polities, then, turn out to be paternalistic semi-dictators such as Lee Kuan Yew of Singapore or Dr Mahathir Mohamed of Malaysia, who fulfil the trust of their people by being trustworthy and governing demonstrably for the good of all, and providing the stability that is so prized in East Asia. Opponents of the movement, of course, are able to point to rather more malign examples of the dictatorial art, such as President Suharto of Indonesia, or President Marcos of the Philippines; even if the ideas underlying Asian values are right, the whole thing depends on getting the right man in in the first place. With a Western-style democracy, it is possible to get rid of the Suhartos of this world;[56] the Asian reply is that it is much harder for democrats to take unpopular but necessary decisions (for example, European governments are too scared of their own internal lobbies to get rid of the Common Agricultural Policy, despite its manifest unfairness and the problems it causes in the developing world).[57]

Indeed, where Westerners do not trust their states to speak for their nations, in Asia it is often the case that the state is trusted implicitly, and the possibility that there may be others who could act in the interests of the people (or, put another way, that the people might have interests other than those of the state) is rejected.

The latest fashion among American and some other Western intellectuals is to believe that when selfish government individuals have
failed to protect common global concerns, the representatives of
civil society and nongovernmental organizations (NGOs) can act
as a better conscience of mankind. In theory this should be so. But
as the battle of Seattle showed at the WTO conference, NGOs and
civil society are no less prisoners of their sectoral interests. They
may find it easy to seize the moral high ground, because in the
American scheme of things nongovernmental representatives
believe they represent the public good better than government
representatives do. But, as demonstrated in Seattle, most Third
World diplomats were mystified by the claims of these NGOs to
speak on behalf of the six billion people when they had little
understanding of or connection with their needs.[58]

Whereas liberalism privileges what we have called the horizontal
relationships in society, Asian values privilege the vertical, the
authority relations. Trust, in many ways, becomes a duty, rather
than an option, as in Western societies. But the prevailing
individualism in the West assumes self-interested behaviour, and
therefore tries to create trust by creating institutions and patterns
of social interaction that *make you see that it is in your interests to
be trustworthy*.[59] Asian values assume that someone in a position
of trust has a *duty* to be trustworthy, because (as with everyone
further down the hierarchy) societal interests come before the
individual's.

One obvious problem is that people might not be trustworthy;
in that case it is hard to produce sanctions. On the international
level, although Asian organisations are based around the slow
accretion of trust and the development of informal networks,[60]
East Asian societies have found it hard to restrain rogue states
like North Korea or Myanmar. A serious problem of trust exists

235

between Japan and the other regional states as a result of their turbulent histories, and Japanese relations with China, South Korea and Russia are bedevilled by Japan's refusal, unlike Germany, to apologise for atrocities committed in the Second World War;[61] the issue of the 'comfort women', Korean ladies forced into prostitution by and for the Japanese army, will not go away,[62] and Japanese Prime Minister Koizumi's visits to the controversial Yasukuni war shrine (which honours Japanese war dead, including convicted war criminals) have not helped diplomatic relations.[63]

However that may be, liberty takes a back seat to social order and stability.[64] Singaporean diplomat Kishore Mahbubani, whose works on Asian values are among the most influential (and from whom I have quoted liberally), has argued that certain abuses of human rights should be overlooked, given their domestic contexts, abuses such as the Tiananmen Square massacre of 1989,[65] or President Fujimori's reversal of democracy in Peru.[66] In particular, Mahbubani accepts the thesis that the press have an awful lot of power to create or destroy trust, and argues that press freedom should therefore be sharply diminished;[67] in the developing world in particular, the US press, he argues, is simply too powerful.

> Power corrupts. The absolute power of the Western journalist in the Third World corrupts absolutely.[68]

In the US there are informal brakes on media power, but these, claims Mahbubani, do not obtain outside. Often the US government sends the media in to do its dirty work for it, but this can backfire when the distorted picture sent back actually affects US public opinion adversely (a serious problem in the most democratic country in the world).[69] Our own discussion of the power of the media, above, came to the opposite conclusion, that its power was overstated. Mahbubani's aim might better be achieved by fostering a free and powerful press. The problem that worries him may have its roots not in the power of the US press, but in the virtual monopoly on news reporting (indeed, on trust in the field of news dissemination) that Western news agencies, such as CNN and the BBC, have created for themselves. When that monopoly is challenged (e.g. by al-Jazeera, the Qatari news channel that presents an Arab-centred view of the world), Western news outlets struggle to retain viewers, and to maintain the Fukuyama-esque vision of the triumph of Western ideas.

Trust in politics will inevitably be a problem. In democracies, mistrust is institutionalised, and checks and balances try to maintain trustworthy behaviour by making untrustworthy behaviour too costly. Individualistic selfishness is assumed, and catered for. Aggressively free presses help keep politicians on the straight and narrow. In the Asian dictatorships (and partial democracies), benign father-figures act in the interests of all. Trust is maintained in the latter by worries about the instability that would follow the disappearance of such strongmen. The advantages and dangers of such uncritical trust can be seen across the region, the illiberal but prosperous and peaceful state of Singapore being exhibit A for the defence, the fissile, unstable and violent mess that is Indonesia being exhibit B for the prosecution.

Moving on

Trust, authority, deference, cooperation, interest and legitimacy: a difficult set of intertwining concepts whose interdependence is strong. Different contexts require different approaches, practices and institutions, and create different problems. In the last few chapters we have discussed the new and virtual world of the Internet, where identities are so fluid; business, where people's interests are often murky; science, where the operation of expertise means that only experts can evaluate their colleagues' claims; and politics, where power, hierarchy and authority can be abused. In all these areas there are problems of trust, and we have set out some of the reasons why. Similarly, in all these areas, many of the supposed deficits of trust are actually rather exaggerated, for whatever reason. The situation is a little more optimistic, if complex, than much of the literature on trust might suggest.

What we have seen in these chapters is a pretty constant pattern, where the standard mechanisms of trust are not perfect, and there are many influential criticisms; however, when we have examined these critical stances more closely, we have not really found their positive suggestions very appealing either.

So, given the diverse background, we must now go on to ask the important questions: is trust declining? And, if so, what can we do about it? Is there to be a one-size-fits-all solution, or will the preservation and extension of trust require careful and pain-staking analysis of the individual context?

CHAPTER NINE

Is Trust Declining?

Declining trust: the evidence

The non-anecdotal evidence for the decline in trust comes from surveys of public opinion. As a recent international example, surveying 15,000 people across 15 countries for the Davos World Economic Forum,[1] showed, our trust in our leaders is low (Figure 11) and declining (Figure 12). Only leaders of NGOs were trusted by more than 50 per cent of the respondents (and even then not with a massive vote of confidence).

Trust in Leaders
Percentage Saying "A Lot" and "Some Trust"
(Average Across All 15 Countries Surveyed)

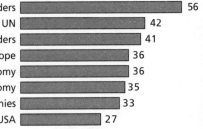

NGO leaders	56
Leaders at the UN	42
Spiritual/religious leaders	41
Leaders of Western Europe	36
Managers of global economy	36
Managers of national economy	35
Executives of multinational companies	33
Leaders of the USA	27

Asked of half the sample in each country

Figure 11. Trust in leaders.

Change in trust levels of leaders in past year
Self-Reported Changes (Average Across All 15 Countries)

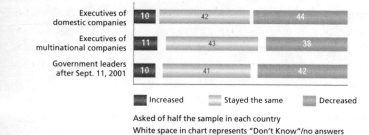

Asked of half the sample in each country
White space in chart represents "Don't Know"/no answers

Figure 12. Change in trust levels of leaders in past year.

Trust in institutions to operate in society's best interests
Global Ratings (*n* = 34,000 Across 46 Countries)

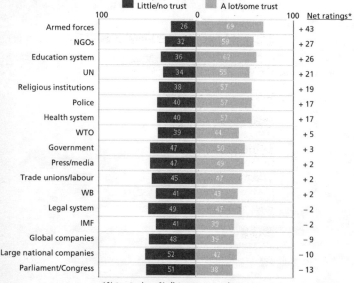

*% trust minus % distrust = net rating

Figure 13. Trust in institutions to operate in society's best interests.

A wider survey, *Voice of the People*, conducted on 36,000 people over 47 countries, found similarly problematic results.[2] Trust in institutions was not high either. Perhaps surprisingly, perhaps not in the post-September 11th atmosphere, it was the armed forces that were most trusted (though this survey predated the Second Gulf War). Multinationals actually did better in the survey than national companies (Figure 13).

Governments and media seem to be more or less equally trusted across the world, though with large variations between regions (Figure 14).

Trust in government vs. media
Percentage Saying "A Lot/Some Trust", by Region

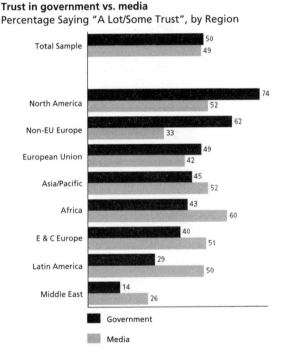

Figure 14. Trust in government vs. media.

Trust in parliament/congress to operate in society's best interests
Regional Results

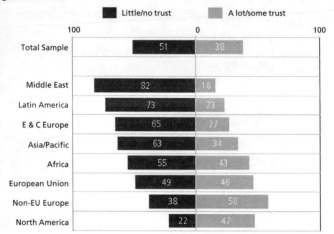

Figure 15. Trust in parliament/congress to operate in society's best
interests.

Parliaments and parliamentarians – and this is certainly worrying
– are not trusted very much at all (Figure 15).

In general, most people think the world is moving in the wrong
direction, and more people think that in 2003 than thought it in
2002, according to the World Economic Forum survey (Figure 16).

These two big surveys, recently published, must make worrying
reading. And other smaller, more focused, surveys provide similar
food for thought. The 2000 European Values Survey, for instance,
reported that only 30 per cent of British people said that most
people could be trusted, down from 44 per cent in 1990. PR firm
Edelman London reported in February 2002 that opinion leaders
(educated adults attentive to the media and government policy –
that includes you and me, I think) in the UK were more likely to
trust the media (26 per cent) than Mr Blair's government (20 per

World is going in the right direction
Percentage Saying "Agree" (n = 1,000 per country), 2002–2003

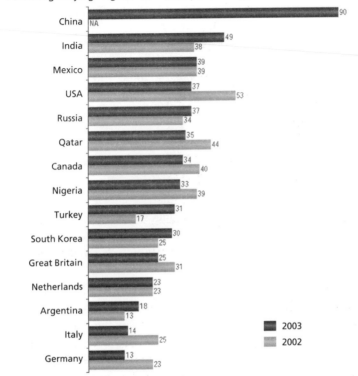

Figure 16. World is going in the right direction.

cent); that has changed since 2001, when Mr Blair won 31 per cent to 17 per cent. ICM and the *Guardian* produced an opinion poll in 1999 showing that scientists, after the GM food debate had begun, were trusted less than policemen, though more than journalists and politicians. Euro RSCG discovered in March 2002 that 15 per cent of Europeans do not trust any company at all.[3]

Much ado?

But are these surveys as convincing as they seem? For example, let's take the last survey, that 15 per cent of Europeans (and indeed as many as 49 per cent of American women) don't trust any company at all. What does that mean? How would *you* respond if asked the question: which companies would you trust? What is involved in trusting a company?

I certainly don't trust Enron; evidence of its wrongdoing is legion (recall Chapter 6). Did I trust Enron before that evidence became public after its collapse in 2001? Well, er, no. But then I had barely heard of Enron. And if I did trust Enron, how could my trust be assessed? I am not an energy dealer, so I wouldn't really come into contact with Enron in order to be able to display any signs of mistrust. How does trust manifest itself for any company? If I buy goods from a company, then I must trust it to some degree, presumably, otherwise why part with my money? But then how do the unfortunate 15 per cent of Europeans who don't trust *any* company get by?

Or, let's take the *Guardian*/ICM poll on trust in scientists and other professions. The respondents were asked whether they trusted particular professions a lot, a little, or not at all. The full results of the poll are these (in rounded percentages which may not total 100 per cent):

Table 2. Trust in professions.

Profession	Trusted 'a lot'	'A little'	'Not at all'	Trust vs. non-trust
Doctors	74	24	3	98–3
Teachers	68	28	4	96–4
Policemen	53	41	6	94–6
Scientists	35	54	12	89–12
Politicians	10	65	25	75–25
Journalists	4	49	48	53–48

Actually, what comes out of this poll is not, as the headline had it, that scientists were taking flak, but rather that levels of trust were astonishingly *high*. No doubt the 48 per cent of people who don't trust journalists at all didn't believe the story, which makes you wonder somewhat why the journalists, having found this out, bothered to print it. But of course, if they weren't trustworthy, they would just have made it up. But then I have just borrowed the report to put in my book – oh my goodness! We can't believe anything!!!

Except that, paradoxically, we do. We believe stories in the papers about how little trusted journalists are (and there are plenty of such stories). Go figure.

And, though the general story is one of decline and crisis, there are anomalies. For example, the European Values Survey showed that young people were the most mistrustful, with over three-quarters of them saying that they did not feel that they could trust others. Oh dear. Thank goodness for the British *Observer/*YouGov poll of 2002,[4] then, which revealed that 90 per cent of British youngsters trust their parents to guide them through adolescence (bless!) and 80 per cent trust their siblings and their teachers, though only 2 per cent trust vicars and priests on the specific topic of sex. Two-thirds gave money to charity, and half of them did voluntary work. Among this constituency, politicians came out ahead of journalists, though they may not be very satisfied with their 2 per cent rating.

As we noted earlier, trust is rather a nebulous phenomenon, and one that exercises some groups of people more than others. Might it be possible that these surveys are not asking questions that are particularly meaningful? Or might we tend to give negative answers, which make us look streetwise, as opposed to positive ones, which make us look naïve? As Reith lecturer Onora O'Neill put it:

The polls supposedly show that in the UK public trust in office-holders and professionals of many sorts is low and declining. ...

Much of the evidence of the way we actively place our trust seems to me to point in quite different directions. We constantly place trust in others, in members of professions and in institutions. Nearly all of us drink water provided by water companies and eat food sold in supermarkets and produced by ordinary farming practices. Nearly all of us use the roads (and, even more rationally, the trains!). Nearly all of us listen to the news and buy newspapers. Even if we have some misgivings, we go on placing trust in medicines produced by the pharmaceutical industry, in operations performed in NHS hospitals, in the delivery of letters by the post office, and in roads that we share with many notably imperfect drivers. We constantly place active trust in many others.

Does action speak louder than words? Are the ways we actually place our trust a more accurate gauge of trust than our comments to pollsters?[5]

When we follow O'Neill's advice and examine people's actions, what we tend to find is that levels of trust seem, on the face of it, extraordinarily robust. For example, many of us use credit cards and mobile phones; as we saw in Chapter 5 each time we use these we provide evidence of our movements and interests, and all these data are logged. Although it is generally claimed by those collecting this stuff that the information is sacrosanct, in fact it is not too difficult for the police or governmental authorities to get their hands on it. And, note, this is not a (perhaps sensible) swap of privacy for security, for instance as a reaction to the terrorist attacks of September 11th. This is swapping privacy for convenience. It is perceived as a genuine swap, too: in general people are not confident that companies will comply with data protection regulation.[6]

Granted, sometimes – as with a public monopoly in, say, water – it is not always possible to take one's business elsewhere, but O'Neill is surely right that the doggedly determined will often if not always find an alternative to something that they genuinely do not trust. The rest of us generally mutter a bit that we will never trust it again – and then do so next time. The intersection of trust and habit is an interesting area, discussed for example by Barbara Misztal,[7] and the balance between the two motive forces may swing over time, but if habit is all that is needed to break through a so-called crisis of trust, then maybe the crisis is not too bad. It may just be the sort of mild disgruntlement that is not strong enough to displace entrenched behaviour, a disgruntlement borne of hope, nicely described by Proust.

> Every time a man about town enters into relations with a banker in such circumstances, the latter leaves him the poorer by a hundred thousand francs, which does not prevent the man about town from at once repeating the process with another. We continue to burn candles in churches and to consult doctors.[8]

This still leaves the question as to the underlying significance of why people *claim* to trust (or not). For instance, if a respondent to a values survey makes a claim to trust people, what does that tell us? Researchers have suggested various answers. A general position is that whether or not people are intrinsically trustworthy, the society of a trusting respondent must contain enough constraints on behaviour, in the form of either a strong and effective legal framework, or a widely shared set of norms of 'fairness', to make it sensible for people to behave in a trustworthy manner.

There are alternative views though. The respondent may simply be culturally disposed to trust.[9] The respondent's answers may reflect his or her trustworthiness rather than that of others; trusting

247

people tend to be trustworthy.[10] Or it may be that the respondent's answers reflect his or her views on the future rather than on others' behaviour. Optimists tend to trust, pessimists don't.[11]

In other words, the survey evidence – the main empirical evidence – is open to quite a few interpretations. Might it be the case that our blithe assumptions about trust, and its decline, could be open to doubt? Maybe the breadth of application of the notion of 'trust', the diversity of its content, should be alerting us to the possibility that there are many social phenomena operating here, and that the relationship between trust and good behaviour has been, on occasion, misconceived. *Inter alia*, culture, street wisdom and naïveté are factors that influence trust and trusting – if these and other such imponderables are important, how easy can it be to drive trust, to create or re-establish trust when we wish to?

The expectation gap

One important parameter of trust is that of *expectation*. If I trust someone to do something, then that has a lot to do with my expectations. For example, if I trust the government to preserve my employment, then I expect that the government will act in order to prevent my losing my job. Then it follows that my trust in government might be lost, not only in the event of the government's being untrustworthy, but also if my expectations are unrealistic. And that might happen in two ways. It may be that the government actually has little or no power to affect my employment prospects; or it may be that I am simply being unrealistic in assuming that the government will act to preserve my job (if, say, the cost of preserving my job is equal to the cost of creating two new jobs elsewhere, then all things being equal it is better for the government to create the new jobs rather than subsidise my old one).

An *expectation gap*, that we expect more to be done for us than is actually feasible or desirable, is beginning to be detectable in a number of sectors of society. One example is an increasing tendency for people to seek compensation after any mishap, even if no one has been negligent, or they have suffered no tangible loss. More serious is the pension problem. Demographically, European populations are currently aging, as people are living longer thanks to improved medical treatment and technology, and fewer babies are being born. In France, for instance, there are currently four pensioners for every ten workers; in 2040 there will be seven. If these trends continue, that will be an unsustainable ratio; the people working in 2040 will have to sacrifice too much of their income to support their economically idle compatriots. Unfortunately, the French are unwilling to change regulations to increase the amount of time people will have to work before they receive a full pension, or to increase the incentives to use private pension plans.[12] The voters do not trust their government on the topic of pensions (or on much else, as shown by the dismal 2002 Presidential election).[13] There was a giant demonstration about pensions in Paris in May 2003, of the size of demonstrations in London opposing war in Iraq, or the Million Man March about the plight of African-Americans in New York. The cause for complaint in Paris? An attempt to make workers work 40 years instead of 37.5 before they were eligible for full pensions![14]

But it may well be that what we have here is not a weaselly government trying to get out of its statutory obligations, but in reality an expectation gap on the part of the French voters. Something has to give; either the demographics have to change and current trends be deviated from (actually, the government is spending €1.2 billion to try to increase birth rates and make that happen!),[15] or people will have to spend less and save more over their working lives, or they will have to work for longer, or future generations will have to pay much more in tax. Those are the options, but the evidence seems to suggest that French voters want their government magically to create another option. In which case they expect too much of their government. Non-European commentators find this expectation gap incredible.[16]

As another example, people are very keen to be consulted on decision-making. Governments, ever willing to oblige, indulge in long 'consultation exercises'. We live in a democracy, goes the argument; we deserve to be consulted about the expenditure of our money. New technologies are seen as a key to consultation.[17] The figures are quite clear, from the *Voice of the People* survey at least, where less than a third of people worldwide believe they are consulted enough (Figure 17).[18]

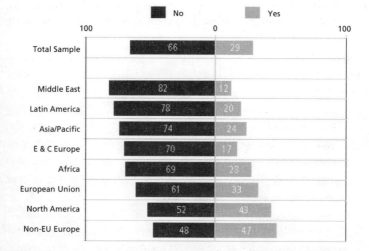

Country governed by the will of the people?
By Geographic Region (*n* = 34,000 Across 46 Countries)

Figure 17. Country governed by the will of the people?

The reality, of course, is different. Consultation exercises often go on at great length, whereupon the government does what it was going to do in the first place (as for example with a series of consultations about airport expansion at various sites across the United Kingdom over the last 40 years or so). Some consultations are obviously spurious: we are invited to present our views over premium rate phone lines by television programmes, Internet sites or Teletext pages. And for what? Other than selecting the winners of pop music competitions or reality shows, what effect do our 'votes' have? Not a sausage. People will speak for hours on end on radio phone-in programmes, often to be insulted or cut off in their prime by rude hosts; they are achieving nothing other than filling the radio station's time cheaply for it. In Britain, prior to the Second Gulf War in 2003, the Prime Minister himself appeared on a television show to try to persuade a group of women of the righteousness of the US-led coalition's cause; he failed, and was humiliated by their giving him a slow hand-clap at the end of the programme.[19] Which achieved: precisely zilch. The war went ahead anyway.

Consultation exercises actually can get in the way of good government, as Mike Goddard, a project manager in Hackney, complains.

> Five years ago Hackney, one of the poorest London boroughs, successfully bid for Single Regeneration Budget (SRB) funding to regenerate its civic heart, the town hall square. Driving this ambition were the ongoing plans to build a new library and museum and a state-of-the-art music venue.
>
> ...
>
> Throughout the process, consultation was a paramount objective. A consultation group was set up. An ideas forum event, set up at a cost of almost £50,000 was held over three days in a marquee

on the square. Over 3,500 people had input in one way or another during that weekend. A magazine was regularly printed and distributed. More cost. A website was built. Exhibitions mounted and an open day organised. Yes, you've guessed it, more cost.

When the project had shape and finally went before the council's regeneration committee for approval, a group of local agitators cried in one voice 'where's the consultation?' Incredulously, they claimed not to have seen any of the previous events. Not one of them received the magazine, they said. 'The internet? For yuppies,' they all cried.

In short, despite enormous costs, despite teams of people working towards gathering input and ideas from as wide a selection of local people as possible, in a few people's eyes that target was missed.

The question I would put to anyone is this: How much money does a scheme have to spend, how much time has to slip, how many costly events need to be staged before that project says 'enough', and actually gets on with the job?

The last four years of my life have been, to a large extent, wasted on doing consultation exercises that achieved nothing. Always attended by the same vociferous groups, each one purporting to be the voice of the ordinary man, yet each having a particular personal axe to grind, never really involving minorities or those people who are content to see local change if it promotes jobs and public safety.[20]

Public consultation is not in itself wrong, but at some point a decision has to be taken, and that decision will – if there is not total agreement amongst voters – have to ignore some people's wishes. There is an expectation gap about what can be achieved via consultation; merely expressing one's views, via opinion polls, radio phone-ins or local referenda, cannot in and of itself deliver the decision one wants. To claim that a consultation exercise is phoney simply because one didn't get one's own way is to expect too much.

There is some evidence that expectation gaps increase with wealth. Superior living standards do not necessarily generate happiness. People habituate very quickly to new-found wealth, and what gave them a buzz five years ago (e.g. air conditioning) becomes a routine necessity. And many experiments have shown that people are concerned not with their absolute level of wealth, but with the level compared with others (and hence that making more money won't make them happier if everyone else makes more money as well). People will not appreciate increases in living standards, even as they work harder and harder to secure them.[21] And this general level of dissatisfaction leaches through into other attitudes. Though trust in one's fellow man increases with education and wealth,[22] Mark Warren argues that:

> In the stable democracies, political institutions and elites are probably no less trustworthy than in the past. Rather, the decline in trust in institutions probably reflects a more general decline in respect for authority that has come with the development of post-material cultures. When people no longer worry for their survival, they do not need to cling unquestioningly to the authorities they hope will ensure their survival. Instead, as material well-being increases, trust in political institutions and elites is likely to decline as publics begin to evaluate their leaders and institutions by more demanding standards.[23]

What may be happening – and not just in the political sphere – is that the new standards are becoming *over*-demanding, at least in some instances. We may have been fostering what O'Neill calls a culture of suspicion.[24] As we get richer and more comfortable –

and the risks affecting us more theoretical and less present – we ratchet up the standards of trustworthy behaviour beyond the realistic. For example, given that one in seven British men and one in eleven British women between the ages of 16 and 44 are unfaithful to their partners *each year*,[25] why do we expect our political representatives to behave any better? Do we *really* think that the journalists and politicians hounding, say, Bill Clinton, are averse to the odd bit on the side themselves? As St Paul sternly admonished the Corinthians:

> And what hast thou that thou didst not receive? Now if thou didst receive it, why dost thou glory, as if thou hadst not received it?[26]

Narratives of doom

Expectations are important for trust. And expectations are formed by our understanding of the likely course of events, which in turn is created by different *narratives*. We have seen (Chapter 7) the importance of narratives in scientific work. Actually they play similar roles in the other domains too, creating stories by smoothing out confusing details, supporting *reputations*. Many of our assumptions about past and future events find their way into such narratives, and equally the structure of these explanatory narratives can influence our thinking, albeit unconsciously, about new circumstances.

There is nothing unusual about creating explanatory narratives. However, as the expectation gap has grown, we are beginning to generate what we might call *narratives of doom*. Optimistic stories are seen as less cool, less streetwise than the cynical assumptions of greed and venality in our representatives and incompetence and hubris in our plans. These narratives of doom need not resemble the likely course of events at all. Recall from Chapter 7 the 'grey goo' theory that is routinely trotted out as a criticism of nano-technology. In the case of the MMR vaccine (discussed briefly in Chapter 7), a single report from Andrew Wakefield linking the vaccine with autism has served to dominate the debate, despite the overwhelming evidence produced since that the result was a rogue one; as Dr Mike Fitzpatrick says, what is extraordinary is that people trust Dr Wakefield, even though he can't even convince his fellow doctors[27] (and recall from the *Guardian*/ICM poll cited above that people claim to trust doctors, even though they appear not to in the face of this particular narrative of doom).

In effect, narratives of doom reinforce expectation gaps. They postulate a disastrous outcome of an uncertain endeavour. Whichever person, company or authority is responsible for the endeavour will necessarily fail to address the assumptions of the narrative of doom, because those assumptions are unaddressable, indeed often impossible. There is then an expectation gap, thanks to the failure of responsible persons to address the problem; never mind that that may be due to the underspecification of the problem, rather than the venality and greed that conveniently fit into and reinforce the narrative.

So, if we take the grey goo narrative, there is little or no scientific story as to how everything might be transformed into grey goo, other than some handwaving about self-reproducing bots on the nano scale. No matter that no one has created such a robot, and that no one (least of all the promoters of the narrative of doom) has the foggiest idea of how it could be done. If specific mechanisms were postulated, then nanotechnologists could address the problem – but then if there were specific plausible mechanisms available that could actually turn everything into grey goo, then we would have a narrative that was scientifically kosher, not a narrative of doom. If *any* mechanism is supposed to have the potential for turning everything into grey goo, then the only way to prevent the narrative of doom from happening is to abandon nanotechnology altogether. There may be good reasons for doing that, but this narrative surely can't be one of them.

Not all such narratives are narratives of doom. The global warming narrative provides lots of good, scientifically reasonable motivation for reducing carbon emissions, and it is a serious problem that no one can convince the Americans in particular of its importance. It is extraordinary that a nation can be full of people convinced they have been kidnapped by aliens, who ignore much more plausible warnings about the future. It is very unfortunate that narratives (of doom or otherwise) lose much of their efficacy when people's wealth may be affected; for example, there is little doubt that public mistrust of GM foods would decline to some extent at least if they were available, clearly and properly labelled as such, at a discount on supermarket shelves.

And not all sensible narratives need, in the end, prove true. In the months prior to the year 2000, a huge amount of corporate and public money was spent dealing with the problem of the *millennium bug*, a little time bomb supposedly lurking in older computer systems that meant that they would be unable to tell 2000 apart from 1900. Fears of the collapse of many critical systems, for example in aeroplanes or hospitals, seem, with hindsight, to have been clearly exaggerated. But there was a risk there, and it is hard to argue that careful governments and companies that attempted to sort out the problem in 1999 weren't being properly cautious, even if in fact the money was wasted.

The grey goo narrative is ridiculous, not because it won't happen, not because it is implausible, but because *there is no reason to think it will happen.*

Transparency and the performance paradox

Another innovation that we have seen here and there in the domains we have covered is that of *transparency*, of the use of strict measures of performance of experts, politicians and other specialists. Performance targets are supposed to enable the evaluation of specialists. However, not only do such targets distort the incentives of specialists,[28] but they could remove the essential conditions for certain types of expertise to function. For instance, it is inevitable that the operation of some types of expertise will occasionally involve dissembling or other difficult moral choices. Doctors, as we have seen, routinely need to resort to relatively harmless deception of their patients[29] – and it has long been said that those who love sausages or the law should never witness either being made. Transparency could actually end up *decreasing* trust in some cases, by exposing minor flaws, insensitivities or petty criminality to a public whose high expectations lead them to be very intolerant.

Appearance seems to matter more than reality. This stems from a well-known problem in management: quite often, when there is some good (or bad) type of behaviour that you want to encourage (or discourage) but that is difficult to measure – trust, value for money, criminality, productivity – there is a temptation to find things you *can* measure that will stand proxy for the hard-to-measure stuff. You infer the hard-to-measure stuff from the easy-to-measure stuff. So, when Mr Blair wishes to know whether a school is providing a good education, he doesn't ask 'is this school providing a good education?' because he knows he will get the empty answer 'yes'. Instead he asks what percentage of students have received particular grades at GCSE or A Level or whatever. This is precise and can't be fudged. When he wishes to know whether a university lecturer is any good or not, he asks how many publications the lecturer has had over the last few years, and in which journals he or she has published. The fact that, under such a regime, Wittgenstein for one would have been out on his ear is not deemed relevant, because Wittgenstein's genius is difficult to assess precisely. When Mr Blair wants to know whether there can be public confidence in the police, he asks about the numbers of arrests and reported crimes. These are easy-to-measure indicators that are not too difficult to discover.

However, the indicators can only be imperfect reflections of the hard-to-measure stuff. Not only that, when the indicators are put in place, things begin to change. The world does not stay still, it is dynamic; economies alter, institutions increase or decrease in reputation, science moves on. So the indicators are likely in general to become gradually less and less effective, to reflect the hard-to-measure stuff less well. Second, we discover new things about the indicators themselves. For instance, as we understand the processes of education a little more, or as the governing theories about what constitutes a good education change, we begin to understand the relation between indicators and what they are indicators of in different ways. Third, most perniciously, as people begin to understand the measurement system, they alter their behaviour in order to hit the indicator targets. A teacher stops worrying about providing a good education, the best education for her charges, and instead nurses them through their exams (and maybe even turns away those bound to fail). A university lecturer devotes less effort to teaching, or to following his creative urges, and instead churns out as many publications that are minor variations of each other as he can find journals for. Policemen direct resources towards those crimes that will affect their figures favourably.

And these professionals do this not because they are bad, but because that is where their incentives are pointing them. There is often tough resistance to such targets from those 'on the ground', but it is the ones who aim at the targets who will get on, who will receive increased funding. By such means is the performance paradox created.

Trust is certainly one of these hard-to-measure things. And if trustworthiness is to be an important part of political discourse, then we shall discover that pretty soon we will be dealing with trust's proxies. Certain traits are associated with trustworthiness. Some may be meaningful, such as particular qualifications, experiences, achievements. Others will be extraneous, such as a sharp suit or a command of currently fashionable jargon ('we are about empowering the citizen by foregrounding her aspirations and enabling dialogue with service providers' is the sort of sentence that will get you far nowadays). A person who wants to be trusted makes sure he or she can hit all the right buttons, and ensures that the indicators are OK. The whole system of performance measurement points them in this direction – merely being trustworthy by itself no longer counts.[30] As Jean Giraudoux famously said, 'the secret of success is sincerity. Once you can fake that you've got it made.'

Going bowling and other cures

There is no evidence that performance targets have increased trust (can performance targets have their *own* performance targets?).[31] Narratives of doom seem, bizarrely, to have a much stronger hold on societies than scientifically grounded narratives (perhaps unsurprisingly, as they are in effect a type of conspiracy theory). Standards for trustworthiness seem to be somewhat awry, and people give equivocal and often contradictory responses to opinion surveys. Our responses to the supposed decline in trust, the increase in accountability and the authorities' attempts to show trustworthiness seem confused and irrational.

We shouldn't be surprised. What is remarkable about trust is how *little* rationality (in the self-interested sense) seems to be involved in our decisions to trust. Trust often recognises reciprocity (as we noted in Chapter 2), and what we might call the pursuit of the common good. To take an example, when people are asked why they give blood, the most common answer is 'I might need blood myself one day.' This is true, but clearly involves no *rational* calculation of advantage – the blood supply of some indeterminate time in the future is in no way affected by giving blood now. The rationality is much wider in scope (indeed, appears to be almost Ciceronian in form – recall Chapter 8), and involves a relatively selfless understanding of the requirements of society as a whole.[32]

But many analyses of trust – particularly trust as it appears in political and public discourse, the trust we are examining in particular in this book – still implicitly assume an over-rational, over-individualised trust that cannot have very much to do with the phenomenon itself (otherwise we would react very differently to transparency, performance targets and narratives of doom).

This insight is quite damaging for a lot of theories. Let us take one example, the social capital theory of Robert Putnam (see Chapter 3). Putnam's theory concerns the transition from local to global trust (using our terminology introduced in Chapter 4), and the support that global trust receives. His idea is that plenty of local trust will underpin global trust, and that if local trust declines, then so will global trust. That would be a problem, because it is global, institutionalised trust that is important economically, that supports complex, interconnected societies.

> People who have active and trusting connections to others – whether family members, friends, or fellow bowlers – develop or

maintain character traits that are good for the rest of society. Joiners become more tolerant, less cynical, and more empathetic to the misfortunes of others. When people lack connections to others, they are unable to test the veracity of their own views, whether in the give-and-take of casual conversation or in more formal deliberation. Without such an opportunity, people are more likely to be swayed by their worst impulses.[33]

Hence, argues Putnam, the decline in activities like bowling, local group activities in America, is worrying, because that may be the first sign of the decline of local trust that will in turn cause a decline in global trust.

But it simply is not clear why there should be such a connection, or, if there is, what direction it goes in. People spend very little time in voluntary organisations, bowling with their fellows in teams, and it seems very unlikely that such a minuscule amount of one's time could produce a marked change in attitudes.

More to the point, the admittedly imperfect evidence seems to suggest that those who have active and trusting connections with others are seeking out people to whom they are similar, with whom they feel affinities, whether of gender, ethnicity, social standing or merely worldview. At best, such connections are irrelevant: 'why are members of bowling leagues more likely to trust members of choral societies than people who stay at home?'[34] In many cases, contacts such as these actually restrict the tendency to trust a wider, more diverse community. One's trust becomes turned inward, one becomes overly trusting of those who are similar, and correspondingly less trusting of outsiders, unconsciously swallowing a group's rhetoric of 'the other'.

It may well be, as the European Values Survey found,[35] that there is a link between voluntarism and trusting. But there is no obvious connection between voluntarism and the more valuable global trust, even if voluntarism happens to produce local trust. Speaking as someone who would *rather* go bowling alone, I for one find that relatively comforting.

Induction on good behaviour

Putnam and others assume that trust is the effect of good behaviour, and that the decline in trust is caused primarily by the decline of trustworthiness on the part of the various authorities. Trust is caused by trustworthiness; you act in a trustworthy way for some unspecified period of time, and then gradually people begin to trust you. They will, over time, learn that you will do what you say you will do, and so they will spend less time watching over you, monitoring your performance.

Conversely, this sort of trust can be broken immediately by any failure of trustworthiness on your part. It can take years to build up, depending on the context, and can be shattered in an instant. If you don't mind me breaking into symbols for a second, the logical structure of this view of trust is that an agent X must establish the following proposition for an audience.

- X will do action A within parameters P if he/she says he/she will.

In other words, the audience has to come to believe that X will achieve the goal of the action within some set of constraints, such as a particular budget, or doing the task by a set time, or doing it without offending anyone. This *prediction* has to be established by *induction*, i.e. by demonstrating individual *past* cases of trustworthy actions, painstakingly.

- X did A_1 within P_1.
- X did A_2 within P_2.

- X did A_3 within P_3.
- X did A_4 within P_4.

And so on.

X is trying to show that he or she will *always* be trustworthy, a proposition universally true over X's lifetime. It is impossible to prove a universal proposition by enumerating individual instances of it, but if X's audience sees X succeed often enough, then they will gradually come to believe the universal proposition, so the theory goes. This creation of trust may be a long process.

Logically, however, it is easy to disprove a universal proposition: all you have to do is exhibit a single counter-instance.

- X failed to do A_n within P_n.

That one counterexample is enough to disprove the universal. That is one reason, perhaps the reason, why trust is so hard to produce, and so easy to shatter.

What is interesting, though, after having surveyed the history and politics of trust, is how rarely trust conforms to this pattern. Some examples: an easy one to begin with is that of Neil and Christine Hamilton. As we saw in Chapter 8, they have certainly lost their association with untrustworthiness, and are tolerated and pretty generally liked, although seen as rather weird. Yet the denials of Hamilton's wrongdoings are not believed, and have not been vindicated in court.

A second example: in late 2001, levels of trust in the US Congress shot upwards, to unprecedented heights. Why was this: had Congress put its partisan bickering aside, and begun pulling together for the sake of the nation? Not really. Actually, levels of trust rose in all levels of US government following the terrorist attacks of 11th September.[36] But, one would think, this external matter – devastatingly serious though it clearly was – had very little to do

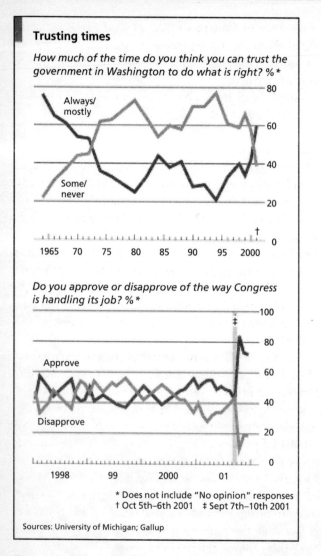

Figure 18. Trust in Washington before and after September 11th, 2001.

with the competence of Congress to do its work. Indeed, many have speculated about the *in*competence of American intelligence agencies as a result. Why then, if trust is so rational, did the attack cause the increase in trust?

A third example, still from politics but an issue of capacity rather than morality: the British Conservative Party had a reputation for economic competence that for most of the 20th century gave them a little head start on their Labour Party opponents. Former Tory chancellor Iain MacLeod famously said that they could always win elections as the harsh and greedy candidates as long as they preserved this reputation. On 'Black Wednesday' in September 1992, this reputation was lost over-night, as Britain was ejected from the Exchange Rate Mechanism, a precursor of European monetary union, despite then-chancellor Norman Lamont's increasingly desperate and expensive attempts to hold the line. The Tories lost the support of the Thatcherite press, and they plummeted to about 30 per cent in the opinion polls, where they have remained ever since. A classic case of the destruction of trust, surely?

Very possibly. But the issue is not as straightforward as all that. For in the late 1980s, Nigel Lawson, another Tory chancellor, engineered an economic boom – for which he received much credit at the time – which helped his party win a convincing victory in the 1987 general election, but which generated high inflation and interest rates of 13.5 per cent. This devastated the British housing market in particular: one in four property owners fell into negative equity in the early 1990s as house prices collapsed, and 400,000 houses were repossessed. This appeared to have little or no effect on the Conservatives' reputation for sound financial management, despite the fact that these dispossessed homeowners might be presumed to be disproportionately Tory voters.

And on the other hand, once John Major had belatedly sacked

'Black Wednesday' chancellor Lamont, the Conservatives, by general consent, actually ran the economy rather well, recreating sound finances and not repeating the error of inducing an inflationary pre-election boom. So appealing, to the political classes at least, were the new economic policies that Labour chancellor Gordon Brown swallowed them more or less whole following Labour's victory in 1997. Yet this four and a half year period of careful management had no effect whatsoever on the Conservatives' fortunes. On the rational model of trust, where it is caused by good behaviour, even if one did not expect trust to be restored completely by such purging, some dent on the poll deficit should have appeared.[37]

Trust doesn't always seem to operate as it is supposed to. The logical structure we sketched above seems actively to get in the way: however many positive instances of 'good behaviour' we see, we can never be *sure* that a bit of bad behaviour won't follow. This problem of induction is an age-old one in philosophy – just because a is F and b is F and c is F and d is F and ... we can never say with full confidence that everything is F. If I see 10, 20, 100 white swans, that still doesn't tell me that the next one I see won't be black. The argument against induction was first produced by Enlightenment philosopher David Hume;[38] he never used the word 'induction', but his analysis of causation showed up the shakiness of the connection from such 'evidence' to a universal conclusion. In my view, Hume's devastating sceptical attack on causation has never been properly refuted.

Of course, an attribution of trust is rarely made with full confidence. But what is so troubling with the inductive view is that there seems to be no guidance at all about how to get from the individual Fs to the universal statement that everything is F. The questions of what trust is, when we are too trusting, and when we are too cynical, remain deeply mysterious on this account.

Indeed, many of our decisions to trust cannot be based on any particular relevant evidence, because there is *no* relevant evidence; so the nature of the transition from the particular to the universal looks even weirder. I often trust a stranger to perform some action, but I cannot in general observe him acting several times before I can place my trust in him, because he is a stranger. I may have observed *other* people acting in a trustworthy manner, but that says nothing about my stranger. In fact, the best interpretation of the rational view of trust as effect is that I draw conclusions about people on the basis of the actions of other people. Clearly my attribution of trust cannot be an *inference* from any behaviour at all, because quite obviously someone I have seen only once will provide me with *no* evidence on which to make that inference.[39] I trust the man next to me on the bus not to pick my pocket – but I have never seen him before! Even though no one else has ever picked my pocket on the bus, I have no evidence about *this* individual man. I should, surely, keep my hand on my wallet!

Trust as cause and trust as effect

What I am suggesting, in a roundabout way, is that the standard view of trust as a rational effect caused by trustworthy behaviour is not always very representative of the trust we actually place in objects, people, processes and institutions. The idea of trust as something we gradually bestow after carefully monitoring behaviour, and which we withdraw when we are betrayed, is (a) rooted in an idea of rationalism that cannot support cooperative and properly trusting behaviour, and (b) reliant on the use of a flawed method of inference, induction. Such a view, as we have seen in this chapter, is not unambiguously in accord with the empirical evidence either. It has led to poorly thought-out policies, such as the use of performance targets. It encourages the proliferation of expectation gaps, where the standards of trustworthiness that are supposed to create trust are placed way too high (for safety's sake); part of this process involves the generation of implausible and irrefutable narratives of doom which are so defined as to preclude the discovery of counter-evidence. It promotes the use of consultation exercises, and of authorities trying to do the most popular thing in order to appear trustworthy. In other words, it is an idea of trust that seems to inveigle people into behaving in ways that may be inimical to the fostering of trust at all.

The standard view takes trust as an effect of good behaviour. Actually, I would like to reverse that idea: trust is, or at least can be, a *cause* of good behaviour. People place trust pretty well automatically, are surprised when that trust is misplaced, and do not lightly withdraw it. To behave badly after being trusted is actually quite hard to do; we are policed by our consciences.[40]

Another way of making the contrast is to say that, on the standard view, the truster is trying to gain some sort of advantage, to work out when it is worth taking a risk on the trustee's goodwill. The truster observes others' behaviour, and tries to work out when it is in his or her interest to trust them. I am contrasting that with the idea that trusting is an act from which the truster doesn't necessarily expect to benefit this side of the grave. It is an act of acceptance of the trustee into a moral community.

And, we should point out, such a moral community is in general pretty diverse, as opposed to the narrower communities that Putnam's social capitalists try to foster. Our trust is placed very widely, and one of the achievements, if such be the correct word, of the radical Islamists of al-Qaeda is that their extreme murderousness and pursuit of 'soft targets' such as night clubs and restaurants have begun to undermine it. Such an understanding of the nature of trust in stable Western societies, in particular of how to use terror to maximal effect in a world jaded by violence, provides further evidence of al-Qaeda's sophistication and modernity.[41]

There certainly can be societies that are low-trust,[42] and in general it is better to live elsewhere. If there is a crisis of trust, that is not necessarily because trustworthiness has decreased, or bad behaviour has shattered trust which now has to be rebuilt. If trust is disappearing, it may be because we are withdrawing it, for whatever reason (and maybe no good reason). Our consciousness of this would explain the answers we give to opinion pollsters, even when such answers plainly contradict our actions. In the long run, this is not a good development. The difficult question to answer is how long it will take to restore trust when that trust has been withdrawn. How delicate a plant is it?

CHAPTER TEN

Re-establishing Trust

The evidence for a decline in trust is equivocal. But there is little doubt that there is an air of crisis, fanned by commentators and opinion polls alike, and not a few high-profile disasters such as Enron or BSE. Does this mean that a decline in trust is inevitable, a self-fulfilling prophecy? What is the nature of the malaise, and how will the relative level of trust affect our lives in the 21st century? And are there any recommendations as to how to maximise trust and trustworthiness?

Back to Tony Blair

Recall the very beginning of this book, the Preface. There I introduced the topic of trust by musing on the problems of Tony Blair, particularly the crisis that beset his government in the summer of 2003. By the time this book is published, it will be known how that crisis ended; Mr Blair may be out of a job, and trousering plenty of dosh on the Clintonian lecture circuit, or alternatively he may have ridden out the storm and have restored his traditionally massive opinion poll lead over the Tories. No point my speculating.

It is generally agreed that Mr Blair's problems stem from plummeting trust in his government; did he lie about the threat from Iraq, did he besmirch the name of a respected scientist and so inadvertently cause his awful suicide?[1] The *Daily Telegraph*'s YouGov poll on 25 July 2003 made, as such articles always say, grim reading for the Prime Minister.[2] Excerpts from this poll include:

Table 3. The 'trust' factor.

The 'trust' factor (per cent)

Do you think the government has, on balance, been honest and trustworthy?

	2001 General Election	May 2003	June 2003	July 2003
Yes, honest	56	29	25	24
No, not honest	30	62	66	68
Don't know	14	9	8	9

Table 4. Trust in the party leaders.

Blair and his successor (per cent)

Who do you think can most be trusted ...?

	All voters	Conservative voters	Labour voters	Liberal Democrat voters
Iain Duncan Smith (Conservative)	27	76	1	4
Charles Kennedy (Liberal Democrat)	26	9	11	79
Tony Blair (Labour)	23	1	73	3
Don't know	24	14	15	14

Trust has rarely been such a serious issue in British politics. And as the *Economist* reported, 'in every political career there is a moment people look back on: that, they say, was when it all started to go wrong. ... Could this be that sort of moment for Tony Blair?'[3]

But hang on. The *Economist* was worrying about the loss of trust in Mr Blair 18 months previously.[4] On that occasion, there was no single issue – certainly no mention of Iraq – but a raft of smaller problems, none of which resonated more than a few weeks later. And 18 months before that, the *Economist* opined that an unwise speech to the Women's Institute, which had led to him being heckled and given a slow hand-clap, was his 'Ceausescu moment' when his personal spell was broken.[5] Actually, Mr Blair has never been trusted. A mere two days into his premiership, the *Economist* was accusing him of 'calculated dishonesty'.[6]

I am neither criticising the *Economist*, nor claiming it is the only journal serially guilty of writing Mr Blair off. I am certainly not claiming that Mr Blair will never be deposed as leader by either his party or the electorate (he may even be before this book is published). But the plain fact is, as the *Economist*'s commentaries have demonstrated, that Mr Blair has *always* been synonymous with spin doctoring, twisting the truth and the media, presenting false pictures. He has been known as a ruthless media manager pretty well since his election as Labour leader in 1994. Unlike in the Hans Andersen story, almost no one believes that this particular emperor has a fine new set of clothes. He has *never* been trusted to tell the unvarnished truth (even if opinion polls have said otherwise). And yet he strolled to two enormous landslide election victories in 1997 and 2001.

Trust is an odd thing. It has become a commonplace in political discussion, perhaps given a big boost by the success of Francis Fukuyama's 1995 book on the topic. And politicians like Blair and

Bill Clinton, charming yet elusive, seem to demand that we trust them against our better instincts. Has it always been the case?

Mr Blair's predecessor, John Major, was perceived as very trustworthy, and was liked by most voters. He was annihilated by the slippery Mr Blair in 1997. Mr Major's successor as leader of the Conservative Party, William Hague, was voted Britain's most honest politician in a 2003 poll for BBC Radio 2.[7] He was annihilated by the slippery Mr Blair in 2001. Mr Major's predecessor, Margaret Thatcher, was also trusted, in a rather different way. No one liked her. Most people generally understood she would manipulate the levers of power unscrupulously.[8] But she was trusted to do what she said, and to handbag the opposition, whether they were socialists, foreigners or Tory wets. Is this a different kind of trust? It certainly never did her any harm.

In fact, if we look at UK elections, what we find is that perceptions of trust don't actually seem to be very relevant or decisive at all. The following table shows all the British elections since the Second World War, together with my (admittedly highly subjective) sketch of the public perceptions of the party leaders (of course I am not saying that these perceptions were *true*). There are only four elections where the winner was perceived as the more obviously trustworthy, Attlee's two victories, Heath's and Major's. In contrast, shifty Harold Wilson won four elections on his own! Similar patterns can be seen in the US, for instance, where many mistrusted men have won presidential elections (Lyndon Johnson, Richard Nixon, Bill Clinton), or France, where Jacques Chirac's shady image did him no harm against plodding Lionel Jospin, or Italy, where Silvio Berlusconi is off the scale. From my position writing in 2003, I would not yet be advising Mr Blair to telephone for the removal vans.

If we really want trustworthy politicians, then we should surely give them the incentives to be trustworthy. But in fact, as our table

Table 5. Trust and post-war British elections.

Year	Conservative leader	Perception	Labour leader	Perception	Winner
1945	Winston Churchill	Raffish, brilliant, always refighting Second World War	Clement Attlee	Principled, boring	Attlee
1950					Attlee
1951					Churchill
1955	Anthony Eden	Decent, stolid, groomed for the job			Eden
1959	Harold Macmillan	Slippery, gets things done, quietly ruthless	Hugh Gaitskell	Raffish, 'champagne socialist'	Macmillan
1964	Sir Alec Douglas Home	Toff, unworldly	Harold Wilson	Two-faced, dishonest, schemer, paranoid	Wilson
1966	Edward Heath	Honest, wooden, humourless			Wilson
1970					Heath
Feb. 1974					Wilson
Oct. 1974					Wilson
1979	Margaret Thatcher	Heartless, determined, ruthless	James Callaghan	Avuncular	Thatcher
1983			Michael Foot	Intellectual, cultured, unworldly, Bolshevik	Thatcher
1987			Neil Kinnock	Windbag	Thatcher
1992	John Major	Nice, ineffectual			Major
1997			Tony Blair	*Spinmeister*	Blair
2001	William Hague	Affable, witty, bit of a 'wally'			Blair

shows, perceived trustworthiness rarely swings an election. We, as voters, are sending out quite the wrong signals – if it is trustworthiness in which we are interested. Mr Blair's popularity soared when he became a father, for the fourth time, to baby Leo in 2000. How did this make him more trustworthy? Maybe trust is not so crucial, in politics at least, after all.

Trust in the 21st century

Trust has different properties and functions in different contexts, of course, as I have argued throughout this book. The four areas that we reviewed in Chapters 5 to 8 were selected quite carefully, to cover as many diverse domains as possible. We chose two domains where much of the trust was local (the Internet and politics), and two where most was global (business and science); we chose two where most relations were horizontal (the Internet and business), and two where some were vertical (science and politics).

What was interesting was that there were problems negotiating trust in *all* these fields. The type of interaction, and the type of relation characteristic of the domain didn't seem to make things any easier. Establishing trust is never a trivial matter.

This shouldn't really be surprising. The relationships out of which mature societies are constructed are changing, and that will clearly have an effect on trust. Such relationships as we have with our fellows are partly constituted by trust, and partly help establish trust; trust both depends on, and helps to strengthen, other bonds in society. So when we reflect on the series of social, political, economic and philosophical changes that have been occurring throughout Western society in the last few decades, we should begin to expect that conditions for placing trust might also be altering as part of that dynamic.

Let me highlight two sets of changes. The first concerns our horizontal relationships, our relations with people where responsibilities are shared. These relationships are thinning out; there seem to be fewer such relationships that are meaningful, and it is thought that the set of social responsibilities we are prepared to support is diminishing. Most major political thought in the mature Western democracies focuses on the autonomy of the *individual*.[9] There has been remarkably little effective opposition to this.[10] Many ideas based on social solidarity of various forms have managed to establish footholds in some marginal areas of social and political life, including green theory,[11] feminism,[12] queer theory[13] and Islamism.[14] A curious creed called communitarianism, the view that the community should be the key focus of analysis and the anchor of the value system, has struggled to make headway in the liberal world, despite some high-profile adherents who see it as a potential cure-all for a number of social problems; it seems that nowadays we prefer our autonomy.[15]

These alternatives to liberalism are simply failing to make much headway, because however much we like the idea in principle of class or religious or racial solidarity (identity-based solidarity), when push comes to shove we also like the freedom to do our own thing. Such solidarity-based nostrums seem largely to appeal to those who do relatively badly from the Wild West that liberalism seems to create, who prefer some social support for their lives, or who wish to define themselves in opposition to the liberal core. The trick that liberalism pulls is that, like other successful creeds, it spreads its benefits reasonably wide, and hence those who feel disadvantaged or alienated are too small in number to affect the mainstream very much.

Solidarity is on the decline, and there are further economic changes that separate us still further from each other; free markets only reward cooperation in specific circumstances, for example.

The quality and quantity of deference-free relations with our fellows are declining as we discover the joys of liberty and autonomy.

A similar story can be told about our vertical relations; we are much less willing to accept someone's authority over us.[16] Our democratising instinct, the idea that authority is very rarely legitimate, and that legitimacy has to be earned, has meant that we are much less likely to assume that we are being well steered from the captain's bridge.

As the quality of our interrelationships both horizontal and vertical has declined, and the guidelines over where and with whom to place our trust have become outdated, our decisions to trust are now exactly that – decisions. No longer can we simply place our trust where we always have done, out of habit, or where our fellows place theirs, out of conformity. Habit and conformity are no longer perceived as good guides for action; we are in a world that prizes innovation and independence. This general social development has shaken up a lot of ways of living – perhaps most obviously with gender relations. No news, then, that it has raised a challenge for our practices of trust.

For a brief few years at least, the need for trust seemed smaller. The end of the Cold War saw the close of what has been called the short 20th century,[17] beginning with the collapse of the 19th-century balance of power that triggered the First World War, and finally ending when the last ripples from the explosion of the Russian revolution expended their energy on the shores of *glasnost*. In the absence of a tangible enemy, our siege mentality dissipated, and we were able to turn our gaze inward, to examine the quality of life we were creating, as opposed to the quality of life we were trying to avoid. Many of us did not like what we saw. But now there may be an enemy once more, and levels of trust in politicians have briefly soared, as we noted in the previous chapter.

George Bush's handling of the economy, national defence and social issues did not notably improve on 12 September 2001; but by then he had gained an opponent, and not coincidentally given himself a boost for his re-election campaign in 2004.

The problem of trust is still pressing, even if the threat from fundamentalism proves to be short-lived. The first notable phenomenon of the 21st century is that of globalisation, the massive increase in connectivity in the world economy, thanks to reduced transport costs, information and communication technologies and a general reduction of tariffs on goods and controls on the movement of capital. Globalisation is highly reversible, certainly not the unstoppable force that many claim, but at the moment it is a key feature in the world economy. It has its own demands for trust, in particular a global trust (no surprise there) robust enough to survive across cultures. Small-scale trusting – favouring those who are most like us – will not help in the diverse globalised economy.

Trust will enable us to get the most out of globalisation, to thrive in the new unprotected environment. But we have to learn how best to place our trust, how to place it intelligently, in systems, in people, in institutions. As our autonomy and individuality increase, we have fewer guidelines to follow. Trust is a habit that we are getting out of, and we are going to have to relearn it, or forego many of the benefits that globalisation can bring. That is a genuine choice; withdrawal from engagement with other cultures is always possible. Such a withdrawal will be brought about if our reluctance to trust becomes embedded in our political, economic and social culture, if our opposition to immigration and asylum, our lack of generosity to poorer countries, our nervousness about Islamic fundamentalism, our desire to protect rich world producers at the expense of those in the developing world, and our aversion to multinationals collectively trump the liberal-capitalist ideology that is globalisation's driving force.

Winding up: crisis ... what crisis?

Trust is often extremely irrational. As Gogol complained:

> What is one to do with man? He doesn't believe in God, but he
> believes that if the bridge of his nose itches he will die; he will
> ignore a poet's work that is as clear as daylight, harmonious
> through and through and pervaded by the spirit of the sublime
> wisdom of simplicity, but he will pounce eagerly upon the work of
> some bounder who confuses, traduces, twists and distorts nature,
> and he will like it very much and he will start crying: 'This is it!
> This is true knowledge of the mysteries of the human heart!' All his
> life he does not care a pin for doctors and ends up by running for
> advice to some wise woman who cures by muttering spells and by
> spittle, or, better still, he himself invents some decoction of
> goodness only knows what rubbish, which for some mysterious
> reason he regards as the only remedy for his ills.[18]

This strange duality still pervades today; we say we do not trust the
people we vote for, yet avuncular middle-aged newsreaders are
among the most trusted people in the land. Trusted to do what?
Faithfully relate the contents of the autocue to us? Actually, as we
noted in our opening chapter, trust has become a blanket term for
many different processes of social cohesion, some that will increase
inclusion, others that focus on 'our' small group and exclude
everyone else, and there is no great reason to think that either our
sampling techniques or our sociological theories can do more than
provide a glimpse of a single aspect of the phenomenon. In short,
the picture is fragmented.

Nevertheless, books should end with conclusions, and, if I can't
solve all the problems of trust that we have uncovered in the course
of our odyssey through betrayal, foolishness, wilfulness and greed,

I can at least close with a few individual ideas that might help illuminate this most shady of social phenomena.

Narratives of doom. We have seen that these narratives often have no serious justification, yet they are amazingly difficult to shift. The big question is: why do we trust narratives of doom? It is important to realise that we are not mistrustful, or getting less trusting. It is that we are more likely to trust doomsters, however wide of the mark they may be. There are a number of reasons why this might be so; perhaps it is more streetwise; perhaps we are keen to show our independence of authority; perhaps we are simply too ignorant of reality, and prefer the internal coherence of the narrative of doom because we can at least understand it. There is no doubt that widening expectation gaps play a part. We may miss real risks as a result of such narratives; for instance, if the nano-technology debate focuses on grey goo, it may be that potentially serious problems, such as the effects on the lungs of objects on the nanoscale, will be ignored.

The precautionary principle. Related to these narratives is the precautionary principle. It is certainly true that we need to be aware of the risks we run, and to put a premium on their investigation, perhaps by changing incentives for politicians, scientists and business leaders. Such a principle would have alleviated the problems of BSE and global warming, for example. On the other hand, when the principle is allied to the pernicious narratives of doom, it makes us not just risk-averse, but positively riskophobic. The precautionary principle, properly applied, would have prevented cavemen from playing with fire. More seriously, it would have prevented the introduction of post-Enron laws to regulate the scandal-prone accountancy industry. Any set of financial regulations will have unintended consequences[19] and the risks to financial conditions (which affect poor and rich alike, of course) are extremely hard to calculate. Such arguments have always been used by the financial community to deter regulators, and are merely instances of the precautionary principle. Surely we should take actual risks and proven benefits more seriously than theoretical risks.

Facts and rationality. It follows from this that we should surely take facts more seriously than the narratives. Narratives of doom often contain a kernel of truth, and they can be of great value by dramatising what may seem very abstruse arguments. But when we begin to concentrate on the husk and not the kernel, on the drama and not the issues, their use has been corrupted. We need to focus on the facts, once our interest has been aroused by narratives. Of course, few of us have the technical abilities to understand many political or scientific processes intimately. But critical thinking is not hard, as long as we are willing to be persuaded. And being properly suspicious of authority does not mean that we should never defer to greater knowledge or experience. Fashionable postmodern nostrums have also under-mined the idea that there may be facts about the world that we can discover. Such nostrums are luxuries that blur the distinction between reality and representation; they are fun for those in the mood, but too frivolous to be made a central part of our political decision-making.

Trust and rationality. Most discussions of trust seem to assume that it is a rational process of induction, that we observe a number of actions, and then, after some threshold is passed, begin to trust that those actions will always be carried out. Trust is therefore easy to lose and hard to win back. Sometimes this is indeed how it works. But in general trust is a wider attitude towards people and institutions that can as suddenly appear as disappear. And we often mistrust for entirely irrational reasons. In looking at a crisis of trust, we should not therefore assume that the cause of the crisis is necessarily the untrustworthy behaviour of those in a position of trust – politicians, scientists, etc. It may well be that the problem lies with those who are supposed to be doing the trusting, placing trust irrationally (as is, after all, their right). And conversely, if we are in a situation where trust is widespread, that does not mean that that trust is well placed, or that those who are trusted are behaving properly or morally.

Trust vs. trustworthiness. Implicit through much of our argument is a little-noticed distinction between someone being *trusted*, and someone being *trustworthy*. There is, no doubt, a correlation between the two, but not a strict one; it is quite possible to be trustworthy without being trusted or *vice versa*. Performance targets, and other attempts at transparency, fail to take account of this important distinction. They seek out the external signs of trust, those characteristics that make people and institutions trusted, and insist that everyone else adopt those signs. But looking like a trustworthy person does not make someone trustworthy, as anyone who has tried to buy a used car from a personable salesman can testify.

Liberty. Trust, as Onora O'Neill argued, is better seen through actions rather than survey responses. It follows that it is better to let people decide for themselves where possible about some things, either through non-interference with markets, or through democratic processes. For instance, the EU has rightly insisted on strict labelling of GM foods, because that is what European voters want. But if European consumers, given these labels, inconveniently buy GM foods in quantity, then that, surely, should also be their right.

Mistakes. Greater trust, by and large, leads to greater prosperity. It is a good thing. But there will be errors of judgement, and mistakes will be made. This is to be expected, it is a corollary of the very idea of trust, which functions in a state of uncertainty. We should understand that, and be aware that one MP being a Jonathan Aitken, one teenager being a mugger, one asylum seeker being a fraud, or one scientist being in thrall to a sinister multinational doesn't mean that they all are.

Regulation. Regulation can help with trust, especially where there are legitimate causes for concern. Such regulation will in general get in the way, resulting in impaired performance. But sometimes it is required, as I argued above in the field of business; sometimes the gains of regulation outweigh the costs. Nevertheless, it is important to note that regulation doesn't *remove* the need for trust, it merely shifts its *object*. The regulatory *system* and its agents still need to be trusted, as we noted in Chapter 4. For example, there is a serious problem in many countries where there is a mass of regulations (because public trust is low) and an unloved, poorly paid bureaucracy to deal with them (poorly paid because trust in the bureaucracy is equally low). The result is a set of officials with little money and much power, a recipe for the Nigerian-style corruption that currently costs Africa $150 billion per year (or about 25 per cent of GNP), on African Union figures.[20]

Trust is a multifarious phenomenon, the by-product of many interactions, cultural effects and institutional practices. We cannot quantify it, except crudely; we do not understand it, except via many different and inconsistent theories. It is easier to destroy than create, though some people remain trusted despite repeatedly betraying those who trust them. Sociologists, economists and philosophers have studied it, and agree on little, except that it is a mystery.

If we radically reconfigure our society in order to promote trust, we will be making a mistake, since we have no idea what *will* promote trust. All I can say is that going around saying 'I want to be trusted' is a great way of not being trusted, in the same way as saying 'I want to be loved' will also defeat its own object.

And even if we could promote trust reliably, would that necessarily be a good thing? What is the use of producing trust if we are not sure of producing trustworthiness?

If there is a crisis of trust in our society, there is only one known potential remedy, and to the chagrin of many it is at the micro-level of individual behaviour, rather than at the macro-level of social engineering. It is for us to attempt to be trustworthy, to the best of our abilities.

And even that might not work.

Notes

1 By Atropos Divorced

1 Dante, *Inferno* (trans. H.F. Cary; J.M. Dent, London, 1908), XXXIII.

2 The pioneer of attempts to get computers to understand 'scripts' of common types of encounter is Roger Schank, for example in Roger C. Schank and Robert P. Abelson, *Scripts, Plans, Goals and Understanding* (Lawrence Erlbaum Associates, Hillsdale, NJ, 1977).

3 Ludwig Wittgenstein, *Philosophical Investigations* (Basil Blackwell, Oxford, 1953).

4 In Book XII.

5 For a brief discussion of this, see George Steiner, *Grammars of Creation* (Faber and Faber, London, 2001), pp. 226 ff.

6 I Corinthians 8:1.

7 B. Traven, *The Treasure of the Sierra Madre* (trans. Basil Creighton; Penguin, Harmondsworth, 1956), p. 193.

8 Capt. W.E. Johns, *Biggles Sweeps the Desert* (Hodder and Stoughton, London, 1942), republished as *Biggles Defends the Desert* (Red Fox, London, 1993), pp. 86–7.

9 Capt. W.E. Johns, 'Savages and wings', in *Biggles Flies Again* (Dean & Son, London, 1935), pp. 90–106, at p. 95.

10 Sax Rohmer, *The Daughter of Fu Manchu* (Cassell & Co., London, 1931), reprinted in *The Fu Manchu Omnibus Vol. 2* (Allison and Busby, London, 1997), p. 168.

11 As chronicled in many places, including Dee Brown, *Bury My Heart at Wounded Knee: An Indian History of the American West* (Random House, London, 1970).

12 Elizabeth Loftus, 'Reconstructing memory: the incredible eyewitness', *Psychology Today* (December 1974), pp. 116–19.

13 'Presidential candidate totals change as Florida recounts votes', *cnn.com Election 2000*, http://www.cnn.com/2000/ALLPOLITICS/stories/11/08/election.president/.

14 Antjie Krog, *Country of My Skull* (Random House, Parktown SA, 1998).

15 Laurel Teo, 'Recycling to meet 15 per cent of water needs by 2010', *Straits Times*, 13 January 2001; Peh Soo Hwee, 'Singapore hopes to quench thirst with recycled water', *Singapore Window*, 6 August 2002.

16 Adam B. Seligman, *The Problem of Trust* (Princeton University Press, Princeton, NJ, 1997), pp. 13–43.

17 Russell Hardin, 'Do we want trust in government?', in Mark E. Warren (ed.), *Democracy and Trust* (Cambridge University Press, Cambridge, 1999), pp. 22–41, at pp. 24–6.

18 Seligman, *The Problem of Trust*, p. 70.

19 Hardin, 'Do we want trust in government?', pp. 38–9.

20 See pp. 104–5.

2 The Development of Trust in the West

1 Francis Fukuyama, *Trust: The Social Virtues and the Creation of Prosperity* (Free Press, New York, NY, 1995) is a controversial whistle-stop tour of some of these.

2 'The fight for God', *Economist*, 19 December 2002.

3 Genesis 6–9.

4 See Chapter 6, pp. 144–55 for more on logos.

5 Raymond P. Scheindlin, 'Introduction', in Raymond P. Scheindlin (trans. and ed.), *The Book of Job* (W.W. Norton, New York, NY, 1999), pp. 9–52.

6 Job 9:22.

7 Job 38:4.

8 Job 42:7–9.

9 Seligman, *The Problem of Trust*, pp. 21–2.

10 Genesis 22:2.
11 Genesis 22:12.
12 Genesis 17:5–8, though this etymology is probably spurious. There are various theories about the significance of the change of name; quite often in the Bible slight changes of name signify points where the bearers are entering a new phase of their life, although perhaps a simpler explanation is that 'Abram' and 'Abraham' are versions of the same name in two different languages.
13 The disputes are (a) whether the nouns *philos* and *philia* refer to relationships that are (more or less) like our current notion of friendship, or include a wider range of affectionate relationships (such as kin relations), and (b) whether *philos* and *philia* denote the same range of relationships or different ones. David Konstan, 'Greek friendship', in *American Journal of Philology*, 117 (1996), pp. 71–94.
14 Aristotle, *The Ethics of Aristotle* (trans. J.A.K. Thompson; George Allen and Unwin, London, 1953), VIII–IX.
15 Aristotle, *Ethics*, IX, 9.
16 Aristotle, *Ethics*, VIII, 3.
17 Aristotle, *Ethics*, VIII, 2–3.
18 Richard Bett, *Pyrrho, His Antecedents and His Legacy* (Oxford University Press, Oxford, 2000).
19 Alan Bailey, *Sextus Empiricus and Pyrrhonean Scepticism* (Oxford University Press, Oxford, 2002), pp. 86–99.
20 See Chapter 7, pp. 157–71 for further discussion of expertise.
21 Xenocrates, fragment B34. We have this fragment of Xenocrates' poetry thanks to Sextus Empiricus who quoted it in his work, *Against the Mathematicians*, VII 49. This translation is from Jonathan Barnes, *Early Greek Philosophy* (2nd edition, Penguin, Harmondsworth, 2001), p. 41.
22 Jonathan Barnes, *The Toils of Scepticism* (Cambridge University Press, Cambridge, 1990).
23 Some major papers relating to this interpretation of Pyrrhonism are collected in Myles Burnyeat and Michael Frede (eds), *The Original Sceptics: A Controversy* (Hackett, Indianapolis, IN, 1997).
24 See Chapter 7, pp. 198–201.
25 See Michel de Montaigne, *The Complete Essays* (trans. and ed. M.A. Screech; Penguin, Harmondsworth, 1991); Edmund Burke, *Reflections*

on the Revolution in France (ed. Conor Cruise O'Brien; Penguin, Harmondsworth, 1968); Michael Oakeshott, *Rationalism in Politics and Other Essays* (expanded edition, Liberty, Indianapolis, IN, 1991); Roger Scruton, *The Meaning of Conservatism* (3rd edition, Palgrave, Basingstoke, 2001); Oliver Letwin, *The Purpose of Politics* (Social Market Foundation, London, 1999).

26 G.E.R. Lloyd (ed.), *Hippocratic Writings* (trans. J. Chadwick; Penguin, Harmondsworth, 1978).

27 Helen King, *Greek and Roman Medicine* (Bristol Classical Press, London, 2001).

28 For his greatest work, see Niccolò Machiavelli, *The Prince* (trans. George Bull; Penguin, Harmondsworth, 1961) – highly readable, even now.

29 Cf. e.g. John F. Danby, *Shakespeare's Doctrine of Nature: A Study of King Lear* (Faber and Faber, London, 1948).

30 Shakespeare, *King Lear*, I, ii.

31 Shakespeare, *Macbeth*, I, v.

32 *Macbeth*, V, viii.

33 Shakespeare, *Richard III*, V, iii.

34 All quotes in this passage from *King Lear*, I, i.

35 Coleridge was the first to put forward this criticism of Cordelia, in his *Lectures on Shakespeare*.

36 Marshall McLuhan, *The Gutenberg Galaxy* (University of Toronto Press, Toronto, 1962), p. 14.

37 Norman Hampson, *The Enlightenment: An Evaluation of its Assumptions, Attitudes and Values* (Penguin, Harmondsworth, 1968).

38 Thomas Hobbes, *Leviathan* (ed. C.B. Macpherson; Penguin, Harmondsworth, 1968).

39 Though this is a thought experiment, there are examples even in recent history of strongmen aspiring to be Hobbesian sources of order in a chaotic world. For a recent, and brilliant, fictionalised account of the regime of Rafael Trujillo of the Dominican Republic which analyses the rights and wrongs of all these issues, see Mario Vargas Llosa, *The Feast of the Goat* (trans. Edith Grossman; Farrar, Straus and Giroux, New York, 2001).

40 See Peter Kropotkin, *Mutual Aid: A Factor of Evolution* (Freedom Press, London, 1987).

41 David Hume, *A Treatise on Human Nature* (2nd edition, ed. L.A. Selby-Bigge and P.H. Nidditch; Oxford University Press, Oxford, 1978).

42 Kant is fearsomely difficult to read; his greatest work is *The Critique of Pure Reason* (1781). A good entry point is Roger J. Sullivan, *An Introduction to Kant's Ethics* (Cambridge University Press, Cambridge, 1994).

43 *The Social Contract*, in Jean-Jacques Rousseau, *The Social Contract and Discourses* (trans. G.D.H. Cole, rev. J.H. Brumfitt and John C. Hall, upd. P.D. Jimack; Everyman, London, 1993), pp. 180–309.

44 Brian Skyrms, *Evolution of the Social Contract* (Cambridge University Press, Cambridge, 1996).

45 Cf. A.C. Grayling, *What is Good? The Search for the Best Way to Live* (Weidenfeld and Nicolson, London, 2003).

46 Adam Smith, *The Wealth of Nations* (Penguin, Harmondsworth, 1982). First publication in the momentous year of 1776.

47 This account of the Enlightenment and rationality is indebted to the entertaining narrative in Martin Hollis, *Trust Within Reason* (Cambridge University Press, Cambridge, 1998).

3 Trust and Social Cohesion

1 Barbara A. Misztal, *Trust in Modern Societies* (Polity Press, Cambridge, 1996), pp. 33–64.

2 Halldór Laxness, *Independent People* (trans. J.A. Thompson; Harvill Press, London, 2001).

3 Emile Durkheim, *The Division of Labour in Society* (trans. G. Simpson; Free Press, New York, NY, 1964).

4 David Blunkett, 'What does citizenship mean today?', *Observer*, 15 September 2002; Mark Leonard, *Britain: Renewing Our Identity* (Demos, London, 1997). Interestingly, in Britain, it is people from ethnic minorities who are more likely to think of themselves as 'British' as opposed to, say, 'English' or 'Scottish': John Carvel, 'Sense of Britishness more prevalent among ethnic minorities, survey shows', *Guardian*, 18 December 2002.

5 Emile Durkheim, *Moral Education: A Study in the Theory and Application of the Sociology of Education* (trans. E.K. Wilson and H. Schnurer; Free Press, New York, NY, 1973).

6 See for instance, Amitai Etzioni, *Rights and the Common Good* (St Martin's Press, New York, NY, 1995).

7 Max Weber, *Economy and Society* (trans. and ed. G. Roth and C. Wittich; University of California Press, Berkeley, CA, 1968).

8 John Cheever, *The Stories of John Cheever* (Vintage, London, 1978).

9 In, respectively, 'The swimmer' (Cheever, *Stories*, pp. 776–88) and 'O youth and beauty!' (pp. 275–85). As well as describing a Weberian world, I have argued elsewhere that 'The swimmer' constitutes an attack on the Kantian view of morality, in Rebecca Hughes and Kieron O'Hara, 'Cheever's "The swimmer" and the abstract standpoint of Kantian moral philosophy', in Andrew Hadfield, Dominic Rainsford and Tim Woods (eds), *Literature and Ethics* (Macmillan, London, 1999), pp. 101–15.

10 'The worm in the apple', in Cheever, *Stories*, pp. 370–74, at p. 374.

11 'The fourth alarm', in Cheever, *Stories*, pp. 830–35, at p. 835.

12 Max Weber, 'Science as a vocation', in *From Max Weber: Essays in Sociology* (ed. Hans H. Gerth and C. Wright Mills; Oxford University Press, New York, NY, 1948), p. 155.

13 Talcott Parsons, *Structure of Social Action* (Free Press, Glencoe, IL, 1949).

14 Jonathan Margolis, 'Expletive deleted', *Guardian*, 21 November 2002.

15 Talcott Parsons, *The Social System* (Free Press, New York, NY, 1951).

16 Misztal, *Trust in Modern Societies*, pp. 66–7.

17 See e.g. Michael Allingham, *Choice Theory: A Very Short Introduction* (Oxford University Press, Oxford, 2002).

18 Hollis, *Trust Within Reason*.

19 James Coleman, *Foundations of Social Theory* (Belknap Press of Harvard University Press, Cambridge, MA, 1990).

20 Misztal, *Trust in Modern Societies*; Jon Elster, *The Cement of Society* (Cambridge University Press, Cambridge, 1989).

21 Roger B. Myerson, *Game Theory: Analysis of Conflict* (Harvard University Press, Cambridge, MA, 1991) is a demanding introduction to this technical field.

22 Skyrms, *Evolution of the Social Contract*.

23 Kroptokin, *Mutual Aid*; Richard Dawkins, *The Selfish Gene* (Oxford University Press, Oxford, 1976); and a vast literature that has developed on this topic.

24 Niklas Luhmann, 'Familiarity, confidence, trust: problems and alternatives', in Diego Gambetta (ed.), *Trust: Making and Breaking Cooperative Relations* (Basil Blackwell, Oxford, 1988), pp. 94–107.

25 Ulrich Beck, *Risk Society* (Sage, London, 1992) is an important theorist here, although he dramatically overstates his case.

26 Niklas Luhmann, *Trust and Power* (John Wiley, Chichester, 1979).

27 Kenneth Arrow, *The Limits of Organization* (Norton, New York, NY, 1974); and Deepak Malhotra and J. Keith Murnighan, 'The effects of contracts on interpersonal trust', *Administrative Science Quarterly*, 47 (2002), pp. 534–59.

28 Robert Putnam, *Bowling Alone* (Simon and Schuster, New York, NY, 2000).

29 Fukuyama, *Trust*.

30 Jean Cohen, 'Trust, voluntary association and workable democracy: the contemporary American discourse of civil society', in Mark E. Warren (ed.), *Democracy and Trust* (Princeton University Press, Princeton, NJ, 1999), pp. 208–48.

31 Fukuyama, *Trust*, p. 270. See pp. 269–281.

32 Misztal, *Trust in Modern Societies*.

33 Misztal, *Trust in Modern Societies*, pp. 95–101. This diagram is an adaptation of a table in Misztal's book, p. 101.

34 Misztal, *Trust in Modern Societies*, pp. 120–39.

4 Trusting Strangers

1 Plato, *Phaedrus*, Stephanus edition 227a–79c. There are several editions of this; I am using the translation by A. Nehamas and P. Woodruff in John M. Cooper (ed.) and D.S. Hutchinson (ass. ed.), *Plato: Complete Works* (Hackett, Indianapolis, IN, 1997), pp. 506–56, and for all my references to Plato in this book I will give the standard Stephanus references together with the page numbers from the *Complete Works*.

2 Eric A. Havelock, *Preface to Plato* (Basil Blackwell, Oxford, 1963).

3 For Xenophon, see Xenophon, *Conversations of Socrates* (ed. Robin Waterfield, trans. Hugh Tredennick and Robin Waterfield; Penguin, Harmondsworth, 1990).

4 Andrew Benjamin and Christopher Norris, *What is Deconstruction?* (Wiley, London, 1989).

5 *Phaedrus*, 274d–5b, pp. 551–2.
6 Walter J. Ong, *Orality and Literacy* (Methuen & Co., London, 1982).
7 Rebecca Hughes, *English in Speech and Writing: Investigating Language and Literature* (Routledge, London, 1996).
8 *Phaedrus*, 275de, p. 552.
9 Colin Brown and Jo Dillon, 'Whitehall rejoices at demise of Jo Moore', *Independent*, 17 February 2002; Steve Richards, 'The tragedy of Mr Byers, a decent minister who became a laughing stock', *Independent*, 29 May 2002. Other than this, there are billions of stories. For instance, Suzanne Goldenberg, 'Big Brother will be watching America', *Guardian*, 23 November 2002; or 'Snared in the web', *The Hindu*, 12 October 2002.
10 Leo Strauss, *Persecution and the Art of Writing* (University of Chicago Press, Chicago, IL, 1952).
11 I have discussed these issues with respect to the *Phaedrus* in Kieron O'Hara, *Plato and the Internet* (Icon Books, Cambridge, 2002), pp. 16–18; and 'Socrates, trust and the Internet', in Masanori Toyota and Judy Noguchi (eds), *Speech, Writing and Context: Interdisciplinary Perpectives* (Intercultural Research Institute, Kansai Gaidai University, Osaka, Japan, forthcoming in 2004).
12 Hughes, *English in Speech and Writing*.
13 Penny Fielding discusses similar phenomena in the context of 19th-century Scottish nationalism in *Writing and Orality: Nationality, Culture and Nineteenth-Century Scottish Fiction* (Clarendon Press, Oxford, 1996), pp. 43–73.
14 E.g. he has a hard time in the *Parmenides* (with, surprise, Parmenides).
15 Fukuyama, *Trust*.
16 Seligman, *The Problem of Trust*, pp. 114–15.
17 See Chapter 6, pages 121–7.
18 Hardin, 'Do we want trust in government?', p. 36.
19 Hardin, 'Do we want trust in government?', p. 22.
20 Bernard Williams, 'Moral Luck', in *Moral Luck* (Cambridge University Press, Cambridge, 1981), pp. 20–39.
21 Marshall Meyer, 'The performance paradox', in B.M. Staw and L. Cummings (eds), *Research in Organizational Behavior Vol. 14* (JAI Press, Greenwich, CT, 1994), pp. 309–69; Onora O'Neill, *A*

Question of Trust (Cambridge University Press, Cambridge, 2002), pp. 48–57.

22 Nick Davies, 'How Britain is losing the drugs war', *Guardian*, 22 May 2003.

5 Cybertrust

1 For ICANN see http://www.icann.org/. For the W3C, see http://www.w3.org/.

2 The connection between liberty and fertility of thought is strongly argued by John Stuart Mill in *On Liberty* (ed. Gertrude Himmelfarb; Penguin, Harmondsworth, 1982).

3 David Manasian, 'Caught in the net', *Economist*, 23 January 2003.

4 Manasian, 'Caught in the net'.

5 'Landmark ruling against Yahoo! in Nazi auction case', *Guardian*, 20 November 2000.

6 Lawrence Lessig, *Code and Other Laws of Cyberspace* (Basic Books, New York, NY, 1999).

7 Cass Sunstein, *republic.com* (Princeton University Press, Princeton, NJ, 2001).

8 E.g. Timothy Casey, *ISP Liability Survival Guide: Strategies for Managing Copyright, Spam, Cache and Privacy Regulations* (John Wiley, New York, NY, 2000); Kevin D. Mitnick and William L. Simon, *The Art of Deception: Controlling the Human Element of Security* (John Wiley, New York, NY, 2002); William R. Cheswick, Steven M. Bellovin and Aviel D. Rubin, *Firewalls and Internet Security: Repelling the Wily Hacker* (2nd edition, Addison-Wesley, New York, NY, 2003).

9 Andrew Leonard, *Bots: The Origin of New Species* (HardWired, San Francisco, CA, 1997); Jeffrey M. Bradshaw (ed.), *Software Agents* (M.I.T. Press, Cambridge, MA, 1997).

10 Anthony Painter and Ben Wardle (eds), *Viral Politics: Communication in the New Media Era* (Politico's, London, 2001).

11 Tim Jordan, *Activism! Direct Action, Hacktivism and the Future of Society* (Reaktion Books, London, 2002); Tania Branigan, 'Net tightens around the hacktivists', *Guardian*, 2 January 2001; Stuart Millar, 'Hackers: the political heroes of cyberspace', *Guardian*, 8 March 2001.

12 A MUD is a Multi-User Domain, in which dispersed users can interact and play with different identities and styles of interaction. The gaming origin of MUDs used to be commemorated explicitly in the first version of the acronym, 'Multi-User Dungeon'. A MOO is just a MUD programmed in a particular (object-oriented) style: it stands for MUD Object Oriented. See Sherry Turkle, *Life on the Screen: Identity in the Age of the Internet* (Simon and Schuster, New York, NY, 1995).

13 Nelson Goodman, 'How buildings mean', in Nelson Goodman and Catherine Z. Elgin (eds), *Reconceptions in Philosophy and Other Arts and Sciences* (Routledge, London, 1988), pp. 31–48; Ken Worpole and Liz Greenhalgh, *The Freedom of the City* (Demos, London, 1996). A spectacular meditation in science fiction form on this and many related themes is Doris Lessing's *Shikasta* (Jonathan Cape, London, 1979).

14 Steven Johnson, *Interface Culture: How New Technology Transforms the Way We Create and Communicate* (Harper, San Francisco, CA, 1997); Lessig, *Code*, pp. 19–60.

15 Patrick Barkham, 'FBI and multinationals no match for 100,000 hackers', *Guardian*, 10 February 2000; Jason Burke and Nick Paton Walsh, 'Supervirus threatens IT meltdown', *Observer*, 7 May 2000; Millar, 'Hackers'; Nick Hopkins, 'Cyber terror threatens UK's biggest companies', *Guardian*, 3 April 2001; Justin Hunt, 'Coded warning', *Guardian*, 19 April 2001; Patrick Collinson, 'Have the hackers got your number?', *Guardian*, 18 May 2002. This is a tiny representative sample – there are zillions of articles like these.

16 Fred B. Schneider (ed.), *Trust in Cyberspace* (Report of the Committee on Information Systems Trustworthiness, National Research Council, National Academy Press, Washington, DC, 1999), pp. 109–50.

17 Karen Winton, 'Security counsel: computer risk', *CFO Asia*, July 2002, http://www.cfoasia.com/archives/200207-08.htm.

18 Clay Shirky, 'Listening to Napster', in Andy Oram (ed.), *Peer-to-Peer: Harnessing the Power of Disruptive Technologies* (O'Reilly, Sebastopol, CA, 2001), pp. 21–37.

19 Mr Kevin Mitnick, Testimony to US Senate Committee on Governmental Affairs, March 2000, http://www.senate.gov/~gov_affairs/030200_mitnick.htm. See also Mitnick and Simon, *The Art of Deception*.

20 Tom Standage, 'The weakest link', *Economist*, 24 October 2002.

21 Diane Savage, 'Buggy code blues', *CIOInsight*, 1 January 2002, http://www.cioinsight.com/article2/0,3959,1530,00.asp.

22 See http://www.gnu.org/philosophy/philosophy.html.

23 Michael Cross, 'Windows opens up', *Guardian*, 23 January 2003.

24 For more on the Internet, see O'Hara, *Plato and the Internet*, pp. 27–31.

25 'Profits at last', *Economist*, 19 December 2002.

26 Beth Cox, 'E-tailers enjoying pre-holiday sales crush', *CyberAtlas*, 17 December 2002, http://cyberatlas.internet.com/markets/retailing/article/0,,6061_1558481,00.html.

27 L. Jean Camp, *Trust and Risk in Internet Commerce* (M.I.T. Press, Cambridge, MA, 2000), pp. 65–77.

28 Lessig, *Code*, pp. 30–42.

29 'The revenge of geography', *Economist Technology Quarterly*, 13 March 2003.

30 Lessig, *Code*, pp. 34–5; Camp, *Trust and Risk*, pp. 79–98.

31 Sharon Gaudin, 'Online fraud growing in scale, sophistication', *Datamation*, 5 December 2002, http://itmanagement.earthweb.com/ecom/article.php/1552921.

32 Fukuyama, *Trust*.

33 Jason Bennetto, 'FBI investigation into child porn spans the world', *Independent*, 14 September 2002.

34 Andy Oram, 'Afterword', in Oram, *Peer-to-Peer*, pp. 393–7, at pp. 393–4.

35 Manasian, 'Caught in the net'.

36 O'Hara, *Plato and the Internet*, pp. 24–7 about the information stored, pp. 38–52 about making sense of it. See also Nigel Shadbolt, 'Someone to watch over you', *IEEE Intelligent Systems*, March/April 2003, pp. 2–3.

37 Lessig, *Code*.

38 'The best thing since the bar-code', *Economist*, 6 February 2003.

39 'Taxman.biz', *Economist*, 20 September 2001.

40 David Manasian, 'No hiding place', *Economist*, 23 January 2003.

41 Manasian, 'Caught in the net'.

42 Ludwig Siegele, 'Gathering steam', *Economist*, 14 April 2001.

43 Nigel Shadbolt, 'A matter of trust', *IEEE Intelligent Systems*, January/February 2002, pp. 2–3.

44 http://www.google.com/.

45 http://www.google.com/technology/index.html.

46 See http://www.aktors.org/technologies/d3e, or http://d3e. source forge.net, or Tamara Sumner and Simon Buckingham Shum, 'From documents to discourse: shifting conceptions of scholarly publishing' at http://kmi.open.ac.uk/tr/papers/kmi-tr-50.pdf, and Paul A. Kirschner, Simon J. Buckingham Shum and Chad S. Carr (eds), *Visualizing Argumentation: Software Tools for Collaborative and Educational Sense-Making* (Springer-Verlag, London, 2003).

47 Yolanda Gil and Varun Ratnakar, 'Trusting information sources one citizen at a time', in *Proceedings of the First International Semantic Web Conference*, and http://www.isi.edu/expect/web/semanticweb/iswc02_trellis.pdf.

48 Jennifer Golbeck, James Hendler and Bijan Parsia, *Trust Networks on the Semantic Web* at http://mindswap.org/papers/Trust.pdf. For the semantic web, see O'Hara, *Plato and the Internet*, pp. 49–52.

49 Marianne Winslett, Ting Yu, Kent E. Seamons, Adam Hess, Jared Jacobson, Ryan Jarvis, Bryan Smith and Lina Yu, 'Negotiating trust on the web', *IEEE Internet Computing*, November/December 2002, pp. 30–37.

50 Theo Dimitrakos and Juan Bicarregui, 'Towards modelling e-trust', *3rd Panhellenic Logic Symposium* (Anogia, Greece, 2001), http://www.math.uoa.gr/pls3/proceedings/dimitrakos.ps.

51 Golbeck et al.'s paper is an attempt to do this.

52 Lessig, *Code*.

6 Crash!

1 Baruch Lev, *Intangibles: Management, Measurement, and Reporting* (Brookings Institution Press, Washington, DC, 2001).

2 Su Chan, John Kesinger and John Martin, 'The market rewards promising R&D – and punishes the rest', *Journal of Applied Corporate Finance*, vol. 5 (1992), pp. 59–66; and George Pinches, V. Narayanan and Kathryn Kelm, 'How the market values the different stages of corporate R&D – initiation, progress and commercialization', *Journal of Applied Corporate Finance*, vol. 9 (1996), pp. 60–69. Though see Baruch Lev, Bharat Sarath and Theodore

Sougiannis, 'R&D reporting biases and their consequences', *The ICFAI Journal of Accounting Research*, November 2002.

3 William J. Baumol, *The Free-Market Innovation Machine: Analyzing the Growth Miracle of Capitalism* (Princeton University Press, Princeton, NJ, 2002), pp. 133–5.

4 Nicholas Kristof and Sheryl WuDunn, *Thunder From the East: Portrait of a Rising Asia* (Nicholas Brealey, London, 2000).

5 'Hurtling towards paralysis', *Economist*, 19 March 1998.

6 Dominic Ziegler, 'Rocky shores', *Economist*, 8 February 2003.

7 'Korean glums', *Economist*, 8 January 1998.

8 Chart taken from Ziegler, 'Rocky shores', and see that article also for lengthy discussion of the attempts to clean up after the bad debt in South Korea, Malaysia and Thailand.

9 Andrew Roberts, *Salisbury: Victorian Titan* (Weidenfeld and Nicolson, London, 1999), pp. 551–2.

10 David Kynaston, *The City of London Vol. 1: A World of its Own 1815–1890* (Chatto and Windus, London, 1994), pp. 425–37.

11 Leeson's own account is the most famous. Nick Leeson, *Rogue Trader* (Time Warner, London, 1997).

12 Kynaston, *The City 1*, pp. 126–30.

13 Kynaston, *The City 1*, pp. 151–64.

14 Neil Bennett, 'The bubble bounces', *Sunday Telegraph*, 19 March 2000.

15 Maury Klein, *Rainbow's End: The Crash of 1929* (Oxford University Press, Oxford, 2001).

16 'Killing Glass-Steagall', *Economist*, 30 October 1999.

17 'Conflicts, conflicts everywhere', *Economist*, 24 January 2002.

18 'Setting the rules', *Economist*, 29 January 2003.

19 Loren Fox, *Enron: The Rise and Fall* (John Wiley, Hoboken, NJ, 2003), p. 108.

20 'The only way is up, maybe', *Economist*, 25 July 2002.

21 'Europe's Enron', *Economist*, 27 February 2003.

22 Larry Elliot, 'Too good to be true', *Guardian*, 13 March 2000; Nina Montagu-Smith, 'Will being nutty about the Net bring regrets?', *Daily Telegraph*, 19 February 2000.

23 Catherine Elsworth, 'Party goes on for internet entrepreneurs', *Sunday Telegraph*, 9 April 2000.

24 Sally White, 'The UK still does not look like a bargain', *Independent*,

8 March 2003; Neasa MacErlean, 'Markets stocked with risks', *Observer*, 26 January 2003.

25 From the Telegraph's online shares page, http://shares.telegraph.co.uk.

26 Francis Fukuyama, *The End of History and the Last Man* (Free Press, New York, NY, 1993).

27 'The only way is up, maybe', *Economist*.

28 Fox, *Enron*, p. 31.

29 Fox, *Enron*, pp. 20–21.

30 Fox, *Enron*, pp. 77–97.

31 Arundhati Roy, *Power Politics* (South End Press, London, 2001); John Vidal, 'A bad business', *Guardian*, 30 November 2001.

32 'A matter of principals', *Economist*, 28 June 2001.

33 Fox, *Enron*, p. 190.

34 Fox, *Enron*, p. 128.

35 Fox, *Enron*, p. 262.

36 Fox, *Enron*, p. 158.

37 Fox, *Enron*, p. 276.

38 Fox, *Enron*, pp. 228–30.

39 Rupert Cornwell, 'Top Enron executive charged with fraud', *Independent*, 3 October 2002.

40 'When the numbers don't add up', *Economist*, 7 February 2002.

41 Arrow, *The Limits of Organization*.

42 Malhotra and Murnighan, 'The effects of contracts on interpersonal trust'.

43 Misztal, *Trust in Modern Societies*, p. 121.

44 Oliver Morgan, 'Open mouth, place foot in', *Observer*, 9 June 2002.

45 Naomi Klein, *No Logo* (Flamingo, London, 2000).

46 Klein, *No Logo*, p. 361.

47 Klein, *No Logo*, pp. 27–61.

48 Sophie Barker, 'The optimist of adland', *Sunday Telegraph*, 25 August 2002.

49 Klein, *No Logo*, p. 52.

50 David Ricardo, *Principles of Political Economy and Taxation* (ed. R.M. Hartwell; Penguin, Harmondsworth, 1971).

51 'The world's view of multinationals', *Economist*, 27 January 2000.

52 'And then there were three', *Economist*, 25 January 2003; 'The great leap forward', *Economist*, 30 January 2003.

53 *Britannica Book of the Year 2002* (Encyclopaedia Britannica, Chicago, IL, 2002), pp. 630, 650.

54 Klein, *No Logo*, p. xv.

55 Klein, *No Logo*, pp. 99–100.

56 *Trust and Governance for a New Era*, report of the annual meeting of the Trust and Government Committee of the World Economic Forum, 23 January 2003, http://www.weforum.org/site/knowledge navigator.nsf/Content/Trust+and+Governance+for+a+New+Era.

57 Klein, *No Logo*, p. 361.

58 As for example in the *Guardian* of 14 April 2003.

59 Cf. Klein, *No Logo*, p. xviii.

60 For example, see 'Listed: Modern Art', *Vogue*, May 2003, p. 264.

61 Misztal, *Trust in Modern Societies*, p. 122.

7 Virus the Small at Last Shall Inherit the Earth

1 Michelene T.H. Chi, Robert Glaser and Marshall J. Farr (eds), *The Nature of Expertise* (Laurence Erlbaum, Hillsdale, NJ, 1988).

2 William J. Clancey, 'Heuristic classification', *Artificial Intelligence*, vol. 27 (1985), pp. 289–350; E.T. Keravnou and J. Washbrook, 'What is a deep expert system? An analysis of the architectural requirements of second-generation expert systems', *The Knowledge Engineering Review*, vol. 4 (1989), pp. 205–33; Nigel Shadbolt and Kieron O'Hara, 'Model-based expert systems and the explanation of expertise', in Paul J. Feltovich, Kenneth M. Ford and Robert R. Hoffman (eds), *Expertise in Context* (AAAI Press/M.I.T. Press, Menlo Park, CA, 1997), pp. 315–37.

3 Neil M. Agnew, Kenneth M. Ford and Patrick J. Hayes, 'Expertise in context: personally constructed, socially selected and reality-relevant?', in Feltovich, Ford and Hoffman, *Expertise in Context*, pp. 219–44.

4 One of the most comprehensive and interesting reflections on the relativity of explanation is Peter Achinstein, *The Nature of Explanation* (Oxford University Press, New York, NY, 1983).

5 'Doctor who posed as surgeon suspended', *Daily Telegraph*, 21 August 2002.

6 Karl R. Popper, *Conjectures and Refutations: The Growth of Scientific Knowledge* (Harper and Row, New York, NY, 1968). For a

defence of Freud against Popper, see Owen J. Flanagan Jr, *The Science of the Mind* (M.I.T. Press, Cambridge, MA, 1984), pp. 74–82.

7 Meyer, 'The performance paradox'; Anthony Browne and Matthew Young, 'A sick NHS: the diagnosis', *Observer*, 7 April 2002.

8 Paul Feyerabend, *Science in a Free Society* (Verso, London, 1978), p. 64.

9 Stevan Harnad, *For Whom the Gate Tolls? How and Why to Free the Refereed Research Literature Online Through Author/Institution Self-Archiving, Now* (Research paper, Dept. of Electronics and Computer Science, University of Southampton), http://eprints.ecs.soton.ac.uk/archive/00005944/01/resolution.html.

10 Feyerabend, *Science in a Free Society*, pp. 96–8.

11 Paul Feyerabend, 'How to defend society against science', *Radical Philosophy*, vol. 2 (1975), pp. 4–8.

12 Steven Shapin, *A Social History of Truth: Civility and Science in Seventeenth-Century England* (University of Chicago Press, Chicago, IL, 1994).

13 Baumol, *The Free-Market Innovation Machine*. We briefly discussed the slightly anomalous position of R&D and other intangible investments in Chapter 6, pp. 125–6.

14 Paul Gompers and Josh Lerner, *The Venture Capital Cycle* (M.I.T. Press, Cambridge, MA, 2002); Geoffrey Carr, 'Climbing the helical staircase', *Economist*, 29 March 2003; 'Money to burn', *Economist*, 25 May 2000.

15 Kenneth J. Arrow, 'Economic welfare and the allocation of resources for invention', in Richard R. Nelson (ed.), *The Rate and Direction of Incentive Activity* (NBER, New York, NY, 1962), pp. 609–25; Baumol, *The Free-Market Innovation Machine*.

16 Information taken from 'Notes on the contributors', in Tony Gilland (ed.), *Science: Can We Trust the Experts* (Hodder and Stoughton, London, 2002), p. ix.

17 *Statesman* (trans. C.J. Rowe), 293b, p. 337.

18 Jennifer Jackson, *Truth, Trust and Medicine* (Routledge, London, 2001), pp. 11–13.

19 *Republic* (trans. G.M.A. Grube, rev. C.D.C. Reeve), 459cd, p. 1087. Recall from Chapter 4 that Plato used the dialogue form. The interlocutors here are Socrates and Glaucon.

20 *Laws* (trans. Trevor J. Saunders), 659e–660a, p. 1351.

21 Jackson, *Truth, Trust and Medicine*, pp. 81, 125, 147–57.
22 Stanley Milgram, *Obedience to Authority* (Harper and Row, New York, NY, 1974).
23 Milgram, *Obedience to Authority*.
24 Misztal, *Trust in Modern Societies*, pp. 131–2.
25 Feyerabend, *Science in a Free Society*, p. 97, n. 28.
26 Miroslav Holub, 'If Kant were around today', in *The Dimension of the Present Moment and Other Essays* (ed. David Young; Faber and Faber, London, 1990), pp. 96–106, at pp. 102–3.
27 Page 152. Klein, *No Logo*, pp. 98–101.
28 Alan Irwin and Brian Wynne (eds), *Misunderstanding Science? The Public Reconstruction of Science and Technology* (Cambridge University Press, Cambridge, 1996); Sue Mayer 'From genetic modification to nanotechnology: the dangers of "sound science"', in Gilland, *Science*, pp. 1–15.
29 David J. Levy, 'Politics, technology and the responsibility of the intellectuals', in Ian Maclean, Alan Montefiore and Peter Winch (eds), *The Political Responsibility of Intellectuals* (Cambridge University Press, Cambridge, 1990), pp. 123–42.
30 Edward Shils, 'Intellectuals and responsibility', in Maclean et al., *The Political Responsibility of Intellectuals*, pp. 257–306, at p. 285.
31 Shils, 'Intellectuals and responsibility'.
32 Andrew Denham and Mark Garnett, *Keith Joseph* (Acumen, Chesham, 2001), pp. 379–80.
33 For example, the case of Hungary is described in Elemer Hankiss, 'The loss of responsibility', in Maclean et al., *The Political Responsibility of Intellectuals*, pp. 29–52.
34 Jonathan Harwood, 'Scientific knowledge as political authority', in Michael Gibbons and Philip Gummett (eds), *Science, Technology and Society Today* (Manchester University Press, Manchester, 1984), pp. 48–63.
35 Sheldon Rampton and John Stauber, *Trust Us, We're Experts! How Industry Manipulates Science and Gambles With Your Future* (Jeremy P. Tarcher/Putnam, New York, NY, 2001). The whole book defends this thesis, and the description of MOP is at pp. 16–17.
36 Cf. Misztal, *Trust in Modern Societies*, pp. 131–2.
37 Jackson, *Truth, Trust and Medicine*, pp. 22–7.
38 Jackson, *Truth, Trust and Medicine*, p. 81.

39 John D. Lantos, *Do We Still Need Doctors? A Physician's Personal Account of Practicing Medicine Today* (Routledge, New York, NY, 1997), pp. 89–90.

40 Bjorn Lomborg, *The Skeptical Environmentalist: Measuring the Real State of the World* (Cambridge University Press, Cambridge, 2001).

41 'Thought control', *Economist*, 9 January 2003.

42 'Misleading math about the earth', *Scientific American*, January 2002. The debate with *Scientific American*, and with other critics, goes on, and Lomborg has produced a series of replies available at http://www.lomborg.org/.

43 Celia Hall, 'Passive smoking may not damage your health after all, says research', *Daily Telegraph*, 16 May 2003.

44 James Meikle, 'New MMR link to autism, claims study', *Guardian*, 21 May 2003.

45 Quoted in Jonathan Schell, 'Our Fragile Earth', *Discover*, vol. 10, no. 10, October 1989, pp. 44–8.

46 Jacek Kurczewski, 'Power and wisdom: the expert as mediating figure in contemporary Polish history', in Maclean et al., *The Political Responsibility of Intellectuals*, pp. 77–99.

47 'Outside the Bell curve', *Economist*, 26 September 2002.

48 Charles Piller, 'Prominent physicist fired for faking data', *Los Angeles Times*, 26 September 2002.

49 Maxime Schwartz, *How the Cows Turned Mad* (trans. Edward Schneider; University of California Press, Berkeley, CA, 2003), pp. 156–7.

50 R.G. Will, J.W. Ironside, M. Zeidler, S.N. Cousens, K. Estibeiro, A. Alperovitch, S. Poser, M. Pocchiari, A. Hofman and P.G. Smith, 'A new variant of Creutzfeldt-Jakob Disease in the UK', *The Lancet*, vol. 347 (1996), pp. 921–5.

51 Douglas Parr, 'Knowing about ignorance', in Gilland, *Science*, pp. 55–74, at pp. 55–6.

52 Schwartz, *How the Cows Turned Mad*, pp. 83–4.

53 Schwartz, *How the Cows Turned Mad*, pp. 98–103, 110–18.

54 Schwartz, *How the Cows Turned Mad*, p. 100.

55 Schwartz, *How the Cows Turned Mad*, pp. 81–2.

56 Schwartz, *How the Cows Turned Mad*, pp. 44, 95.

57 Schwartz, *How the Cows Turned Mad*, p. 199.

58 Schwartz, *How the Cows Turned Mad*, pp. 42–3.

59 Schwartz, *How the Cows Turned Mad*, pp. 106–9.

60 Schwartz, *How the Cows Turned Mad*, p. 209, n. 1.

61 Schwartz, *How the Cows Turned Mad*, p. 95.

62 Schwartz, *How the Cows Turned Mad*, p. 95.

63 O'Hara, *Plato and the Internet*.

64 Schwartz, *How the Cows Turned Mad*, p. 136.

65 Thomas S. Kuhn, *The Structure of Scientific Revolutions* (2nd edition, University of Chicago Press, Chicago, IL, 1970).

66 Schwartz, *How the Cows Turned Mad*, p. 199.

67 Schwartz, *How the Cows Turned Mad*, pp. 146–9, 189–91.

68 The Phillips Report (*Return to an Order of the Honourable the House of Commons Dated October 2000 for the Report, Evidence and Supporting Papers of the Inquiry into the Emergence and Identification of Bovine Spongiform Encephalopathy (BSE) and Variant Creutzfeldt-Jakob Disease (vCJD) and the Action Taken in Response to it up to 20 March 1996*), vol. 2, chap. 3, para. 3.52.iii, http://www.bseinquiry.gov.uk/index.htm, mentions the tigers, though in the context of wondering how they got the TSSE in the first place, not whether they might have found their way into meat and bone meal fed to cattle. Their case is discussed in D.F. Kelly, H. Pearson, A.I. Wright and L.W. Greenham, 'Morbidity in captive white tigers', in R.J. Montali and G. Migaki (eds), *The Comparative Pathology of Zoo Animals* (Smithsonian Institute Press, Washington, DC, 1980), pp. 183–8, and now downloadable from the Phillips Inquiry website, http://www.bseinquiry.gov.uk/evidence/mbundles/mbund1.htm.

69 Schwartz, *How the Cows Turned Mad*, p. 151.

70 Schwartz, *How the Cows Turned Mad*, p. 152.

71 Schwartz, *How the Cows Turned Mad*, p. 139.

72 Karl R. Popper, *The Logic of Scientific Discovery* (Hutchinson, London, 1959).

73 Paul Feyerabend, *Against Method* (Verso, London, 1975).

74 Imre Lakatos, 'Falsification and the methodology of scientific research programmes', in Imre Lakatos and Alan Musgrave (eds), *Criticism and the Growth of Knowledge* (Cambridge University Press, Cambridge, 1970), pp. 91–196; A.F. Chalmers, *What is this Thing Called Science?* (3rd edition, Open University Press, Milton

Keynes, 1999); Richard W. Miller, *Fact and Method: Explanation, Confirmation and Reality in the Natural and the Social Sciences* (Princeton University Press, Princeton, NJ, 1987).

75 Schwartz, *How the Cows Turned Mad*, p. 40.

76 James Meikle, 'Spread of CJD slows but threat remains', *Guardian*, 28 February 2003; Roger Highfield, 'Forecast of human BSE deaths cut again to 500', *Daily Telegraph*, 7 May 2003.

77 http://www.bseinquiry.gov.uk/report/volume1/execsum2.htm #669592.

78 Guus Schreiber, Hans Akkermans, Anjo Anjewierden, Robert de Hoog, Nigel Shadbolt, Walter Van de Velde and Bob Wielinga, *Knowledge Engineering and Management: The CommonKADS Methodology* (M.I.T. Press, Cambridge, MA, 2000), pp. 187–214.

79 Shadbolt and O'Hara, 'Model-based expert systems'.

80 Ian Gibson, 'Restoring trust', in Gilland, *Science*, pp. 39–54.

81 Anne Stevenson, 'Clovenhoof's-bane', in Anne Stevenson, *A Report From the Border* (Bloodaxe, Tarset, 2003), p. 29.

82 Tony Gilland, 'Introduction', in Gilland, *Science*, pp. xi–xxii, at pp. xvii–xviii.

83 Anthony Giddens, *The Consequence of Modernity* (Polity Press, Oxford, 1990); Ulrich Beck, *Risk Society* (Sage, London, 1992).

84 A.L. Poole, *Domesday Book to Magna Carta 1087–1216* (2nd edition, Clarendon Press, Oxford, 1955), pp. 445–58, especially p. 448. For another brief rebuttal of the risk society thesis see Onora O'Neill, *A Question of Trust: The BBC Reith Lectures 2002* (Cambridge University Press, Cambridge, 2002), pp. 15–16.

85 Parr, 'Knowing about ignorance'.

86 Schwartz, *How the Cows Turned Mad*, p. 41.

87 Schwartz, *How the Cows Turned Mad*, p. 69.

88 Schwartz, *How the Cows Turned Mad*, pp. 46–50.

89 Schwartz, *How the Cows Turned Mad*, p. 154.

90 Schwartz, *How the Cows Turned Mad*, p. 155.

91 Schwartz, *How the Cows Turned Mad*, pp. 58–66.

92 Schwartz, *How the Cows Turned Mad*, pp. 68–9.

93 Schwartz, *How the Cows Turned Mad*, p. 71.

94 T.A. Holt and J. Philips, 'Bovine spongiform encephalopathy', *British Medical Journal*, vol. 296 (1988), pp. 1581–2.

95 Schwartz, *How the Cows Turned Mad*, pp. 155–6.

96 Jonathan Coe, *What a Carve Up!* (Viking, London, 1994), pp. 241–60 (in editions with different pagination, this is the chapter entitled 'Dorothy').

97 Major, *Autobiography*, p. 657.

98 Anthony Seldon and Lewis Baston, *Major: A Political Life* (Weidenfeld and Nicolson, London, 1997), p. 642.

99 Daniel Litvin, 'Cows and the British disease', *Die Zeitschrift der Neuen Zürcher Zeitung*, March 1997.

100 'Science not helped by the media', *Guardian*, 4 September 2002.

101 Puffery from the Foresight Institute, http://www.foresight.org, quoted in Mayer, 'From genetic modification to nanotechnology'. Note that the Foresight Institute has no connection whatsoever with the UK Office of Science and Technology's Foresight programme (http://www.foresight.gov.uk), whose projects on cybertrust and on cognitive systems I have worked on.

102 'Beyond the nanohype', *Economist Technology Quarterly*, 15 March 2003.

103 George Gamow, *Thirty Years That Shook Physics: The Story of Quantum Theory* (Dover, New York, NY, 1985).

104 Patrick McGee, 'Sizing up nanotechnology', *Wired News*, 26 June 2000.

105 Bill Joy, 'Why the future doesn't need us', *Wired*, April 2000.

106 Mayer, 'From genetic modification to nanotechnology', p. 13.

107 Mayer, 'From genetic modification to nanotechnology', p. 10.

108 K. Eric Drexler, *Engines of Creation: The Coming Era of Nanotechnology* (Oxford Paperbacks, New York, NY, 1986).

109 *New Scientist*, 21 June 2003, p. 104.

110 E.g. Michael Crichton, *Prey* (HarperCollins, New York, NY, 2002).

111 'Prince sparks row over nanotechnology', *Guardian*, 28 April 2003.

112 Schwartz, *How the Cows Turned Mad*, pp. 133–4.

113 Norman Myers, 'Genetically modified foods: the political debate', in Charles P. Trumbull (ed.), *2001 Britannica Book of the Year* (Encyclopaedia Britannica, Chicago, IL, 2001), pp. 150–51.

114 'Better dead than GM-fed?', *Economist*, 19 September 2002.

115 Sarah Boseley, 'Study finds no autism link to MMR', *Guardian*, 7 November 2002.

116 James Meikle, 'Error warning over separate MMR jabs', *Guardian*, 10 February 2003.

117 Alison Holt, 'Measles – the comeback', *Guardian*, 29 April 2003.

118 Feyerabend, *Science in a Free Society*; Irwin and Wynne, *Misunderstanding Science?*; Rampton and Stauber, *Trust Us, We're Experts!*

119 Paul Brown, 'Trade war fear as public resists GM food', *Guardian*, 7 May 2002.

120 John Vidal, 'Global GM market starts to wilt', *Guardian*, 28 August 2001.

121 Parr, 'Knowing about ignorance'.

122 Pru Hobson-West, '"Needle politics": risk, trust and anti-vaccinationism', in *Proceedings of the Political Studies Association 2003*, http://www.psa.ac.uk/cps/2003/Pru%20Hobson-West.pdf.

8 'A Plague on Both Your Houses'

1 Shakespeare of course, but of much application to politics, for example as the epigraph to Sidney Gilliat's political comedy of 1959, *Left, Right and Centre*. The reputation of this movie has declined somewhat, and it certainly isn't top notch, but it is a lot better than most critics claim.

2 Cicero, *On Obligations* (trans. P.G. Walsh; Oxford University Press, Oxford, 2000).

3 Cicero, *On Obligations*, 1.41.

4 Cicero, *On Obligations*, 2.33–4.

5 Cicero, *On Obligations*, 3.27.

6 Cicero, *On Obligations*, 1.101.

7 Recall Chapter 2, pp. 36–42.

8 'The future is Texas', *Economist*, 19 December 2002.

9 Recall Chapter 6, pp. 133–44.

10 Michael Crick, *Jeffrey Archer: Stranger Than Fiction* (2nd edition, Fourth Estate, London, 2000).

11 Luke Harding, David Leigh and David Pallister, *The Liar: The Fall of Jonathan Aitken* (Penguin, London, 1997).

12 'A mountain to climb', *Economist*, 10 April 1997.

13 Ed Vulliamy and David Leigh, *Sleaze: Corruption in Tory Britain* (Fourth Estate, London, 1997).

14 'Al Fayed's Pyrrhic victory', *Economist*, 23 December 1999.

15 Sir Gerald Nabarro, *NAB 1: Portrait of a Politician* (Robert Maxwell, Oxford, 1969).

16 Joy Copley, 'Bell dented by ding-dong on the heath', *Daily Telegraph*, 9 April 1997; Sandra Barwick, 'Loyalty of the wife who never wavers', *Daily Telegraph*, 9 April 1997.

17 Christine Hamilton, *The Book of British Battleaxes* (Robson Books, London, 1998).

18 Mark E. Warren, 'Introduction', in Mark E. Warren (ed.), *Democracy and Trust* (Cambridge University Press, Cambridge, 1999), pp. 1–21, at p. 1.

19 Theodore H. White, *The Making of the President 1960* (Atheneum House, New York, NY, 1961), p. 79.

20 White, *The Making of the President*, p. 79.

21 Hardin, 'Do we want trust in government?', p. 36.

22 Misztal, *Trust in Modern Societies*, p. 122.

23 The front cover of *The Sun*, 9 April 1992.

24 John Andrews, 'High and mighty', *Economist*, 14 November 2002.

25 'After the cataclysm', *Economist*, 25 April 2002.

26 'At last they are waging war', *Economist*, 28 September 2000.

27 Pierre Péan and Philippe Cohen, *La Face Cachée du Monde* (Edition Mille et Une Nuits, Paris, 2003).

28 Roland Dumas, *L'Epreuve, les Preuves* (Michel Lafon, Paris, 2003).

29 Sarah Spencer and Brian Micklethwait, 'Should we be forced to vote?', *Guardian*, 19 June 1999. Tom Watson and Mark Tami, *Votes for All: Compulsory Participation in Elections* (Fabian Society, London, 2000) puts the case in the British context.

30 Andrew Tucker, *Why Trust Has No Part in Modern Politics* (Centre for Reform, London, 1999), pp. 50–54.

31 Arrow, *The Limits of Organization*.

32 Rom Harré, 'Trust and its surrogates: psychological foundations of political process', in Warren, *Democracy and Trust*, pp. 249–72.

33 Harré, 'Trust and its surrogates', pp. 267–8.

34 'The war that never ends', *Economist*, 16 January 2003.

35 James C. Scott, 'Geographies of trust, geographies of hierarchy', in Warren, *Democracy and Trust*, pp. 273–89, at p. 274.

36 Stuart Millar, 'Beauty spot bypass "proving a failure"', *Guardian*, 12 July 1999. Simon Festing, *End of the Road: Managing Newbury's*

Traffic to Reduce Congestion and Pollution Without a Western Bypass (Friends of the Earth, London, 1995) and Gordon Rollinson, *Only Just: A History of the A34 Newbury Bypass 1979–1998* (Gordon Rollinson, 1997) put the anti and pro case respectively.

37 Joseph Raz, 'A right to dissent (1): civil disobedience', in *The Authority of Law: Essays on Law and Morality* (Clarendon Press, Oxford, 1979).

38 The example and analysis is taken from Norman Fairclough, *New Labour, New Language?* (Routledge, London, 2000), p. 23. Fairclough's book is full of such examples. However, it needs to be used with care; it is marred by its explicit ideological antipathy to Blair and all his doings. Fairclough is commendably explicit about his opposition (pp. 15–16), but it undermines the splendid linguistic analysis of New Labour newspeak.

39 Recall Chapter 7, p. 159.

40 Mark E. Warren, 'Conclusion', in Warren, *Democracy and Trust*, pp. 346–60, at pp. 358–9.

41 Anna Grandori, *Organizations and Economic Behavior* (Routledge, London, 2001), p. 185.

42 'Walkout by angry Democrats halts work at Texas House', *Houston Chronicle*, 12 May 2003.

43 'In praise of Iowa', *Economist*, 17 October 2002.

44 See for example Richard Crossman, *The Diaries of a Cabinet Minister Volume 3: Secretary of State for Social Services 1968–1970* (ed. Janet Morgan; Hamish Hamilton/Jonathan Cape, London, 1977), e.g. entries for 7 June 1969 (pp. 506–7) or 19 June 1969 (pp. 530–31). The extent of the fierce all-party opposition to this measure can be gauged by remarks in, say, the entry for 20 July 1969 (p. 582).

45 Recall Chapter 3, pp. 55–8.

46 Anthony Giddens, *Politics and Sociology in the Thought of Max Weber* (Macmillan, London, 1972), p. 18.

47 Patrick Dunleavy, *Democracy, Bureaucracy and Public Choice: Economic Explanations in Political Science* (Prentice Hall, Harlow, 1991).

48 Giddens, *Politics and Sociology in the Thought of Max Weber*, p. 33.

49 Associated most strongly with Singapore, particularly under Prime Minister Lee Kuan Yew. See the second volume of his memoirs, Lee Kuan Yew, *From Third World to First: The Singapore Story 1965–*

2000: Singapore and the Asian Economic Boom (HarperCollins, London, 2000).

50 Fukuyama, *The End of History*.

51 On the BBC Radio 4 programme, *Analysis*, 'With friends like these …', 1 May 2003, transcript available at http://news.bbc.co.uk/nol/shared/spl/hi/programmes/analysis/transcripts/01_05_03.txt.

52 Chapter 6, p. 127.

53 Fukuyama, *Trust*, pp. 69–95.

54 Ronald Inglehart, 'Trust, well-being and democracy', in Warren, *Trust and Democracy*, pp. 88–120, at p. 93.

55 Kishore Mahbubani, 'The West and the rest', in Kishore Mahbubani, *Can Asians Think? Understanding the Divide Between East and West* (Revised and expanded edition, Steerforth Press, South Royalton, VT, 2002), pp. 40–57, at p. 50.

56 'What would Confucius say now?', *Economist*, 23 July 1998.

57 Mahbubani, 'The West and the rest', pp. 55–7.

58 Kishore Mahbubani, 'UN: sunrise or sunset organization in the twenty-first century?', in Mahbubani, *Can Asians Think?*, pp. 166–84, at p. 179.

59 Hollis, *Trust Within Reason*; Cicero, *On Obligations*.

60 Kishore Mahbubani, '"The Pacific impulse"', in Mahbubani, *Can Asians Think?* pp. 137–57, at pp. 154–7.

61 Kishore Mahbubani, 'Japan adrift', in Mahbubani, *Can Asians Think?*, pp. 118–36, at pp. 129–30.

62 'NGOs stand up for "comfort women"', *Korea Herald*, 24 April 2003.

63 'Koreans lash out at Koizumi over third visit to war shrine', *Korea Herald*, 18 January 2003.

64 Kishore Mahbubani, 'An Asian perspective on human rights and freedom of the press', in Mahbubani, *Can Asians Think?*, pp. 58–79, at pp. 74–5.

65 Kishore Mahbubani, 'The dangers of decadence: what the rest can teach the West', in Mahbubani, *Can Asians Think?*, pp. 92–8, at p. 95.

66 Mahbubani, 'An Asian perspective on human rights and freedom of the press', p. 73.

67 You don't have to be Asian to advocate restricting press freedom on the grounds that the press undermines trust. See O'Neill, *A Question of Trust*, pp. 92–5.

68 Mahbubani, 'An Asian perspective on human rights and freedom of the press', p. 62.
69 Mahbubani, 'Japan adrift', pp. 121–2.

9 Is Trust Declining?

1 *Declining Public Trust Foremost a Leadership Problem* (Press release, World Economic Forum, 2003), http://www.weforum.org/site/homepublic.nsf/Content/Annual+Meeting+2003%5CResults+of+the+Survey+on+Trust. Figures 11, 12 and 16 are taken from this survey.
2 *Trust Will Be the Challenge of 2003: Poll Reveals a Lack of Trust in all Institutions, Including Democratic Institutions, Large Companies, NGOs and Media Across the World* (Press release, World Economic Forum, 2003), http://www.weforum.org/site/homepublic.nsf/Content/Annual+Meeting+2003%5CResults+of+the+Survey+on+Trust. Figures 13, 14, 15 and 17 are taken from this survey.
3 Nicola Hill, 'Sharp decline in social trust', *Guardian*, 15 December 2000; Julia Day, 'People "trust media more than Blair"', *Guardian*, 12 February 2002; Alan Travis, 'Scientists take flak over food scares', *Guardian*, 8 June 1999; Julia Day, 'People lose faith in corporations', *Guardian*, 15 March 2002.
4 Ben Summerskill, 'Whatever happened to teen tearaways?', *Observer*, 21 July 2002.
5 O'Neill, *A Question of Trust*, pp. 11–12.
6 Perri 6, Kristen Lasky and Adrian Fletcher, *The Future of Privacy Volume 2: Public Trust in the Use of Private Information* (Demos, London, 1998).
7 Misztal, *Trust in Modern Societies*, pp. 102–20.
8 Marcel Proust, *The Guermantes Way*, in C.K. Scott Moncrieff and Terence Kilmartin (trans.), *Remembrance of Things Past Vol. 2* (Penguin, Harmondsworth, 1983), p. 420.
9 Fukuyama, *Trust*; Toshio Yamagishi and Midori Yamagishi, 'Trust and commitment in the United States and Japan', *Motivation and Emotion*, vol. 18 (1994), pp. 129–66.
10 E. Glaeser, D. Laibson, J. Scheinkman and C. Soutter, 'What is social

capital? The determinants of trust and trustworthiness', *Quarterly Journal of Economics*, vol. 65 (2000), pp. 811–46.

11 This view is supported by statistical analyses of various US values surveys by Eric M. Uslaner, *The Moral Foundations of Trust* (Cambridge University Press, Cambridge, 2002).

12 'It has to happen – but will it?', *Economist*, 24 April 2003.

13 See Chapter 8, pp. 218–20.

14 John Lichfield, 'Raffarin's reform strategy in ruins as half a million march', *Independent*, 26 May 2003.

15 'Keep it up', *Economist*, 1 May 2003.

16 Mahbubani '"The Pacific impulse"', p. 141.

17 Painter and Wardle, *Viral Politics*.

18 *Trust Will Be the Challenge of 2003*.

19 Polly Toynbee, 'Blair won't be forgiven, even if Iraqis dance in the streets', *Guardian*, 12 March 2003.

20 Mike Goddard, 'The hidden costs of public consultation', *Guardian*, 4 July 2001.

21 Richard Layard, *The Lionel Robbins Memorial Lectures 2003: Happiness – Has Social Science a Clue?* (London School of Economics), available from http://www.lse.ac.uk/cgi-bin/cached_xslt?xml=2003/01/06/20030106t1439z001.xml&xsl=events_wrapper.xsl. or it may be easier to go to http://www.lse.ac.uk/events and click on the link to 'events transcripts' where Lord Layard's talks can be found.

22 Inglehart, 'Trust, well-being and democracy', pp. 89–96.

23 Warren, 'Introduction', p. 8.

24 O'Neill, *A Question of Trust*, pp. 18–19.

25 Robert Uhlig, 'Truth stranger than *EastEnders* fiction', *Daily Telegraph*, 15 May 2003.

26 I Corinthians 4:7.

27 Quoted in Hobson-West, 'Needle politics'.

28 Meyer, 'The performance paradox'.

29 Jackson, *Truth, Trust and Medicine*.

30 O'Neill, *A Question of Trust*, pp. 63–79.

31 O'Neill, *A Question of Trust*, pp. 51–2.

32 R.M. Titmuss, *The Gift Relationship: From Human Blood to Social Policy* (Allen and Unwin, London, 1970). See Hollis, *Trust Within Reason*, pp. 144–50 for a discussion of this.

33 Putnam, *Bowling Alone*, pp. 288–9.
34 Uslaner, *The Moral Foundations of Trust*, p. 41.
35 Hill, 'Sharp decline in social trust'.
36 'What September 11th really wrought', *Economist*, 10 January 2002. The diagram overleaf is taken from this article.
37 The respective chancellors defend themselves in Nigel Lawson, *The View from Number 11* (Bantam, London, 1992) and Norman Lamont, *In Office* (Little, Brown, London, 1999). Michael J. Oliver puts forward the heterodox view that the Tories lost their reputation for economic competence after the 1987 stock market crash and the Lawson Boom in 'The macroeconomic policies of Mr Lawson', *Contemporary British History*, vol. 13 (1999).
38 *Treatise on Human Nature*, I. iii.
39 Uslaner, *The Moral Foundations of Trust*, pp. 14–50.
40 Seligman, *The Problem of Trust*, pp. 124–46.
41 John Gray, *Al Qaeda and What it Means to be Modern* (Faber and Faber, London, 2003).
42 As described, for example, in Edward Banfield, *The Moral Basis of a Backward Society* (Free Press, New York, NY, 1958); and Fukuyama, *Trust*.

10 Re-establishing Trust

1 Andrew Grice, 'Blair must regain trust or be remembered solely for the suicide of a leading scientist', *Independent*, 30 July 2003; Patrick Wintour, 'We lost your trust, Blair admits', *Guardian*, 31 July 2003.
2 Toby Helm, 'Public's trust in Blair hit by Kelly affair', *Daily Telegraph*, 25 July 2003.
3 'Bliar?', *Economist*, 5 June 2003.
4 'Do you trust Tony Blair?', *Economist*, 21 February 2002.
5 'The Ceausescu moment', *Economist*, 8 June 2000.
6 'Now reveal yourself', *Economist*, 3 May 1997.
7 'Hague's time will come', *Daily Telegraph*, 2 July 2003.
8 Magnus Linklater and David Leigh, *Not With Honour: The Inside Story of the Westland Scandal* (Sphere Books, London, 1986).
9 Michael Freeden, *Ideologies and Political Theory: A Conceptual Approach* (Clarendon Press, Oxford, 1996), pp. 139–314; Robert

Eccleshall, 'Liberalism', in Robert Eccleshall, Alan Finlayson, Vincent Geoghegan, Michael Kenny, Moya Lloyd, Iain MacKenzie and Rick Wilford (eds), *Political Ideologies: An Introduction* (3rd edition, Routledge, London, 2003), pp. 18–45; Matthew Festenstein, 'Contemporary liberalism', in Adam Lent (ed.), *New Political Thought: An Introduction* (Lawrence and Wishart, London, 1998), pp. 14–32.

10 Moya Lloyd, 'The end of ideology?', in Eccleshall et al., *Political Ideologies*, pp. 218–41.

11 Michael Kenny, 'Ecologism', in Eccleshall et al., *Political Ideologies*, pp. 152–79; John Barry, 'Green political thought', in Lent, *New Political Thought*, pp. 184–200; Freeden, *Ideologies and Political Theory*, pp. 526–50.

12 Rick Wilford, 'Feminism', in Eccleshall et al., *Political Ideologies*, pp. 182–215; Moya Lloyd, 'Feminism', in Lent, *New Political Thought*, pp. 163–83; Freeden, *Ideologies and Political Theory*, pp. 488–525, 548–50.

13 Tamsin Spargo, *Foucault and Queer Theory* (Icon Books, Cambridge, 1999).

14 Phil Marfleet, 'Islamist political thought', in Lent, *New Political Thought*, pp. 89–111.

15 Amitai Etzioni, *The Spirit of Community: Rights, Responsibilities and the Communitarian Agenda* (Crown Publishers, New York, NY, 1993); Elizabeth Frazer, 'Communitarianism', in Lent, *New Political Thought*, pp. 112–25.

16 Ronald Inglehart, 'Postmodernization brings declining respect for authority but rising support for democracy', in Pippa Norris (ed.), *Critical Citizens: Global Support for Democratic Government* (Oxford University Press, Oxford, 1999), and http://wvs.isr.umich.edu/papers/postmod.shtml.

17 Eric Hobsbawm, *Age of Extremes: The Short Twentieth Century 1914–1991* (Abacus, London, 1996).

18 Nikolai Gogol, *Dead Souls* (trans. David Magarshack; Penguin, London, 1961), p. 217.

19 As argued on pp. 130–33.

20 'Small place, big wave', *Economist*, 19 September 2002.

Credits

The author and publisher wish to thank the following for their permission to reprint copyright material:

Jonathan Barnes (trans.), *Early Greek Philosophy* (Penguin, Harmondsworth, 2001). Copyright © Jonathan Barnes 1987. Reproduced by permission of Penguin Books Ltd.

Extracts from *The Stories of John Cheever* by John Cheever published by Jonathan Cape and Vintage. Used by permission of The Random House Group Limited.

Paul Feyerabend, *Science in a Free Society* (Verso, London, 1978). Reproduced by permission of Verso.

Naomi Klein, *No Logo* (Flamingo, London, 2000). Reproduced by permission of HarperCollins Publishers Ltd. Copyright © Naomi Klein 2000.

Anne Stevenson, *A Report from the Border* (Bloodaxe Books, 2003). Reproduced with permission.

Andrew Tucker, *Why Trust Has No Part in Modern Politics* (Centre for Reform, London, 1999). Reproduced with permission.

P.G. Walsh (trans.), *Cicero, On Obligations* (Oxford University Press, Oxford, 2000). Reproduced by permission of Oxford University Press.

Figures 5 and 18: Copyright © The Economist Newspaper Limited, London (2003, 2002).

Figure 6: Courtesy of Financial Express and FTSE.

Figure 7: Reproduced with permission of HarperCollins Publishers Ltd.

Figure 9: Reproduced with permission of The Sun Newspaper.

Although every effort has been made to contact copyright holders, there are instances where we have been unable to do so. If notified, the publisher will be pleased to acknowledge the use of copyright material in future editions.

Index

Vaz, Keith 214
vertical relations 278; Asian values
    235; authority 91, 92, 235; politics
    93–4, 207, 276; reciprocity 156;
    science 93–4, 166, 276
viruses 99–100, 101, 103, 105–6
Voice of the People 241, 250
voluntarism 261–2
Vonnegut, Kurt 196–7
voting, compulsory 221–2

Wakefield, Andrew 255
Wakeham, Lord 143
Wall Street Journal 152
Warren, Mike 253
weapons of mass destruction 2, 3,
    195–6
Weber, Max 56, 59, 229–30

Welles, Orson 217
whistleblowing 176–7
Wilson, Harold 229, 274, 275
witnesses 83
Wittgenstein, Ludwig 12, 258
Wolfe, Humbert 217–18
World Economic Forum 152–3,
    239–40, 242
World Wide Web 95, 113–14,
    117
WorldCom 133, 135, 141
writing/speaking 76–84

Xenocrates 33, 289n21
Xenophon 77

Zambia 199
Zimbabwe 151